Born Again

Born Again

The Christian Right Globalized

JENNIFER S. BUTLER

Pluto Press

LONDON • ANN ARBOR, MI

First published 2006 by Pluto Press
345 Archway Road, London N6 5AA
and 839 Greene Street, Ann Arbor, MI 48106

www.plutobooks.com

British Library Cataloguing in Publication Data
A catalogue record for this book is available from the British Library

ISBN-10 0 7453 2243 3 hardback
ISBN-13 978 0 7453 2243 8 hardback
ISBN-10 0 7453 2242 5 paperback
ISBN-13 978 0 7453 2242 1 paperback

Library of Congress Cataloging in Publication Data applied for

10   9   8   7   6   5   4   3   2   1

Designed and produced for Pluto Press by
Chase Publishing Services Ltd, Fortescue, Sidmouth, EX10 9QG, England
Typeset from disk by Stanford DTP Services, Northampton, England
Printed and bound in the United States of America by
Maple-Vail Book Manufacturing Group

Contents

Acknowledgements

I'd like to thank Jean Hardisty and Political Research Associates who first encouraged me to write about this topic, as well as James Paul of the Global Policy Forum for publishing my first article. I especially thank Roger van Zwanenberg at Pluto for his energetic support and enthusiasm.

I am indebted to Kirstin Isgro and Glenn Zuber for their insights on early drafts and challenging my thinking on many of the issues in this book. I could not have finished this book without the support of dedicated research assistants: Christina Holder, Christie Brewer Boyd, Rachel Pederson and Ricarda Velez Negron, all of whom also brought unique insights to this work. I'm grateful to Sara Lisherness and the Peacemaking Program of the Presbyterian Church for faithfully supporting my work.

I am also grateful to Austin Ruse of the Catholic Family and Human Rights Institute, who graciously opened doors for me to interview many of his colleagues.

And to Max Café at 123rd and Amsterdam for coffee, croissants, and a place to focus.

Introduction

T HE FIRST TIME MEMBERS OF the Christian Right appeared at a United Nations women's conference in 2000, they planned their entrance to maximize their exposure. Like Jake and Elwood in the film, *The Blues Brothers* (1980), they were on a mission from God and they wore the dark suits to prove it. In March 2000, I was sitting in the balcony of a United Nations conference hall with other leaders in the global women's movement listening intently to the opening speeches of the Beijing+5 conference, given by government representatives. U.N. staff and NGO leaders (representatives of non-profit or activist organizations) sat below us in the plenary hall. As I listened to a speech by Charlotte Bunch, a leader in the women's movement, a crowd of men from Mormon and Catholic groups suddenly began streaming through the backdoors of the conference hall as if on cue. They represented a contrast in every way from the traditional crowd of activists that attended this kind of conference to observe and lobby governments.

The newcomers were mostly male, white, young, conservative, and religious, while we were female, (mostly) middle-aged, racially diverse, liberal, and (mostly) secular, or at least private about our religious beliefs. It's worth mentioning how the young group of men and women stood out visually in the crowd in almost every way, because it gives you an appreciation of how their mere presence at first unnerved the old-timers like myself. Many of the American women at the conference favored colorful, free-flowing dresses and carried book bags picked up at previous U.N. world conferences. The book bags were covered with the symbols and slogans of women's empowerment, and were stuffed full of conference flyers. Their hair was often graying; many had joined the global women's movement in the 1960s and 1970s. When a group of young, conservatively dressed men suddenly enters this arena, they can easily cause a stir. The men had a contrasting look reflecting their emergence from a very different culture. They wore professional business suits like the ones bankers and lawyers prefer. Their hair was short and clean-cut. The few women among them wore power suits and perfectly coifed hair. All of them wore bright campaign buttons emblazoned with a single word: "motherhood." One of the young men on the ground floor approached the platform and just glowered at Charlotte Bunch, as if the intensity of his gaze might silence her. He and his compatriots had come to stop, or at least register a protest against, the women they believed had attacked motherhood. They planned to do so through symbolic protests and infiltrating U.N. conferences.

This dramatic entrance proved to be only the first of a series of unusual spectacles that we saw during that conference. The men employed religious practices and symbols to defeat the feminist threat and that choice of tactics only exacerbated the underlying tensions. If they had asked the women they now opposed about their background, the men would have learned that many had actually grown up in religious households, but they remembered when all the mainstream options (Jewish, Catholic, and mainline Protestant) had prohibited women leaders. Many of the women who stayed in those communities often felt estranged and at odds with the leadership. The aggressive use of religious symbols only made a difficult situation worse. After one meeting concluded, the women streaming out of a conference room found themselves surrounded by robed monks with full, long beards. There was no warmth in their face as they softly prayed for the soul of their captured conference participant. One woman told me she only managed to get away by slipping into a bathroom. The experience proved so unnerving that she sought counseling afterward. The monks also made their presence known in subtler, but no less unnerving ways. In some meetings, the monks sat in the back of the room silently moving their lips in prayer while others made sure to arrive early to that they could sit in the chairs in the form of a cross.

When conference participants witnessed these scenes, submerged anxieties developed into apocalyptic fears for the future. A committed feminist who has read her history will tell you that she often wonders if Margaret Atwood's novel *The Handmaid's Tale* (1985) will become reality in her own time. In Atwood's harrowing story, a nuclear cataclysm leads to a militaristic society where women and their aspirations are violently suppressed. Advocates of women's rights often wonder if the gains of this generation might be reversed – and when chanting monks pray to save your feminist soul such fears are heightened. When I first told people I was going to write an essay on the origins of these groups, and interview their leaders, the question that many women asked me – "Do you fear for your life?" – came from this deep fear of what the future might hold.

Christian Right groups are also targeting NGO caucuses for takeover. When government representatives met to debate new treaties and agreements, NGO caucuses or subcommittees often met simultaneously. Over the next two years the Christian Right coalition grew larger, more confident and more professional. By 2001 their man George W. Bush was in the White House. There was clearly a complete change in conservative organizing tactics by the time the U.N. Special Session on Children was held in the spring of 2001. Christian Right NGOs became more strategic and more understated.

For example, at the second preparatory meeting for the Special Session on Children, Christian Right youths actually took over the leadership of the Youth Caucus. These young leaders had first trained at a conference in Alberta, Canada organized by the World Family Policy Center and World Youth Alliance. The NGO Organizing Committee for the Special Session had originally organized the Youth Caucus to provide a discussion forum for young people to share ideas and discuss how to best express their views at government meetings. Seeing this as a strategic opportunity, "pro-family" NGOs allocated most of their NGO slots to register youths for the meeting. The right-wing youths, many of whom had trained together prior to the conference, attended the caucus but sat in different seats around the room. Unbeknownst to the other young participants, who came from different NGOs, they were outnumbered by a well-trained voting bloc. Adult right-wing leaders sat around the periphery of the room, monitoring their protégées and occasionally coaching them. Hoping to address this problem, caucus members and leadership raised the issue of whether or not people over 18 years of age should remain in the caucus. Conservative youths opposed the removal of participants who were over 18 (which would have removed many of their members) and easily outmaneuvered the other participants on this issue. Frustrated, and feeling they were being manipulated, the chair of the caucus and many others abandoned the caucus in a walkout demonstration. The conservative young people quickly engineered the election of a new leader and took over the caucus. Once they assumed control, they walked through a well-rehearsed procedure and outlined their agenda to submit a statement representing the voice of the world's youth to the world's governments.

These stories graphically illustrate how dramatically the usually staid NGO conferences at the U.N. have to adjust to the new activism of Christian Right groups. Moreover, these events show how Christian Right groups are experimenting with their organizing tactics.

In order to fully tell this story, this book traces the changing Christian Right presence at the U.N. between the 2000 U.N. Beijing+5 Conference and the U.N. Declaration on Human Cloning adopted in 2005. It investigates the organizing strategies of the Christian Right at the U.N., and assesses its potential as a global movement as well as its potential impact on international law and the effort among nongovernmental organizations to build a global democracy and civil society.

Purposes of the Book

The story of how the Christian Right is globalizing has not received the attention it deserved; it remains under-researched both by those who study the Christian Right and the political scientists who study international movements. The Christian Right is building a global, interfaith coalition, advocating policies at the United Nations through government allies, establishing offices around the world, catalyzing regional networks and holding international conferences. It has had the support of powerful religious and political leaders from Pope John Paul II to President George W. Bush. Its pro-family message in many ways resonates with deeply religious evangelical, Catholic, and Muslim communities around the world who hold traditional social values, particularly on the subject of homosexuality. The goal of strengthening the family resonates all the more among communities in the developing world because family life struggles to survive the immense poverty, urbanization, conflict and cultural disintegration wrought in great part by globalization. Even though the Christian Right does not directly seek to address these obstacles to family life, their stated support for family connects with those who struggle to survive with their families' dignity intact.

This book fills a gap in the scholarship by assessing the prospects of the globalizing Christian Right. The book explores the origins and outlines the organizing strategies of the Christian Right at the U.N. as illuminated through interviews with key leadership and their progressive opponents as well as through direct observation of their activism. This book asks why the Christian Right is globalizing; what strategies have given them a measure of success thus far, and what this development holds for global civil society. By focusing on its movement-building strategies and resources, it is designed to complement the book by Doris Buss and Didi Herman, *Globalizing Family Values*, which details the political rhetoric and theological origins of the Christian Right at the U.N.[1]

My Research Methods

I write as a participating observer in this story. For almost a decade I represented the Presbyterian Church (USA) and ecumenical bodies at the U.N. My church and many others had been active at the U.N. since its founding after World War II, and advocated a largely progressive social agenda especially around women's rights, including a nuanced version of the right to choose an abortion, and children's rights. The historic or mainline churches that belong to the World Council of Churches and National Council of Churches sent delegations to many of the U.N. women's conferences and efforts that complemented their own. For example, the 1985 conference held in Nairobi sparked a movement in the World Council of Churches called the Ecumenical Decade of Churches in Solidarity with Women.[2]

As one of the leaders of a coalition called Ecumenical Women 2000, I organized an interfaith, feminist religious voice the same year that the Christian Right brought hundreds of activists to the U.N. to oppose a liberal feminist agenda at the fifth-year review of the 1995 U.N. Women's Conference held in Beijing. Ecumenical Women brought women church leaders from all over the world to lobby delegates to support the women's rights platform. We held events to analyze the role of religion in women's lives, both for good and for ill. Although I had little knowledge of the Christian Right, I soon found myself at Ground Zero in the volatile encounter between Christian Right activists and women's rights activists, both church based and secular. Being at the center of the storm around religion and women's rights at the

United Nations gave me a unique chance to interview both Christian Right and feminist leaders as they both came to grapple with the new situation they faced.

Guiding Themes

The Return of Religious Influence on International Affairs

This examination of the globalizing Christian Right provides a small window into the often under-explored role of religion in world affairs. While world attention has focused on Islam after the terrorist attacks on the U.S. on September 11, 2001, Christianity, as both a regressive and progressive political force, has received far less attention.[3] There are a few important exceptions. Some scholars have explored the relationship between American Evangelicalism and American Empire, U.S. fundamentalism and the expansion of neoliberal capitalism, and Catholic communities and movements to stop the further expansion of women's rights.[4] Unfortunately, though, secular liberals too often see Christianity monolithically as the religion of the oppressor, rather than as a diverse, dynamic religion. There is less scholarship that evaluates the multiple kinds of "Christianities" that are reshaping the world, even the several forms of conservative Christianity.[5] As we rightly struggle to identify the diversity that exists throughout the Muslim world, we must also aim to see the many manifestations of Christianity in a global context.

While rejecting the stereotype that Christianity is the religion of the oppressor, there is no doubt that there are some interesting historical parallels between the contemporary Christian Right's activism in U.N. forums and, say, the role of evangelicalism in creating the British empire of the nineteenth century. Take for example, the fact that British evangelicalism developed an interest in overseas missions at the same moment in the nineteenth century that British government leaders began promoting the idea of empire. While John Wesley and his circle of Methodists spread the Evangelical Revival in the first half of the eighteenth century, a second wave began in the 1790s that shaped and guided Britain's imperial expansion.[6]

This second wave of evangelical fervor not only influenced all sectors of British religious culture but provided a new impetus for Christians to organize overseas missions to save the "heathens" in other lands. This missionary impulse quickly resulted in an important, if sometimes implicit, justification for Britain's imperialism. In a recent essay, Peter Van der Veer remarks, "There can be little doubt that the simultaneous evangelical activities of Bible societies, missionary societies, and Sunday schools created a public awareness of a particular kind of world and of an imperial duty of British Christians in the empire." The influence of evangelicalism on British nationalism, however, spread beyond the boundaries of specific religious communities. Van der Veer sees the influence of evangelicalism in how British leaders such as Prime Minister William Gladstone formulated a broad national mission to "civilize" other peoples: "In Gladstone, there is a liberal view of progress instead of the usual evangelical views of damnation and the end of times, but added to this is the notion that progress is the Christian improvement of society and that in such progress we see the hand of God." The combination of these evangelical and liberal ideas, he concludes, led "to the quite general emphasis on the moral character of the English people and their duty to lead the world."[7]

The Christian Right activism today can be both compared and contrasted with that of evangelicals in the making of the British empire. For example, a mixture of religious belief and moralism plays an important role in how some U.S. intellectuals and politicians conceptualize the role of America in the world. These intellectuals (neoconservatives, for example), politicians (President Bush and other Republican leaders), and activists (Catholics, evangelicals, and Mormons) stand on a broad platform that emphasize the need to recognize absolute values if not particular religious beliefs that transcend any one tradition like U.S. evangelicalism. The fact that the Christian Right involves so many different kinds of Christians, representing many nationalities and races, suggests the limits to the above historical analogy. This is particularly true when one considers the fact that Christian Right activists have occasionally joined forces with Muslims in the Middle East and Catholics in the developing world. Evangelicals in Victorian Britain did not form these kinds of international alliances. So while the historical analogy between Victorian evangelicals and the new religious activists at the U.N. illuminates aspects of this story, especially in answering why the Bush administration and its allies would express its goals in a religious idiom, it does a poor job in accounting for the international, interracial, and interfaith character of this new group of activists.

Christian Diversity and Dynamism

The course of Christianity, like all religions, is not pre-determined, or even easily categorized. Leaders and events often shape its political course. Related to this theme is the book's emphasis of conservative evangelicals as being a diverse constituency with a range of interests.[8] The Christian Right cannot be conflated with the constituencies in whose names it speaks: it is not nor should not be the sole arbiter of the voice of religious conservatives in the U.S. or globally. The statements and projects of conservative Protestants constantly should remind us that behind the media stereotypes and confident claims of Christian Right leaders is the fact that conservative Christians are not inflexible ideologues, wedded to a two-point agenda.

Consider the following examples. On October 18, 2004, a hundred representatives of evangelical organizations from around the world gathered at the United Nations for a press conference. Speaking for the World Evangelical Alliance of 3 million churches, Gary Edmonds declared, "Governments are given by God and have a moral responsibility. Christians need to hold their governments responsible."[9] The purpose of the press conference: To endorse the Micah Challenge, a campaign to halve global poverty by 2015 as called for in the U.N. Millennium Development Goals (MDGs). The campaign, representing 267 Christian relief organizations, the Baptist World Alliance and World Evangelical Alliance, plans to rally 25 million Christians to support the MDGs, which include eradicating hunger, reducing child mortality, empowering women, combating AIDS, improving maternal health, and ensuring environmental sustainability.

Or think about the significance of the following event: After a recent event hosted by my office at Beijing+10, a major U.N. meeting on women's rights, a Nigerian Pentecostal took us to task – not for the fact that our panel of church leaders spoke about the need for sex education and supporting gay rights, but for the fact that we didn't have more resources available for her to take home. The sympathetic attitude of this Pentecostal brought home to me the need for feminists to better reach out to religious communities. To cite another example of how outdated our common stereotypes of rigid religious conservatives can be, consider how conservative Mormon, Catholic, evangelical and Muslim organizations and governments are experimenting with creating workable coalitions on major issues. While some view this in exclusively cynical terms, calling this union of conservative religious players an "unholy alliance," this book instead seeks to unpack the complex meaning of such a trend and its implication for global democracy.

Secularization as Ideology

While the purpose of this book is to focus on the Christian Right, it is impossible to understand the success and potential of the Christian Right without knowing more about the context in which it has emerged. Many scholars and activists have explored fundamentalism as a response to secularization and modernity. This book takes this a step further in examining ways in which the U.S. political Left, by embracing secularity as an ideology, unnecessarily exacerbates a polarization that strengthens the hand of the Christian Right.

An Emerging Global Culture War

This book explores the possibility of the emergence of a global culture war by looking at the growing involvement of the Christian Right at the United Nations and in global civil society. The book ponders the question of whether the American culture war might be exported, in particular through the U.N., and suggests that a culture war can be avoided and its dynamics actually disrupted.

The definition and existence of a "culture war" is the subject of much debate. The term "culture wars" was coined by sociologist James Davison Hunter in his 1991 book *Culture Wars: The Struggle to Define America*, and then popularized by Pat Buchanan in his controversial speech at the 1992 Republican National Convention. The term suggests that Americans are deeply polarized over moral and religious concerns, which have supplanted the classic economic struggles that dominated American politics for most of the twentieth century.[10]

Hunter also posited that American culture was undergoing a fundamental realignment in which Americans were no longer polarized by multiple competing religious and cultural identities, but by two opposing moral visions: orthodox and progressive. For the orthodox, moral authority comes from above once and for all time. For progressives, moral authority tends to be defined by a spirit of modernity, rationalism and subjectivism. These two moral visions were at the heart of issues like abortion, values in schools, homosexuality and other issues over which Americans are deeply divided. Hunter recognized that communities historically antagonistic toward one another were now finding themselves in alliance with one another because of their common worldview. Orthodox wings of Protestantism, Catholicism and Judaism were forming associations with each other, as were the progressive wings of each faith community.[11] This book explores the international implications of such new alliances and suggests that through the U.N. and international organizing, the American culture wars are going global.

But this book also builds on the work of those who question whether a culture war actually exists. Morris Fiorina suggests it is the elite that are polarized and polarizing, while the majority of Americans find themselves trapped between loud activists on both sides.[12] Political leaders, activists and media capitalize on divisiveness and conflict as they seek respectively to win elections, raise funds and increase ratings. Respectful of these claims to some extent, this book suggests that the culture wars are also used by elites to cloak unpopular policy objectives.

Are culture wars being waged? I think they are. In my travels home to Atlanta and to churches across the country I have never failed to encounter and participate, often times unwillingly, in the unfolding of these wars, which have pitted family members and congregants against one another. Those who theorize that the wars are concocted fear also that the culture wars might be a "self-fulfilling prophecy as a polarized political class abandons any effort to reach out toward the great middle of their country."[13] Theories that the culture wars are an invented concept are helpful in that they suggest, as does this book, that the culture wars may be avoided. Reframing issues and building new, creative alliances for instance can lessen polarities. Choices made by liberal and conservative leaders as well as unforeseen events may well prevent the culture wars from intensifying and globalizing.

This book builds on the work of others who have suggested that powerful political and economic interests benefit from the culture wars, which serve to distract the public from an economic agenda that harms a majority of the world's population. My findings echo the work of political scientist Rosalind Petchesky who pointed out that the polarization of some U.N. conferences over the issue of reproductive health and sexuality actually drains resources from NGOs focused on social development and poverty. In a related instance, the culture wars serve as a smokescreen behind which the U.S. in international forums can take unpopular stances on poverty and child welfare. Such culture war debates inordinately consume the energies of progressives of all stripes. In Petchesky's view, feminists put disproportionate energy into "combating the fundamentalist and traditionalist attacks on reproductive, sexual and other women's human rights and less towards assuring the structural and macroeconomic conditions for those rights."[14] She observed that both the Vatican and women's rights groups put less effort into U.N. meetings on poverty and more into those meetings that address reproductive health and women's rights as a central concern.[15] Similarly, Thomas Frank in *What's the Matter with Kansas?* explores how the culture wars have led struggling working class Americans to vote for the agenda of the nation's economic elites in the mistaken belief that they are effectively resisting the nation's media and cultural elites.[16] In both of these works, the culture wars are actually not removed from economic conflicts, they have simply obscured the operation of economic interests.

The Next Global Divide

Both Samuel Huntington in his book *The Clash of Civilizations* and Philip Jenkins in *The Next Christendom* theorize that religion and culture will play a major role in structuring the new world political order and determining the next global conflict. Huntington suggested that this new global clash of civilizations or cultures would be between Islam and Christianity. Philip Jenkins conjectures that the next great global divide might be between a global secular North and a global religious South. This case study of the Christian Right at the U.N. offers some insight into both of these theories.

While Huntington speculated that the culture wars would be between the West and Muslim world, in the realm of social and family concerns, a different alignment is possible. Despite geopolitical tensions, conservative religious actors are busy experimenting with new kinds of alliances. Conservative evangelicals are willing to work alongside Muslim leaders to advance the traditional family in international law. Mormons are planning conferences with Muslim governments. A think tank in the American heartland unwittingly catalyzed a Mexican "pro-family" network. There is always the possibility that geopolitics and economic concerns will unravel this tentative religious coalition of conservative Catholics, Muslims, Mormons and evangelicals, but so far this has not happened. On the contrary, it seems possible that civil-society connections among conservative religious leaders might continue to increase over decades. As a result, Jenkins's theory that the next global divide might be between a secular North and a religious South helps to explain the larger forces that I saw at work at the U.N.

What is The Christian Right?

The Christian Right is one of the major influences in the U.S. culture wars. The term "Christian Right" refers to the *organizations* and *leaders* that mobilize key constituencies to a conservative social agenda motivated by religious values. This distinction is critical to this book's premise that conservative religious communities have diverse interests and alliances and do not belong necessarily to the Christian Right. Christian Right leaders form part of the political elite that continues to seek to polarize Americans in ongoing culture wars.

In the late 1970s, evangelical leaders like Jerry Falwell and Pat Robertson mobilized white conservative evangelicals around social issues like abortion, homosexuality and the defense of the traditional family. Conservative evangelicals, alarmed by Supreme Court decisions over prayer in schools and abortion, and awakened by the election of southern evangelical Democrat Jimmy Carter in the 1970s, were wooed by New Right leaders to their coalition in the Republican Party. While they initially mobilized primarily white conservative evangelicals, Christian Right organizations and leaders now draw significant numbers of conservative Catholics and Mormons. The roots of the Christian Right can be traced back to the fundamentalist controversy of the 1920s in which fundamentalists opposed the growing tendency of church leaders to embrace a liberal interpretation of scripture and the social gospel, urging the church to support government involvement in social welfare. Dismissed by the press after their defeat at the famous Scopes trial that took place over the teaching of evolution in public schools, fundamentalists began to build their own parallel institutions. Many of these same institutions provided the infrastructure for the Christian Right (what some call the New Christian Right) to emerge in the late 1970s.[17]

The involvement of Christian Right leaders at the United Nations is a relatively new phenomenon that at first glance seems to be a surprising development. Buss and Herman distinguish the Christian Right at the U.N. from the domestic Christian Right because the former diverges in many ways from traditional Christian Right activism. They point out that Christian Right's involvement in the U.N. system as well as their willingness to form coalitions with "pariah" states, especially post-9/11, significantly diverges from the traditional patriotism and anti-Muslim sentiment in the domestic Christian Right. Because this coalition seems exceptional, Buss and Herman also do not see the Christian Right at the U.N. as a transnational or global social movement, although they believe it has the makings of one.

In my view the Christian Right at the U.N. is the culmination of several trends in religion and civil society over the past few decades. The Christian Right is anti-U.N. just as it is anti-government. Yet just as its opposition to government did not significantly impede its participation in U.S. politics, so its opposition to global governance has not impeded its activism at the U.N. As Buss and Herman themselves astutely observe, although some of its rhetoric may indicate otherwise, the Christian Right is not against the state, rather it is against the state that currently exists, one that is secularist, humanistic and liberal.[18] In the same way it is against a U.N. that is liberal. Their involvement at the U.N. is no more unusual in some respects than is their seeking to impose religious values in abortion law or advocating that the federal government intervene in a Florida judicial decision to withdraw a feeding tube from a brain-dead woman despite her husband's wishes to do so. Since the 1970s, the Christian Right has joined forces with Catholics and Mormons, particularly in opposing the Equal Rights Amendment.

Christian Right coalition building at the U.N. then could be seen as a natural progression in the movement. Buss and Herman recognize that leading domestic Christian Right actors are active at the U.N.: Focus on the Family, Family Research Council and Concerned Women for America.[19] The involvement of three of the five main Christian Right NGOs would suggest that the U.N. project is becoming integral to the Christian Right's agenda and fits naturally with their pragmatism and evangelistic zeal.

Therefore this book simply refers to the Christian Right at the U.N. as the Christian Right, not as a subcategory or distinct entity of the Christian Right. While the Christian Right works with Muslim governments, it still has weak ties to Muslim civil society. While partnerships with Mormons and Catholics are quite strong, moreover, it has weak connections with Jewish organizations. Therefore this book uses the term "Christian" rather than "religious" right. Still, this book seriously considers the possibility of this becoming a religious right coalition.

The Christian Right Supports Rights for Women, But Not "Women's Rights"

The Christian Right platform at the U.N. is always evolving – more so than its opponents often recognize. Their positions also vary somewhat depending on the NGO's religious orientation. Buss and Herman have written an excellent book, *Globalizing Family Values,* which explores in depth the nuances and differences of opinion among the Christian Right NGOs at the U.N.[20] For the purpose of this book though, I will summarize three different areas of concern for the Christian Right: their suspicion for the U.N., their opposition to women's rights (as defined by feminists) and reproductive rights, and their pro-family platform.

Conservative white evangelicals have traditionally viewed the U.N. with suspicion. Their thinking is influenced by American conservatives in general as well as by deeply held religious convictions. First, during the Cold War the fact that the Soviet Union was a member of the global institution deeply disturbed American conservatives who believed that "godless communists" should not be allowed to join the international body. The U.N. has also traditionally been viewed as both a threat to U.S. sovereignty and the epitome of "big government" which American conservatives oppose. Among conservative white evangelicals in particular, apocalyptic beliefs intensify these broader concerns. The prophecy writing works of Pat Robertson (*The New World Order,*

1991) and Hal Lindsey (*The Late Great Planet Earth*, 1994) and more recently Tim LaHaye's best selling *Left Behind* fiction series all place the U.N. at the center of end times scenarios and the coming of the anti-Christ. Say Buss and Herman, "whether in fiction or prophecy-writing genres, premillennial conservative Protestants predict, in graphic terms, that catastrophic consequences will result from movements for world peace and global unity, much of this represented by developments at the U.N." While conservative Catholic NGOs and Muslim NGOs do not share this history of anti-U.N. sentiment or apocalyptic literature they disagree with some U.N. policies and critique the dominant influence of liberal western NGOs.[21]

A series of U.N.-sponsored world conferences during the 1990s sought to tackle a host of global issues from human rights to the environment. Two conferences in particular gave birth to a new wave of Christian Right organized opposition to the U.N. and its policies: the U.N. Fourth World Conference on Women held in Beijing in 1995, and the U.N. International Conference on Population and Development held in Cairo in 1994. Progressive NGO activists, in particular feminist organizations, were instrumental in shaping these conference's agenda and outcomes, which catalyzed broader government support for women's rights and reproductive health. Not only was the Christian Right alarmed by the substance of those two conferences, but also by the fact that liberal activists were successfully advancing their agenda through such bodies and exporting that agenda to other parts of the world.

Christian Right organizations viewed these conferences as undermining the family and hence, the very foundations of society. For American religious conservatives, social revolutions of the 1960s and 1970s undermined the family and foundations of society. The advent of birth control and legalization of abortion encouraged sexual freedom, licentiousness and divorce. Women's liberation drew women away from their roles as mothers and wives and weakened the role and authority of fathers. Feminism not only enticed women out of the home, it devalued motherhood. An emphasis on individual fulfillment and ethical relativism led to irresponsibility and a lack of personal and social responsibility. All of these developments, for conservatives and especially religious conservatives, threatened the very fabric of society. American culture seemed to become more secular and the

Supreme Court outlawed school prayer. The Christian Right views liberal activists as using the U.N. as a vehicle to continue this very social revolution.

While conservative religious concerns about these issues can be traced to the 1960s, their views have also evolved over time. Conservative religious views on abortion are perhaps the least transient. All three sectors of the Christian Right movement at the U.N. clearly oppose abortion. Catholics also oppose birth control, while evangelicals usually do not. However Mormons and conservative evangelicals do share with Catholics a reticence about making birth control or sex education widely available, especially to sexually active youth, and emphasize abstinence for unmarried people. Believing life begins at conception, Christian Right NGOs also oppose both human cloning and therapeutic cloning.

The most change can be seen in Christian Right views of feminism and the advancement of women. Rather than simply oppose these, they have begun to articulate a less defensive, more proactive platform for women. In fact, many Christian Right NGOs state that they are not anti-feminist, but are opposed to the way liberals define feminism. This shift might be seen as a tactical move or a sign that feminist viewpoints have become so mainstream that they cannot be directly countered. However, it might also be simply the capacity of religious conservatives to integrate new ideas when encountering new developments. As religious conservatives have tackled sex trafficking, for instance, many have become more aware of the need to work for women's advancement and legal protections for women.

Most members of the Christian Right coalition, including Concerned Women for America leaders and Austin Ruse of C-FAM, argue that they do not oppose feminism, but instead oppose *radical* feminism. Organizations like CWA regularly use the language of women's rights. An article on its website is entitled "Hijacking a Nobel Cause: How Modern Feminism has abandoned its founders."[22] It posits that feminism has been hijacked by liberals who have led it astray from its original more biblically centered objectives. The article contrasts today's feminism with that of Lucretia Mott and Elizabeth Cady Stanton who campaigned for women's right to vote and asserts: "Unlike the early feminist goals, modern feminism's agenda is based on a foundation of separation and anger rather than equality and fairness." It concludes, "early and modern feminism are two separate movements." Likewise

Howard Center President Allan Carlson says "a certain sort of feminism" stood as a foe of the family (not feminism per se). [23] He makes a distinction between equity or liberal feminists and social feminists or maternalists. Carlson's version of feminism recognizes that "men and women should be equal in political and property rights, but are different in reproductive, economic and social functions, differences which must be accommodated in policy and law."[24]

Many Christian Right NGOs follow the Vatican's careful stance on human rights and women. The Vatican distinguishes between the "human rights of women," for which it advocates, and "women's rights," which it opposes. The Vatican posits that women should be protected under existing human rights agreements, rather than a separate category of rights. In contrast, during the 1990s international feminist and women's groups began arguing, "women's rights are human rights." They argued that international human rights law had failed to address the human rights needs of women. Therefore the U.N. needed to rethink international human rights, which assumed masculine norms about the nature of human rights, and outline gender specific rights for women. Christian Right NGOs argue that "women's rights" is a dangerous concept because it represents "new" rights that have not been agreed to through democratic means. These rights move international policy "into private areas traditionally reserved first to families and religious institutions."[25] Their purpose is to denigrate the "importance of motherhood" and promote "homosexuality, abortion-on-demand, and removal of parental rights."[26] Similarly, the concepts of sexual and reproductive rights are viewed as advancing an individualist concept of sexuality when sexual expression should only take place in the context of the family. Catholic NGOs in particular and the Holy See stress the theory of complementarity – the idea that men and women have different and complementary roles in the family and society – and reject the concept of "equal rights." These roles are determined by the divine order and revealed in what they see as clear biological differences. To religious conservatives, the concept of "equal rights" implies women and men are the same. The U.N. should instead advocate for equal "dignity."[27]

Likewise the definition and value of the concept of gender is another contested area. Feminists advocate that gender roles are socially constructed and fluid changing over time and different among different cultures rather than biologically pre-determined. Based on this understanding, feminists have successfully advocated that governments work to eradicate gender stereotypes that marginalize or oppress women. Religious conservatives believe gender is rooted in biology, not defined by upbringing, culture and social norms. They assert that feminists in relativising gender are encouraging role confusion and perversion. They remain suspicious of gender as a veiled reference to homosexuality.[28]

Just as the Christian Right opposes the legal concept of women's rights, so too it opposes children's rights as creating a new category of rights that threatens to undermine the family. In their view, child rights undermine the rights of parents and unnecessarily invite government to intervene in the private affairs of the family.

Buss and Herman rightly argue that while focused on the specific policies of rights for women, gays, and lesbians, the Christian Right's argument and motivation should be seen more broadly as a protection of family and religion from the dangers of secularism. As evidenced by the fact that Christian Right NGOs chose most often to define their activism as "pro-family," this perhaps is the most unifying aspect of Christian Right activism and the one that resonates in other parts of the world, in particular the Muslim world.

Like Buss and Herman, this book resists the simple characterization that Christian Right NGOs are "anti-woman" or "anti-feminist."[29] When I refer to the Christian Right as being against women's rights for instance, this is to say that they are against women's rights as currently defined by feminists and the global women's movement at U.N. conferences.

Chapter Overview

The globalization of the Christian Right grows out of several trends in world religion: the revitalization of religion around the world, in particular conservative religion; the growing strength of fundamentalist movements in response to globalization, and in the U.S. the realignment of religious identities around positions on social and cultural issues. Chapter 1 addresses these themes setting the context for how and why the Christian Right began to globalize at this point in history.

Chapter 2 provides one of the first detailed accounts of the nature, origins and impact of the Christian Right's activism at the United Nations and its efforts to build a global, even an interfaith, movement.

The Christian Right's work at the U.N. is a reaction against the perceived hijacking of the U.N. by social liberals, and a proactive response to the leadership of key religious leaders like the Pope and Catholic and Jewish neoconservatives who have urged conservative evangelicals to be more engaged in international policy.

Chapter 3 analyzes the impact of the Christian Right on global democracy by looking at its effect on U.N. debates on women's rights, children's rights, human cloning and the International Criminal Court. Scholars and activists view international movements for justice and peace – such as those set on improving the environment, ending poverty, or banning landmines – as democratizing the world by being a counterbalance to the power of governments and multinational corporations. This chapter points out that just as the Christian Right may both contribute to and diminish this emerging global democracy, its ultimate impact will be shaped by how well progressives respond to this new global alliance.

Chapter 4 explores the Christian Right's growing international alliances and interfaith partnerships and the ways in which geopolitical dynamics enhance and detract from their coalition building. The true measure of the Christian Right's ability to globalize will be its ability to extend its global presence by developing international networks.

In the Conclusion, I examine the seven organizing areas in which the Christian Right excels and progressive organizing has deteriorated. Examining these areas is intended to lay out the fundamental differences that characterize each side and to provoke some debate among progressives about a thorough overhaul of their organizing and rhetorical strategies.

The story of the Christian Right's entrance into the U.N. is a story of dramatic changes caused by a rapidly globalizing world and the growing importance of the U.N. in our new global society. From being among the most strident critics of the U.N., Christian Right NGOs have entered and joined in unexpected coalitions to change international law and the NGO world. From having a free hand at the U.N. to promote change, progressive NGOs have found themselves entering a new period of having their activism vigorously challenged, especially around women's issues and rights. The coming together of the Christian Right and progressive NGOs at U.N. forums will change the nature of all three, as well as the nature of global civil society.

1

Born Again: Three Reasons the Christian Right is Globalizing

JOURNALISTS, ACTIVISTS AND SCHOLARS HAVE predicted the demise of the Christian Right several times since the 1970s. Needless to say, the Christian Right never died out. Each time the end was predicted, Christian Right leaders defied the journalists and experts by finding new causes to champion. Rather than collapse in the face of modernity, the Christian Right's influence has grown over the past decade and its interests have broadened. Once concerned largely with state and national issues, the Christian Right, just like many other social and political movements, is now developing international networks, initiatives and interests.

The Christian Right's most surprising shift in tactics is its recent decision to advocate its concerns at the United Nations, an organization that some continue to demonize as one of the possible stomping grounds of the Antichrist. Christian Right NGOs such as Focus on the Family and Concerned Women for America are now accredited with the U.N. so that they can attend and influence U.N. meetings. Christian Right leaders now lobby U.N. Ambassadors and rent offices in the U.N. neighborhood rather than solely working in Washington to block funding for the U.N.

The Christian Right's interest in the U.N. is not a temporary or isolated foray into international organizing: it is part of a trend of growing Christian Right involvement in international concerns. Over the past two decades, conservative evangelicals have expanded their concerns from a focus on anti-communism to an interest in global concerns ranging from the AIDS pandemic, sex trafficking, and opposition to reproductive rights, human cloning and the expansion of women's rights language in treaties, to support for Israel and religious freedom.

As they have expanded their vision, Christian Right leaders have continued to build new alliances, laying the foundation for a global, possibly even an interfaith movement. The Christian Right is no longer a handful of leaders and their organizations with a largely evangelical membership: it is now led by a number of organizations, many of which are Catholic and Mormon as well as evangelical. And its membership is equally distributed among all three communities. This is especially the case in the loose Christian Right coalition operating at the U.N. Not only is it ecumenical: it is increasingly international. Some leaders even hope to make it interfaith by bringing Muslims into the coalition.

Why and how did the Christian Right begin to globalize? A complete answer requires not only understanding the background of these organizations, but also the persuasive assumptions that resulted in these organizations not being noticed until recently. Simply put, one must first problematize commonly held beliefs about religion and modernity that have been held by scholars and intellectual elites for decades. The theory of secularization held that as societies modernized, they would become more secular. Even those who were its foremost proponents are now questioning this theory. In fact, some would say modernity carries within it the seeds of religious revitalization. The rise of fundamentalist movements in all world religions is one of the major developments that called the theory of secularization into question.

Second, it is important to reexamine a common misperception that Christianity is moribund. On the contrary, Christianity, particularly in the global South, is experiencing a revitalization that may rival that of Islam. As the center of Christianity moves to the global South, its global leadership is becoming more socially conservative. Related to this point, despite being a modern superpower, the United States itself remains very religious. While the liberal wing of media and progressive activists often express surprise at the Christian Right's continued influence, religious activism ought not be viewed as an aberration in American politics. From Prohibition to the civil rights movement, evangelicals have long been influential in important social movements. Many journalists tend to cover the Christian Right through the lens of church–state issues, portraying the culture war as a conflict between fundamentalists and secularists. They therefore often overlook a second dimension of the conflict: the struggle within Christianity itself. Both the media and the Christian Right tend to characterize Christianity as being defined by the conservative social views expressed by the Christian Right rather than being a faith characterized by diversity.

Finally, globalization is helping to extend the Christian Right's influence. Once the Christian Right is no longer viewed as an anomaly that somehow survived modernity, its global expansion can be seen as a result of the all-encompassing strength of the forces of globalization itself. A brief examination of conservative evangelical and Christian Right activism on issues of religious freedom, the global AIDS pandemic and sex trafficking reveals that such activism may have progressive as well as conservative results.

Reason 1: Secularism (Despite Predictions) Never Completely Banished Religion

Secularization Theory Reexamined

In the 1940s and 1950s sociologists generally asserted that religion would increasingly play less of a role in both politics and modern life. Social theorists largely doubted that religion could survive the impact of the Age of Reason: scientific research, humanistic education, pluralism, democracy, technology, bureaucratic organizational life among other elements would undermine societal interest and need for religion.[1] As one sociologist reflected, "From its inception, [sociology] was committed to the positivist view that religion in the modern world is merely a survival from man's primitive past, and doomed to disappear in an era of science and general enlightenment. From the positivist standpoint, religion is, basically, institutionalized ignorance and superstition."[2] At best, religion was a relic of barbarism treasured by the less educated, part of a prior stage of human evolution that would crumble under the weight of this post-Enlightenment trend towards secularization.

Even some theologians during the social revolutions of the 1960s and early 1970s proclaimed "God is dead," holding that Westerners no longer found the idea of a radically transcendent God meaningful and that particular change in attitude could be seen in a positive light. Secularity, if not secularism, was to be embraced.[3] An enthusiastic style of religion (Baptists and Pentecostals) in particular was held suspect in favor of more rationalized, philosophical or post-Christian versions of religious practice (such as mainline Protestantism, Buddhism, New Age religion). In the name of cultural sensitivity, African-American religious experience might be tolerated, or even Islam, but Christianity was viewed categorically as the religion of Western colonial oppressors.

Secularization theory was the reigning paradigm in intellectual circles until the mid-1980s. A number of significant events in the 1970s and 1980s revealed that religion had failed to follow the script that social scientists and cultural elites had written for it.[4] World events proved that the secularization theory had to be revised: religion reemerged as a political force in nearly every region and major world religion. In 1979 the Ayatollah Khomeini, a Shi'ite Muslim, ousted the Shah of Iran and established a theocracy. During the 1980s the Mujahadeen waged a battle against communism in Afghanistan and in the 1990s the Taliban wrested much of Afghanistan from the Mujahadeen. Hindu fundamentalism provoked political violence in India. Latin American liberation theology challenged repressive governments. A decade later Pentecostalism began to challenge the hegemony of Catholicism in Latin America. Africa also experienced an evangelical explosion. The Catholic Solidarity movement in Poland helped overthrow communism. The Christian Right in the United States helped elect President Ronald Reagan. As the reality of world events and the predictions of secularization theory increasingly could not be matched up, some critics of the theory pointed out that it had never been based on a body of research findings. Some scholars even suggested that the theory had been an ideology rather than a scientific theory all along, a value judgment rather than an analytical tool.[5]

Secularism's Nemesis: Global Fundamentalism

Religious traditionalism or fundamentalism is said to be on the rise in all of the world's religions, yet debates continue over how to define the phenomenon.[6] First, the term "fundamentalism" is a relatively new term. During the early part of the twentieth century, Protestant evangelicals who wanted their churches to return to the "fundamentals" of the faith called themselves fundamentalists to distinguish themselves from liberal evangelical Protestants. In 1979, the term was appropriated by the mass media to label the Iranian Shi'ite followers of Ayatollah

Khomeini who led an Islamic revolution in Iran and ousted the Shah of Iran.[7] It quickly caught on as a term to describe radical Muslim groups throughout the Middle East (despite objections both from the Muslim world and fundamentalist leaders in the United States). The term has been broadly applied to diverse movements in many different religious traditions as well as used pejoratively as a term synonymous with "backwards," or "crazy."[8]

Some have even suggested that defining fundamentalism has been challenging because such efforts are rooted in the scholarly tendency to see religious vitality as aberrant, rather than the norm. Well-known sociologist Peter Berger once quipped, "The difficult-to-understand phenomenon is not Iranian mullahs but American university professors – it might be worth a multi-million-dollar project to try to explain that!"[9]

Despite the term's limitations, scholarship on fundamentalism can provide insights into the globalization of the American Christian Right. Fundamentalists oppose at least three dimensions of modernity: its preference for secular rationality, the adoption of religious tolerance with accompanying tendencies towards moral relativism, and individualism.[10] As societies modernize, religion becomes more compartmentalized. For instance, state constitutions separate religion and state, or create public school systems that displaced the centrality of religious instruction. Fundamentalists oppose this, seeking to restore religion to a central place in society. Accelerated and dramatic changes wrought by globalization threaten traditional cultures, social structures and livelihoods. Responding to rapid change and the destabilization of traditional cultures and family structures, fundamentalist movements offer stability by reclaiming and protecting religious and cultural identity.[11] Ironically, the very process of secularization inspires fundamentalist movements.

While fundamentalists oppose modernity, they are in many ways paradoxically modern, choosing to fight modernity often with the best of modern tools at their disposal. Religious identity thus renewed becomes the exclusive and absolute basis for a recreated political and social order that is oriented to the future rather than the past. While at times choosing to withdraw quietly from modern society, more often fundamentalists fight back.[12] They fight modernity in God's name, seeking to replace it with a "pure," idealized reconstruction of the past. The struggle and enemies are viewed in cosmic, dualistic and apocalyptic terms. Strongly held beliefs, clearly identified enemies and the cosmic nature of the struggle help reinforce the group's identity (thus making it impenetrable) and unify its members.

When the Christian Right seeks to restore prayer in public schools or speaks of America as a Christian nation, it is opposing the secularizing tendencies of modernity. Its enemies are those who seek to secularize society: secular humanists, academic elites, feminists who upset traditional gender roles, judges who mandate secular classrooms, the federal government and the like. It seeks to return the nation to a mythic past (sometimes represented by the Victorian age, or the 1950s) in which society was Christian and operated along more strict moral lines. Its leaders seek to save Christianity itself from liberal interpreters and to embrace orthodoxy or what they view as the true faith of Jesus Christ.

The Christian Right draws millions of supporters with its response to modern twentieth-century concerns like abortion, individual liberties and the welfare state. It appeals to groups alienated by rapid urbanization and industrialization, in particular those deeply disturbed by the 1963 Supreme Court decision to ban prayer in schools and the 1973 Supreme Court decision making abortion legal. In many ways its response to modernity – its cutting-edge usage of radio, the internet and television – is more innovative than that of the secular Left's.

Gender and Fundamentalism

One of the most striking components of fundamentalism is that it defines tradition and evil in gendered terms, resulting in a zeal to circumscribe women's roles in society. In many societies, women are viewed as bearers of culture because of their role in raising children, and in many cultures, the changes wrought by modernity are most visible in women's changing social roles. When these changes provoke reaction, "the modern woman" often becomes a symbol for fundamentalist movements of the evils of modernity and secularization. In the case of colonized nations in particular, where aspects of modernity were imported and often imposed by communism and/or Western powers, women's liberation often became identified with colonization or occupation. Here, the "modern woman" is feared because she is the Westernized woman. In restricting women's role in society, fundamentalists dramatize their effort to rid society of the vestiges of domination by outsiders and return to an ideal past (one which may never have existed). The control of women is viewed as the key to controlling what is the essential building-block of many societies: the family. The Taliban's treatment of women in Afghanistan may be the most dramatic and visible recent example. Highly educated Afghan women, who helped lead the country under the Soviet Union's puppet regime, found their modern lives and freedoms stripped away when the Taliban took over Afghanistan and sought to rid the country of all aspects of the former communist regime.

Surprisingly women themselves embrace and even lead fundamentalist movements, a fact still under-explored in the academy and by activists.[13] For instance, Concerned Women for America, which describes itself as anti-feminist and pro-family, is not only one of the largest Christian Right organizations in the U.S.; it is also one of the largest women's advocacy organizations in the country.[14]

Feminists have largely failed to come to terms with conservative and religious women, often viewing them as "dupes" or "pawns" of a "patriarchal system." Women's leadership and involvement in conservative movements cannot be so easily dismissed, however. While neither conservatives nor feminists truly address economic strains faced by today's American families, conservatives rhetorically appeal to Americans by addressing family concerns, the area where economic pressure is most keen. The agenda of feminist movement leaders in the U.S. is focused on reproductive and sexual rights rather than economic discrimination. Feminists tend to characterize modernization as granting women greater freedoms rather than having a mixed impact due to such strains as rapid urbanization and social fragmentation. This may blind them to the burdens experienced by women trying to support and raise families under immense economic and social pressure. While they have programs designed to help poor single mothers with children, few domestically focused feminist organizations analyze the economic stress on American families in general.[15]

In the developing world, the impact of modernity on women's lives may wreak greater havoc. Rapid urbanization often tears families apart as economic changes force spouses and even children to leave close-knit communities and support systems to work in cities. Tensions wrought by globalization with its attendant economic, political and cultural strains may lead to conflict, health crises and the assimilation of traditional cultures and communities. Women from the developing world have helped to challenge many of the assumptions of white feminists from industrialized countries and this might happen again on economic issues. Perhaps this North–South debate over the economic benefits of modernity may help Western secular feminists better understand the perspectives of their opponents among Western conservative women.

Reason 2: Demographic and Political Shifts Favor Conservative Religious Movements

The Resurgence of Conservative Christianity in the Southern Hemisphere

At the beginning of the twenty-first century, Islam is the religion that has garnered much of the world's attention. However, one of the most important yet overlooked trends of this century is the advent of revolutionary change occurring within global Christianity. These changes are bound to have a significant impact on world affairs. First, the center of gravity in Christianity is moving southward, from Europe and North America to Africa, Asia and Latin America.[16] Those in secular Europe or secular areas of the U.S. often tend to think of religion, Christianity in particular, as moribund. On the contrary, the heart of Christianity is simply shifting. As one Kenyan scholar observed, "the centers of the church's universality [are] no longer in Geneva, Rome, Athens, Paris, London, New York, but Kinshasa, Buenos Aires, Addis Ababa and Manila."[17] By 2050, only about one-fifth of the world's 3 billion Christians will be non-Hispanic whites. Soon, says religion scholar Philip Jenkins, the phrase "a white Christian" may sound like a curious oxymoron, as mildly surprising as "a Swedish Buddhist."[18]

Not only is Christianity moving south, it is growing exponentially in Africa, Latin America and Asia. Contrary to predictions by Samuel Huntington, whose book *The Clash of Civilizations and the Remaking of World Order* proposed that Christianity would be supplanted by Islam, Christianity will actually have a massive lead. By 2050, there will be three Christians for every two Muslims worldwide. In Africa, Christianity survived the post-colonial era, contrary to some expectations, and by the 1960s Christians grew to outnumber Muslims.[19] Catholic growth has been dramatic in Africa. Today, there are 120 million African Catholics and by 2025 there could be 230 million: one-sixth of all Catholics worldwide. In Tanzania, the number of Catholics has grown 419 per cent since 1961. Protestantism is also growing rapidly in Africa in both the mainstream and independent churches.

In Latin America, where Catholicism once dominated, Protestants or *evangélicos* have been growing at an average annual rate of 6 per cent since 1960.[20] Today Protestants make up around one-tenth of the whole population. They are strongest in Guatemala and Chile, representing around 25 per cent.[21] Throughout the global South, older mission churches remain influential, yet no longer constitute the whole picture. Scholars agree that the most spectacular Christian expansion in recent decades, particularly in Latin America, has occurred in new independent – usually Pentecostal – denominations. In Latin America, for instance, Pentecostals account for 80 or 90 per cent of Protestant growth. Some of these independent churches are affiliated with denominations in the Northern Hemisphere, but many are not. They are indigenous churches with their roots in Africa, Asia and Latin America.

The dominant flavor of Christianity in the global South is traditionalist, orthodox and supernatural.[22] This orientation is reshaping the moral stances of both Catholic and Anglican churches and hence the politics of morality. The Roman Catholic population in Africa more than doubled between 1976 and 1995 and in Asia increased by 90 per cent, while Europe's Catholic population grew by less than 10 per cent. The election of Pope John Paul II in 1978 and Benedict XVI in 2004, with their emphasis on the Catholic Church's conservative social views, is partially attributed to the growing influence of Southern voices in the church. Over 40 per cent of cardinals eligible to vote in Papal elections are from the Third World.[23] As priests who first embraced Vatican II retire, they are being replaced by a generation of priests that is more socially conservative.[24] One scholar describes religious conservatives in the Catholic hierarchy, as "looking southward with happy expectations."[25]

A similar trend can be witnessed in the Anglican Church. As the world's Anglican bishops gathered in 1998 for their decennial meeting known as the Lambeth Conference, bishops from the Church of England, the Episcopal Church and Anglican Churches of Canada and Australia found themselves outnumbered for the first time by their counterparts in Africa and Asia. Liberal Episcopal Church leaders, having won battles in the U.S. on issues of sexuality, found they held the minority view while U.S. conservatives found new allies among leaders from Africa and Asia. The Conference adopted a conservative, non-binding statement on homosexuality, opposing the blessing of same-sex unions by priests. Since that time, the U.S. Episcopal Church (the American arm of Anglicanism) has continued to soften its stance on homosexuality. In 2003 a gay Episcopal bishop was ordained in New Hampshire, an action that has caused some churches to split, and others to break completely with the U.S. Episcopal Church and join Anglican dioceses in Africa and South America whose leaders still view homosexuality as a sin. Even though these kinds of alliances are rare, they are indicative of a larger trend that shapes the Christian Right's strategies at the U.N. Such an alliance echoes the actions of Christian Right organizations which are seeking partnerships with like-minded organizations in Latin America, Canada and Africa.

In a recent interview, religion scholar Philip Jenkins asked an interesting question: "What if a global North, secular, rational and tolerant, defines itself against the rest of the world as Christian, primitive, and fundamentalist?"[26] The specter of churches in Texas linking up with allies in Africa is illustrative of such a divide. The clash of Left and Right at the U.N. and the Christian Right's international networking are two developments that will influence the outcome of this possible polarity. Christian Right leaders at the U.N. portray themselves as defending the religious, family-oriented global South against the secular, liberal West. While it does not embrace all issues of concern to the global South, the Christian Right has been able to draw religious leaders in the global South into its policy making efforts at the U.N. Christian Right NGOs also offer leaders in the global South resources, support and connections, not the least of which is their connection with the White House and hence the U.S. Embassy at the U.N.

Jenkins' prediction has two implications: not only is Christianity becoming more conservative and shifting to the South, but also progressive elites in the North are defining themselves in opposition to religion. Indeed the political Left is often reticent to engage with religious communities and prefers a value-neutral language because it is both more comfortable with secularity as well as an academic model of discourse.[27] Such an orientation intensifies the polarization Jenkins observes and thus strengthens the efforts of those who use religion toward conservative ends. Given the resurgence of religion in the political discourse and its continued strength in shaping cultural values, one might question whether political movements which categorically reject religious values can reach large numbers of people. Clearly progressive choices regarding the role of religion in society will be a factor in determining whether the polarization between a secular West and religious global South becomes a reality.

Left v. Right in American Politics

Some have tended to think of religiosity as exclusively the property of the developing world; indeed, secularization theory proposed that as societies modernized and developed they would become more secular. Yet the world's superpower remains very religious, a fact that continues to blindside the American Left. The outcome of the 2004 presidential elections and the Christian Right's role in garnering massive support for President George W. Bush sparked a major debate about the Democratic Party's lack of outreach to religious communities. The debate was long overdue. The Democratic Party in recent times had tended to neglect or reject the use of religious imagery and values. Evangelicals "perceive Democrats as contemptuous of their faith," says *New York Times* columnist Nicholas Kristof. "And frankly, they're often right. Some evangelicals take revenge by smiting Democratic candidates."[28]

Gallup polls report that more than 90 per cent of Americans believe in God. Three-fourths of Americans believe in the possibility of life after death and in the messianic divinity of Jesus of Nazareth, while 50 per cent believe in hell. Ninety per cent of Americans pray and about two-thirds claim membership in a religious congregation. And according to Gallup, little about these statistics has changed significantly over the course of half a century. Globally, Western Europe stands out like a sore thumb, an island of secularity in a largely religious world.

Why are Americans so religious? One prevailing theory asserts that America is a "marketplace of religions," in which churches compete for members much as corporations compete for consumers and market share. Free from restrictions on religious proselytism or state-sponsored religion, the United States has become fertile ground for new religious movements and religious competitiveness that keeps religious institutions alive and vital.

Religion remains an influential force in American politics. A study by the Pew Forum on Religion and Public Life just before the fall presidential elections reported that "nearly twice as many respondents to a recent poll on religion and politics say there has been too little reference to religion by politicians (41 per cent) as say there has been too much (21 per cent)." Those surveyed, both Democrats and Republicans, also wanted to see religion play a more prominent role in policy making: "In fact, more than 70 per cent of Democrats and 50 per cent of liberal Democrats hold strong personal religious attitudes. That means that Democrats are more religious than the overdrawn popular perception suggests, and that connecting with a majority of these voters probably will require appealing in a convincing fashion to their religiously informed moral convictions."[29] Moral values were cited by pollsters as being the top defining issue of the recent presidential elections. Church attendance was also a strong indicator of political preference.[30] Of those who attend church more than once a week, 61 per cent voted for Mr. Bush and 39 per cent for Mr. Kerry. Nearly one-quarter of the electorate was made up of white evangelical and born-again Christians. They voted four to one for Mr. Bush.

Who Is the Christian Right?

While many on the Left tend to call the Christian Right "extremist," Clyde Wilcox, professor of government at Georgetown University, calculates that should the Christian Right succeed in appealing to its potential constituents, it will have the backing of nearly a quarter of the American citizenry,[31] a figure that can hardly be labeled as outside the mainstream. This potential constituency includes half of white evangelicals,[32] a third of white Catholics, less than a third of white mainstream Protestants, and a quarter of black evangelicals. If this potential were realized, the Christian Right would then be substantially larger than the feminist or civil rights movements of the 1960s and 1970s.

The Christian Right has made significant inroads in reaching the first three constituencies. While polls in the 1980s showed only 25 per cent of white evangelicals supported the Moral Majority, polls in 1994 showed that the Christian Coalition and similar groups were rated favorably by 56 per cent of white evangelicals. Still, social class remains a challenge to the Christian Right's ability to draw all white evangelicals. One University of Chicago study found that the one-fifth of white Americans who belong to "fundamentalist" churches (Southern Baptist, Assembly of God, Holiness, Pentecostal and Missouri Synod Lutheran) are surprisingly pluralistic in their political and social attitudes.[33] A majority (about 52 per cent) of poor Southern white evangelicals voted for John Kerry in the 2005 presidential elections while only 12 per cent of affluent Southern white evangelicals did.[34]

A small percentage of evangelicals are progressive. Religion scholar Robert Wuthnow even conjectures that evangelicals could possibly have been wooed as a voting bloc by the Left and by Democrats had they recognized its potential as an ally.[35] Until the 1970s, leadership in the evangelical community actually drifted left, challenged by the Vietnam War and Civil Rights Movement. Today, moderate and liberal evangelicals like Jim Wallis, Tony Campolo and Ron Sider continue to draw numbers of white evangelicals to address economic justice and peacemaking.

The Christian Right today has strong alliances with conservative Catholic leaders and appeals to conservative Catholics, a dynamic clearly seen in the coalition operating at the U.N. Because of their opposition to abortion and the Equal Rights Amendment, conservative Catholics and evangelicals often found themselves working together during the 1970s and 1980s. In the 1990s, recognizing the need to broaden their support base, Christian Right leaders established more intentional initiatives to reach conservative Catholics. For instance, the Christian Coalition under Ralph Reed's leadership established strategic initiatives to expand ecumenically and sought to avoid the anti-Catholicism of earlier Christian Right periods.

Large numbers of Catholics share viewpoints with conservative evangelicals on abortion, school vouchers, school prayer, homosexuality and feminism. However, fewer Catholics agree with Christian Right stances on creationism, protecting the environment and economic issues. Catholics as a whole are markedly more liberal on the death penalty and war. The Vatican, for instance, opposed the Iraq war while most conservative evangelicals supported it. A study of Virginia politics indicated that Christian Right organizations that avoid such issues more easily attract conservative Catholics.[36] While Catholics may not be as willing to join well-known Christian Right organizations with largely evangelical bases, they are willing to form coalitions on particular issues on which they agree.

The goal of reaching African Americans is admittedly more challenging, although efforts are under way by strategists of the New Right. Many new Christian Right leaders such as Ralph Reed clearly perceive African-American evangelicals, who are conservative on social issues like abortion, school prayer and homosexuality, as a potential constituency for the right.[37] African-American evangelicals are more liberal on political and economic issues and oppose the Christian Right because of its historic opposition to civil rights and affirmative action and its position on economic and welfare issues.

Of equal importance and often overlooked is the Latino population, the U.S.'s fastest growing minority group. Here Christian Right prospects are brighter; they are much more open to voting Republican than are African Americans. The U.S. Census Bureau reported that in 2003 Hispanics made up over 13 per cent of the population, surpassing African Americans.[38] One analysis of Latino voting in ten states in the 2002 election found that about a third of Latinos voted for Republican Senate candidates and half for Republican governors.[39] In the 2004 elections, Democratic presidential candidate John Kerry only garnered 56 per cent of the Hispanic vote, down from Al Gore's 65 per cent showing in 2000. President Bush managed to win 44 per cent, exceeding the milestone set by the president's strategist Karl Rove. Republicans accomplished this feat by exploiting a largely unheralded fact: among minority groups, Hispanics rank with the most religious.[40] The Christian Right coalition at the U.N. has built major partnerships in Latin America, especially in Mexico.

Members of the Mormon Church or the Church of Jesus Christ of Latter Day Saints (LDS), as it is more formally known, resonate with the Christian Right's family values platform and lesser known but significant Christian Right NGOs are led and financed by Mormon supporters. The LDS Church is now the richest one in the United States per capita, with over $25 billion in estimated assets and $5 billion in estimated annual income.[41] It is growing so rapidly that sociologist Rodney Stark projects that, during the present century it will become the most important world religion to emerge since the rise of Islam in the sixth century.[42] With over 10 million members, the LDS Church is poised to surpass the Church of God in Christ and the Evangelical Lutheran Church in the U.S. and become the fifth-largest denomination behind Roman Catholics, Southern Baptists, United Methodists and National Baptists.[43] A generation ago, Mormons were concentrated primarily in the United States. Today, less than half live in the U.S. and Canada and over one-third live in Central and South America.[44]

This striking coalition building by Christian Right organizations both domestically and internationally is yet another example of a broader trend in American religion identified by religion scholar Robert Wuthnow in his ground-breaking book *The Restructuring of American Religion*.[45] In recent decades, denominational identity has grown more fluid. Americans now define their religious identity less by what denomination they belong to, and more by whether they are conservative or liberal on social issues. Conservative Presbyterians or Methodists are therefore more likely to find they have more in common with conservative Catholics and Mormons than with people from their own denominations. The Christian Right has been able to take advantage of this trend, and perhaps has contributed to amplifying it as well. While conservatives used to fight one another over doctrine, they are now uniting to oppose a common enemy: liberals. This book provides additional evidence that this trend has led not just to the diminishing importance of denominational barriers (between, say Methodists and Presbyterians) but of once firm divisions between religions as well. This new realignment in American religion has given impetus to Christian Right leaders to build alliances across ideological lines and internationally – including alliances with orthodox Jews and Muslims. Such coalition building continues despite the terrorist attacks of September 11, 2001 and despite the Bush Administration's War on Terrorism.

The Christian Right's Impact on U.S. Politics

The political strength of the Christian Right has waxed and waned since its larger public recognition with the election of Ronald Reagan in 1980, yet most would agree that it is now a long-lasting and powerful political and cultural influence. In 1994, the Christian Right reached new heights, helping the Republican Party to gain control of Congress. The Christian Right has been gradually taking over state Republican parties in the South and on the West Coast. In 1994, *Campaigns and Elections* reported that the Christian Right dominated the party in 18 states and had substantial influence in 13 others.[46] It helped elect President George W. Bush in 2000 and was the linchpin in the 2004 elections as well. With their friend Bush in the White House and his party dominating Congress, the Christian Right has arrived as never before. As Jean Hardisty put it in *Mobilizing Resentment*, the Christian Right is no longer just the tail on the dog, it is the tail wagging the dog.[47]

The Decline of a Progressive Religious Voice in American Politics

Progressive religious communities were the most organized religious voices in America until the 1970s.[48] Mainstream churches were at the height of their membership and African-American and white Protestants were consistently in the news for their views on civil rights, Vietnam and poverty.[49] Mainline church leaders through their offices in Washington and through the National Council of Churches were accustomed to representing the American Churches – and on paper at least, they represented 50 million Protestants. Conservative evangelicals, because they lacked a strong, unified public presence seemed less in the mainstream than they probably were. The Christian Right remained marginalized in American public life, despite a growing infrastructure that under President Reagan would garner greater media attention.[50]

The ascendancy of the Christian Right has attracted a lot of media attention in recent years, while the decline of the national voice of mainliners, liberal Catholics and African-American churches has rarely been explored in the media. Yet this decline is as important to understanding religion and politics in America and internationally. The problem is not that progressive and liberal beliefs are dying out; they are just not as well organized.[51] Several historical developments unwittingly contributed to making the Christian Right stronger than the Christian Left.

First, progressive religious leaders never managed to build strong parachurch organizations[52] that represented a wide constituency while being able to move quickly in a fast-paced media and advocacy climate. Absent are progressive versions of Family Research Councils and Concerned Women for America. Conservatives have cynically suggested that this is because progressive faith leaders have no existing or potential constituency, that they are liberal elites without a power base. Progressives often offer their own self-critique, saying that organizing progressive religious communities is impossible due to the independent spirit of progressives. Some have compared organizing progressive churches to "herding cats."[53] Neither of these theories seems to suffice. One need only to recall the strength of the civil rights and anti-apartheid movements, or examine the power of faith-based organizing networks like DART, PICO,[54] Gamaliel and Interfaith Worker Justice to get a sense of the potential power of well-organized progressive faith leaders.[55]

It's more likely that the current scattered progressive religious voice is the result of recent history: progressives have held onto traditional, outmoded national structures, theories of evangelism, and communication and organizing strategies. A brief look at the mainline churches can provide a case study of what has happened over the past few decades. Liberal mainline national justice and social welfare programs, including advocacy offices in Washington, DC, flourished from the 1920s until the 1960s. During this period, which followed the Scopes trial and public defeat of fundamentalism, mainline members of the National Council of Churches dominated national media. Yet American religious conservatives did not simply withdraw from the world: conservative evangelicals built institutions and communities that grew rapidly over the next decades and enabled them to organize across denominational lines and outside denominational structures.[56] Bible colleges, Christian bookstores, creation institutes and advocacy organizations nurtured conservative belief systems. Although in a few cases groups of fundamentalists started their own denominations, many conservatives remained members of mainline churches while joining conservative organizations like the Billy Graham Evangelistic Association.[57]

Progressive Christians never built such a large infrastructure, perhaps because they remained at home and confident with their national church leadership and felt little impetus to build alternative organizations to represent them.[58] By advocating progressive values largely through denominational structures, progressive religious activists failed to build an infrastructure that could sustain their vision. Denominations are not advocacy organizations but are communities of faith and worship that do advocacy as one part of their mission. Church denominations therefore are not able to be a direct counter-voice to the Christian Right because their constituency represents a diversity of viewpoints. In contrast, a parachurch advocacy organization represents people who joined it to support a particular issue or worldview.

In addition, denominational bureaucracies, once the cutting edge of corporate life, have changed far too little since the early part of the century.[59] One scholar put it rather bluntly: "… the mainline churches' attachment to old denominational forms – and bureaucratic ways of doing social ethics are often regarded by observers as outmoded, stubborn and even arrogant."[60] Yet another asserted that in an era of rapid change and declining church resources, "Reflection and evaluation must take place both in the national offices of the mainline denominations and among the leaders of local congregations."[61] Reform is drastically needed. Meanwhile, conservative parachurch organizations draw from the best of both worlds: the flexibility, focus and innovation of parachurch organizations, and access to the resources and memberships of established churches and denominations.[62]

During the 1960s while conservative white evangelicals experienced a strengthening in their institutions, mainline operations suffered serious setbacks. In the 1960s, mainstream church membership and financial resources went into a steady decline, a phenomenon we will explore below.[63] At the same time, as church leaders took stances on important issues of the day like civil rights and the anti-war movements in the 1960s and feminism and sexual liberation in the 1970s, churches became increasingly polarized.[64] Elite denominational leaders lost their ability to directly reach their constituency.[65] As memberships declined and liberal church activism was contested, denominational and the National Council of Churches in Christ (NCCC) office budgets were drastically cut. Meanwhile, the new Christian Right emerged, after years of quiet rebuilding, as a nationally unified public voice.

Members of the New Right joined forces with conservative evangelicals who sought to retake their denominations and turn them back to theological orthodoxy and away from liberal causes. Several corporate leaders saw value in such endeavors because they feared progressive church activism would have a negative impact on their businesses. For example, J. Howard Pew of Sun Oil Company established the Presbyterian Lay Committee in the late 1960s to oppose and reverse the liberal social justice policies of the Presbyterian Church.[66] The Institute on Religion and Democracy, established in the 1960s, funds conservative organizations that seek to undermine the progressive activism of the Presbyterian, Episcopalian and United Methodist Churches. This backlash further weakened the prophetic voice of the mainline churches.[67] Progressive religious leaders found their theological witness marginalized.

From the 1970s onward, New Right leaders continued to build strong partnerships with the Christian Right while progressives and the Democratic Party, largely subscribing to a secularist view of society, distanced themselves from religion.[68] Subscribing to over-zealous interpretations of the separation of church and state, many progressives sought to ban all religious expression from public life. This alienated many Americans, who were willing to tolerate such expressions as prayer at football games. It also deprived the Democratic Party of a rich resource of ideas and inspiration.

Liberal mainline leaders themselves came to accept the values underlying secularization theory. While explaining why Presbyterians showed little interest in church growth, a colleague once told me that he had been taught in seminary that religion had lost its once-prominent role in society and that church membership and clergy status would continue to decline. He simply accepted his church's decline as a trend he had to accept. Though anecdotal, the comment was revealing to me. Rather than reorganizing like conservatives to resist this marginalization, liberals simply gave up. How could someone resist what university scholars said was inevitable? Mainline church-based social justice advocates often down play their religious basis for activism rather than speaking to issues in biblical and theological terms. The lack of progressive religious messages in the public sphere has left a vacuum that conservative religious messaging has readily filled.

While the ground changed beneath them, the mainstream churches failed to adapt. Historic churches have in some cases casually abandoned the very tools that could help them get their message to the public. One of the strongest examples is that when the Federal Communications Commission (FCC) started requiring churches to buy radio airtime in the 1970s, many mainline institutions simply decided not to do so, while conservative evangelicals saw an opportunity for evangelism and fundraising.[69] When the media environment became more competitive, mainlines failed to develop strong communications and public relations units.[70] This was a far different strategy than that depicted by New Right architect Richard Viguerre, who compared television, radio and communication as tools comparable to what the printing press was for the Reformation.[71] Just as it expected new members would always find their way through birth or happenstance, so the mainline churches expected to remain at the center of public life with little effort. Once the predominant organizations of civil society, progressive religious NGOs sometimes struggle to find their unique role among the plethora of humanitarian and advocacy organizations that now exist.[72] On the international scene, church development and humanitarian agencies have been cut due to a lack of funds while conservative evangelical and Christian Right organizations continue to expand international ministries. This trend is enhanced by new funding streams which have been opened to them as a result of the Bush Administration's predilection for faith-based, especially conservative, evangelical ministries. Several Christian Right and conservative evangelical NGOs, including Concerned Women for America, a newcomer to international fieldwork, have received hefty grants from the federal government to run programs that curb sex trafficking. In contrast, progressive NGOs, which have worked on the issue for decades, are not being funded at a comparable level.[73]

Mainline Decline and its Impact on American Civil Society

The causes of the decline of progressive Christianity's public voice run far deeper than historical developments and conservative backlash. Today most major Protestant denominations struggle to maintain their own membership and are therefore besieged by financial shortfalls, budget cuts and shrinking national programs.[74] Once referred to as the mainline churches because they were the wealthiest, largest and most historic churches, many now jokingly call them the "old line" churches. Mainline memberships are aging and their congregations failing to attract new generations. A 1999 Presbyterian Panel survey found that the median age of the Presbyterian Church was 55.[75] Almost 40 per cent of Episcopalians are over 60. Grasping for some bit of good news, the 2003 *Yearbook of American and Canadian Churches* shared, "In the most recent data, the mainline churches have all reported a remarkably stable rate of decline, hovering around half of one percent."[76] Presumably the writer was celebrating the fact that the decline is at least not accelerating. As mainline denominations shrink, so do their great ecumenical institutions, the World Council of Churches and the National Council of Churches (NCC), both of which played major roles addressing the important social justice issues of the twentieth century. In 1999 the NCC cut its staff by one-third.

Theories on mainline decline are hotly debated. Complicating the picture is the dynamic that theories of decline are often strongly influenced by the theorists' own political and theological persuasions – whether conservative or liberal. In fact, the literature on this decline itself appears oddly captive to the wider American culture wars. On the one hand, theories by conservative leaning scholars and church leaders posit that mainliners are dying because they have lost their moral fortitude and exclusive claim to salvation. Conservative literature taunts liberal mainliners over denominational "decay" and expresses disdain for their lack of religious fervor as "weakness" and "nihilism."[77] In other words, they are dying because they are not conservative and therefore fail to offer a clear, distinctive moral outlook or worldview to their members.

On the other hand, liberal-leaning leaders and scholars have come to terms with their declining place in American society by claiming that it is due to wider societal factors beyond their control such as declining birthrates, secularization or the social revolutions of the 1960s.[78] But these arguments fail to explain why conservative churches are growing. Others prefer not to even discuss the problem, as to do so would acknowledge the "tyranny of aggregate data"[79] and would lead to denominations "los[ing] their hard-won theological bearings and tack[ing] precipitously to the right." [80] The underlying ideological battle not only prevents clarity when seeking the causes of mainline decline; it also prevents mainliners from taking their decline seriously and finding solutions.[81]

Sifting through the ideology is difficult, but one can point to a number of trends that undercut the ability of mainline Protestants to maintain their membership base and cultural influence. In the past Protestants tended to move up a social ladder of churches (the poor Baptist became a middle-class Methodist and then a wealthy Presbyterian or Episcopal) as they earned more money and attained a higher level of education.[82] This migration pattern in Protestant membership changed in the 1960s. Poor evangelicals who attained higher levels of education simultaneously stopped switching to more socially elite denominations. At the same time, mainline Protestants as a group experienced the prevailing 1960s crisis of authority at all levels. Ministers lost faith in the social and religious value of their calling and went into teaching and other professions. Young people went to college, found themselves attracted to Eastern and alternative religions, and never found conventional Christianity relevant again. Absorbed by the social issues of the late 1960s – poverty, civil rights, and Vietnam – mainline churches generally quit starting new churches. The crisis of mainline self-confidence continues to the present with devasting results and a growing legacy of missed opportunities. In fact, some wear this lack of self-confidence as a badge of honor. To be mainline means to participate in a culture of low expectations, particularly when it comes to outreach. Mainliners now define themselves in opposition to the organizing creativity of their conservative counterparts.

Protestants were less likely to remain in one denomination – in fact they are likely to change several times in the course of a lifetime. It seems likely that the mainline or historic churches, accustomed to maintaining their memberships through birth and restrained by slow-to-change bureaucracies, have for the most part failed to learn how to maintain and recruit members. Repulsed by the evangelical zeal of conservatives, they failed to find an alternative model of outreach. Ironically, as conservative churches experiment with new forms of worship, outreach and attractive programming, progressive churches resist such changes and hold firmly to tradition. As a result, conservative church memberships grow while churches with more progressive theologies languish. While many progressives try to blame this fact on the seductive simplicity of conservative theology, it is also true that mainline churches have, compared with conservatives, placed less emphasis on membership recruitment, particularly to younger generations.

The outcome of the struggle for progressive religious leaders to regain their voice will have a major, even profound, impact on the issues both progressives and conservatives care so much about. For decades progressives asserted that the way to curtail the extremes of religion was to insist on a high wall of separation between church and state – a wall so high it seemed often to suggest that religion had no role to play in civil society. Rather than view the Christian Right's near-hegemony over the moral voice of the U.S. as a failure to enforce the separation of church and state, activists and scholars might instead choose to draw more attention to a more diverse range of moral perspectives in politics. The last presidential elections in the United States (2004) caused a great deal of soul-searching among progressives. Newly established progressive organizations such as the Center for American Progress and Res Publica have worked to revitalize progressive faith communities and to learn from their values. Evangelical Jim Wallis' bestseller, *God's Politics: Why the Right Gets it Wrong and the Left Doesn't Get it*, further contributed to a growing awareness of the importance of religion in the public sphere.[83] Just as it took decades to galvanize the Christian Right, it will take a long-term commitment to rebuild the religious Left. And it will take a commitment to humanity to rebuild in a way that fosters greater unity in the U.S. rather than further polarization.

Reason 3: The Rise of Global Civil Society as a Political Opportunity for Conservatives

The Third Force

To set the context for the new activism of the Christian Right at the U.N., it is important to examine the exponential growth of global civil society after the end of the Cold War. Just as globalization has led economic markets to become increasingly integrated and interdependent, so civil society has also begun to organize itself in globally integrated coalitions and networks.

Many are optimistic that global civil society can be a "third force" that counterbalances the other global powers, that is, government and multinational corporations.[84] Others view global civil society as having a mixed impact on global democracy, in much the same way as government and the corporate world do. Because of the increasing impact of NGOs, a growing body of scholarship has sought to further define and measure the successes and challenges posed by NGO organizing. While global civil society's impact is still being assessed, its influence is significant: NGOs were the driving force behind the Ottawa Treaty banning landmines,[85] the International Criminal Court, the Jubilee 2000 debt relief campaign and the Fourth World Conference on Women.

The building-blocks of global civil society are nongovernmental organizations – what U.N. Secretary General Kofi Annan has poetically called the "conscience of humanity." Broadly defined, NGOs are neither governments nor corporations. By most definitions, they include humanitarian, human rights, advocacy and development organizations, as well as religious groups, cultural organizations, organized labor, hospitals, professional societies, social clubs, self-help groups and universities. They focus on a wide range of concerns affecting citizens: education, health, the environment, human rights, population, labor rights, aging, children, development, disarmament and peace are a few examples. Most often, NGOs work in coalitions around various issues compounding their power and access. Their work includes identifying and drawing attention to problems, proposing solutions and policy measures and pressuring governments to take up causes or change policies and practices. Humanitarian NGOs, because of their expertise and access to remote communities, often are able to advise and alert governments and the U.N. to crises they would have overlooked.

NGOs can obtain consultative status with the U.N., a status that entitles them to attend many U.N. meetings and to lobby governments. NGOs influence the U.N. by lobbying member states and working with U.N. staff both at headquarters and in the field as they implement international policies.

Political scientists and activists are asking important questions that relate to this book's exploration of Christian Right NGOs. Many NGOs claim to represent the voice of the people, yet are such claims authentic? What gives them the right to make such claims? To whom are NGOs accountable? Do NGOs always contribute to making societies more democratic? How should their involvement at the U.N. be structured? Should all NGOs be granted entry to such an important body? Are NGOs by definition peaceful? For example, could terrorist organizations be defined as neither states nor corporations, but clearly as groups attempting to make a political statement? Are NGOs by definition politically progressive? These key questions help inform this study of the Christian Right in global civil society.

Religious NGOs

Across from the United Nations compound in New York City stands a building that tells one part of the history of NGOs at the U.N.: the Church Center for the U.N. For decades the Church Center has been the hub of NGO organizing at the U.N. Today scores of NGOs, both secular and religious, have offices in that building and gather there for strategy meetings and educational events focused on influencing the U.N. The idea to construct such a building in 1969 came from the United Methodist Women's Missionary Association which envisioned that churches in particular, and civil society more broadly, would want to have a role in shaping the U.N. Today only about 9 per cent of NGOs registered with the U.N. are religious NGOs, yet clearly religion and religious NGOs have played a significant if sometimes quiet role at the U.N. and in international affairs.[86]

In the growing body of literature on NGOs, little has been written regarding the historic role religion has played in shaping global civil society.[87] Yet the literature does recognize that many of the first major transnational NGOs were religious organizations, for example, the Red Cross, the YMCA (Young Men's Christian Association) and the Salvation Army. In the 1800s the Quakers, Methodists, Presbyterians and Unitarians brought a deeply religious, evangelical and philanthropic spirit to the abolitionist movement and drew on a vast supply of religious zeal created by the Protestant revival movements of the early nineteenth century.[88] The world antislavery conferences held in London were among the first world gatherings of civil society leaders. The women's suffrage movement which began in the late nineteenth century also drew on religious revivalism, and had networks in Latin America, the Middle East and Asia. Missionary activity led to early campaigns against foot-binding and female circumcision in the late nineteenth and early twentieth century. In the last half of the twentieth century churches provided leadership and lent moral authority to the civil rights movement in the U.S. and the dismantling of apartheid in South Africa.

These early progressive NGO movements can trace their roots to a theological belief known as the social gospel. Social gospel followers believed that churches should respond to the social ills of the industrial era and sought to apply principles of social justice from the gospels. In the U.S. during the 1920s, social gospel proponents were challenged by religious leaders who embraced premillennialism, the belief that the world would continue to worsen before the return of Christ. Premillennialists believed that engagement in politics and social issues was futile and even contrary to the will of Christ. They called the churches to return to the "fundamentals" of the faith, and were therefore called "fundamentalists." They urged social gospel leaders to focus on saving souls rather than focusing on social concerns, and to reject modernist tendencies reflected in historical biblical criticism and embrace biblical literalism. During the 1920s the fundamentalists lost the public debate, but rather than retreat from the battle altogether as was once believed, they quietly built their own institutions and support systems. These laid the groundwork for the New Christian Right to emerge in the 1970s.

The confrontation of progressives and conservatives on the national and international scene over the past few decades is in some ways a new battle in an old war. Only this time, it is the progressive, social gospel-leaning religious leaders who seem to be slowly fading into the background. At the beginning of the twenty-first century, the number of Christian NGOs with a conservative view of the world is growing rapidly as the size and influence of more progressive-minded Christian NGOs, including the World Council of Churches, the World YMCA and YWCA, diminishes. This often-overlooked trend will have a major impact on global civil society just as its influence is heightened.

Conservative Religious NGOs: A Changing Landscape

While this book focuses on Christian Right activism at the U.N., that activism has evolved as part of a growing trend to be more active on international concerns among conservative religious NGOs. The impact of such NGOs is more complicated than many believe. The following overview illuminates the complex impact of conservative religious NGOs on international policies. Many would agree that conservative evangelical activism on issues such as sex trafficking and AIDS has mobilized greater resources and political will for addressing such problems. Yet it has also resulted in the imposition of restrictions on how the U.S. government can address such issues.

This can in part be explained by the fact that Christian Right NGOs like Concerned Women for America have a different focus than humanitarian-focused conservative evangelical organizations such as the International Justice Mission and Samaritan's Purse. While both operate out of conservative social perspectives, Christian Right NGO activism focuses on advancing solely conservative social policies, while humanitarian evangelical NGOs are active in direct service to victims and more concerned with addressing a broader problem.

In the late 1990s conservative evangelicals began to expand their once-narrow interest in international concerns beyond anti-communism and the Middle East. A new interest in religious freedom, raised in part by evangelical relationships with churches in Sudan, laid the foundation for involvement in addressing sex trafficking and the global AIDS pandemic. In addition, key religious and political leaders saw the potential impact of white evangelical involvement and sought to engage this specific constituency.

Religious Freedom

The issue of religious freedom was the first to attract conservative evangelicals to international organizing. In 1996, Nina Shea, the founder of Freedom House; well-known Jewish neoconservative Michael Horowitz of the Hudson Institute, and the National Association of Evangelicals (NAE) convened a conference of Christian leaders to combat persecution of Christians.[89] The effort culminated in 1997 when at the urging of conservative evangelicals, Senator Arlen Specter and Representative Frank Wolf, both Republicans, sponsored The Freedom from Religious Persecution Act, which established an office to monitor religious persecution and to sanction countries that systematically persecute any religious group. The Act became law in 1998. The cause captured the imagination of Christians across the country. Richard Cizik of the NAE concluded, "Human Rights is now no longer the prerogative of only the Left. Believe it or not, the Religious Right is making a distinctive contribution to American foreign policy."[90]

The Christian Right and Sex Trafficking

Feminist and children's rights NGOs and Catholic and Protestant churches mobilized to address the trafficking of women and children in the 1980s.[91] However, it was only when Christian conservatives joined progressive NGOs in lobbying the Bush Administration that the issue caught fire.[92]

Interestingly, conservatives and progressives worked together to advance helpful legislation to help victims of trafficking. For instance The Trafficking Victims Protection Act (TVPA) (2000) came about through the unified efforts of sworn political enemies like feminist icon Gloria Steinem and the born-again former Nixon official Chuck Colson, Concerned Women for America and the feminist National Organization for Women, the Family Research Council and Catholics for a Free Choice.

Despite such coalition building, the issues of sex trafficking and AIDS remain a battleground on which conservatives and liberals fight out their war over sexuality. Even among progressives, the issue of sex trafficking has always been a divisive affair. Some feminists view prostitution or sex work as a choice women should be allowed to make. They advocate that prostitution be legalized so that women can have the full range of labor rights and legal protections from traffickers and abusive johns. Other feminists view prostitution as a form of violence against women and therefore oppose attempts to legalize it.

The 2003 reauthorization of The Trafficking Victims Protection Act (HR 2620), supported by conservative Republican Congressman for New Jersey Chris Smith, restricts funds from groups that "advocate or support the legalization of prostitution," even with their own money. The bill was supported by abolitionist feminist organizations like Coalition Against Trafficking in Women and Equality Now, as well as conservative religious organizations. Other feminists call it the equivalent of the "global gag rule," which bars reproductive health agencies that advocate or perform abortions the right to receive U.S. government funding.

HIV/AIDS

In the winter of 2002, Senator Jesse Helms, the well-known staunch conservative Republican from North Carolina, attended an evangelical international conference on HIV/AIDS sponsored by Franklin Graham's (the son of the famous evangelist) humanitarian organization Samaritan's Purse. Helms, who once blocked HIV/AIDS funding stood before the audience of evangelicals and repented of his callousness towards the HIV/AIDS pandemic, saying contritely, "I am ashamed that I have done so little."[93] Days later he published a column in the *Washington Post* promising to secure $500 million to prevent mother-to-child transmission of the disease. An article in the *Post* that same day hailed the development as possibly having dramatically changed the political landscape on HIV/AIDS.

Just a few months later President Bush in his State of the Union speech shocked members of his own party by committing $15 billion over the next five years. In May 2003 Congress adopted The United States Leadership Against HIV/AIDS, Tuberculosis and Malaria Act of 2003. The result largely of years of lobbying from both progressive NGOs and conservative religious relief organizations, the Act was the first comprehensive articulation of U.S. policy toward the global HIV/AIDS epidemic. Holly Burkhalter, director of U.S. Policy and of the Health Action AIDS campaign at Physicians for Human Rights, recognized the valuable contribution of conservative religious NGOs:

> Thanks to recent activism by conservative political and religious groups, AIDS has finally started to gain foreign policy attention commensurate with its substantive importance. Prodded by its conservative evangelical base, the Bush Administration has pushed AIDS to the forefront of its international agenda, backing record increases in U.S. assistance for AIDS treatment abroad and beginning to address issues such as sex trafficking and the dangers of HIV transmission from unsafe injections and blood transfusions.[94]

Christian conservative activism also came with a price.

Christian Right and social conservatives recognized this as both a threat and an opportunity. They sought to impose the "Mexico City" global gag rule on all the new HIV/AIDS programs.[95] The controversial global gag rule prevents foreign NGOs that receive U.S. government money from accepting private funds for abortion-related activities. In the words of Austin Ruse, "pro-family" groups would make sure "proabortion groups and abortion providers do not get any of this money. Not even a nickel."[96] In the end, the Bush Administration was apparently unable to find ways of imposing this ideological litmus test without disqualifying groups it needed in order to accomplish its objectives. It also did not want abortion politics to get in the way of the bill. The global gag rule was not imposed.

Not to be deterred, the Christian Right denounced the AIDS bill and released a statement of demands through Republican Congressman Joseph Pitts for Pennsylvania, the chair of the House Pro-Life Caucus. They were able to achieve nearly every one of these policy objectives. One of their first priorities was making abstinence a priority in U.S.-funded HIV/AIDS prevention programs. The Christian Right made its case by drawing on Uganda's success in lowering HIV/AIDS prevalence rates during the 1990s after adopting the "ABC approach": "*Abstinence*," "*Be* faithful" and "use Condoms." The teaching of abstinence had a small though not major effect on Uganda's declining HIV/AIDS prevalence rates. Social and religious conservatives found and created a body of "scientific" research that "proved" abstinence was the driving factor. The House of Representatives adopted the Pitts amendment, which reserved at least one-third of prevention funds for "abstinence-until-marriage" programs.

Despite their broad ideological differences, liberal and conservative groups have been able to make headway on issues of common concern as well as learn from one another. The image of Jesse Helms standing beside rock star Bono (of U2) on the issue of HIV/AIDS and Gloria Steinem standing with Chuck Colson to address sex trafficking is for some, a picture of heaven, for others, the picture of hell. But to most, it is the picture of a democracy at work.

2

The Christian Right's Challenge to Global Democracy

IN ITS COVERAGE OF THE massive global protests against the Iraq War in February 2003, the *New York Times* declared, "there are two new superpowers in the world, the United States, and global public opinion."[1] The increasing capacity of citizens to organize mass global movements to advance common objectives around pressing world issues is fast becoming one of the hallmarks of globalization and the post-Cold War era. Recognizing the power of such movements, a panel on United Nations reform recently observed "Nowadays, non-State actors are often prime movers – as with issues of gender, climate change, debt, landmines and AIDS."[2]

The power of such movements did not escape the notice of the New Right. Describing to its conservative constituency its rationale for seeking consultative status at the U.N., the Heritage Foundation, one of the largest American New Right think tanks and one that works closely with Christian Right NGOs, explained, "Our presence will break the 'Liberals Only' roster of present NGOs – and as the skunk at the U.N. Party, we will be in a much stronger position to influence media coverage and public perception."[3] Conservative organizations like Heritage continue to register as NGOs with consultative status at the U.N. Although Christian Right and other likeminded conservative organizations make up a minority of NGOs, and clearly view themselves as outsiders, they quickly learned the system and have a great deal of influence on the biggest player of all at the U.N.: the United States.

This chapter argues that Christian Right NGOs challenge global democracy on several levels. The first two levels are perhaps more obvious than the last. First, Christian Right NGOs often cast suspicion on the legitimacy of global civil society itself by calling into question the activities of progressives. Second, they have challenged the progressive hegemony of NGOs at U.N. conferences. For instance, at U.N. conferences on women, they have made it increasingly difficult for NGOs to appear to speak with a unified voice, slightly undermining the claims and authority of the global women's movement.

Finally, and more complex, they challenge our very definition of global civil society. Christian Right NGO views on homosexuality, abortion and religion are clearly shared by a large percentage of global civil society. These NGOs claim they are defending the developing world from a secular, liberal, and feminist agenda that will tear families and nations apart. The fact that they have been able to forge international and interfaith alliances adds some weight to their claim to represent millions, even if those alliances are nascent and unstable. Activists and scholars who shape and define global democracy cannot underestimate the numbers throughout the world who agree with the conservative agenda, and they will have to take these constituencies and views seriously.

While the Christian Right challenges how we think of global democracy, their lobbying strategies are changing as well. During the 1990s, the Christian Right at the U.N. focused on symbolic protests and blocking progressive agendas. Today, it also advances its own proactive agenda through the U.N. General Assembly. Each new success has gradually moved Christian Right organizations to a higher level of engagement and investment in the U.N. as an institution. The progression of its involvement can be seen by comparing its strategies at three official U.N. meetings: Beijing+5 (2000), the Special Session on Children (2002) and the International Year of the Family+10 (2004). While the Christian Right has influenced other U.N. meetings (some of which are discussed in Chapter 3), each of these meetings provides a convenient benchmark of a different level in Christian Right effectiveness. Furthermore, the Christian Right's involvement in efforts to undermine the International Criminal Court and delegitimize progressive NGOs illustrates how the Christian Right is able to accomplish its ends because it strategically allies its efforts with those of other sectors of the New Right, including neoconservatives. This development is not without a paradox: even as the Christian Right seeks to alter the U.N. system, it is altered by the system itself. We may witness the flowering of a more responsive and effective global democracy from the seeds of this paradox.

Stage 1: Symbolic Protest (2000–01) – Arising to Fight for Faith and Family at Beijing+5

In the months leading up to the five-year review of the Beijing Platform for Action slated for June 2000, Austin Ruse, director of the Catholic Family and Human Rights Institute (C-FAM) sent out a call to action to Christian Right allies. In his rallying cry, Ruse summoned hundreds of "pro-family and pro-life advocates" to come to the U.N. to fight against "the Beijing Platform for Action … one of the most radical and dangerous documents you can imagine." His call took on biblical proportions as Ruse promised his people: "You will work alongside Catholics, Evangelicals, Jews, Muslims and Mormons … We are the children of Abraham arising to fight for faith and family."[4] Ruse rallied 300 activists, a significant presence in this forum of 3,000 NGO advocates dominated by progressive organizers.[5]

The change in civil society at this U.N. meeting was visible and unsettling for many women activists. A group of long-bearded friars wearing grey robes and carrying rosaries openly prayed in meeting rooms and hallways, and even surrounded key feminist leaders to "pray for their souls." Their prayer activity also slowed feminist leaders as they tried to move from one meeting to the next and this unnerved many of them. Christian Right activists attended NGO educational or side events to insert their perspectives. In at least one instance, they arranged themselves in the shape of a cross in one of the meeting rooms. Coming into the caucus designed by women's movement leaders to focus on different aspects of the Beijing Platform for Action, they overwhelmed the meetings and managed to stymie the discussion. The discussion in the reproductive health caucus in particular bogged down and consequently never reached a consensus.[6]

Besides these symbolic protests, activists explored the possibility of a "pro-family" bloc of nations. Austin Ruse (C-FAM) had strategically observed that since the U.N. member states usually reached agreements by seeking consensus (rather than voting), a voting bloc of ten countries could stall the negotiating process at most U.N. meetings. He announced this strategy at a gathering of Christian Right leaders: "I propose that we establish a permanent U.N. pro-family bloc of twelve states. And upon these we lavish all of our attention."[7]

Ruse observed to colleagues that "conservative countries often also feel pressured by other governments to go along with the language proposed by the governments of Europe and North America."[8] He reasoned that he did not actually have to convince governments to embrace conservative positions; rather, all he had to do was to ask conservative governments not to abandon their conservative inclinations when they attended U.N. meetings. He envisioned that a small group of activists could have a dramatic impact on proceedings with little effort. At Beijing+5, the nucleus of the bloc that progressives enjoyed calling the "unholy alliance" included the Holy See as well as the "rogue states" of Sudan, Iran, Syria and Libya. It was certainly a coalition of strange bedfellows, especially given the fact that conservative evangelicals in the U.S. were on record as condemning the Islamic regime in Khartoum for persecuting Christians in southern Sudan as well as objecting to the U.N. allowing Sudan to hold a seat on the U.N. Commission on Human Rights.[9]

During Bejing+5, the Christian Right failed to get some key Catholic countries on board, and most Latin American governments held firm in their commitments to women's rights. Still, Ruse's bloc did manage to slow negotiations at the Beijing+5 meeting, holding firm against the pressure of most of the other member states, even the U.S. (then under the Clinton Administration). Government debates bogged down over issues of abortion and homosexuality, preventing discussion and more advanced government commitments to address other issues affecting the world's women like violence and poverty. Governments nearly failed to reach a consensus on a final outcome document, arriving at an agreement in the wee hours of the morning a day after the session should have ended. While they once regularly expected to make advances at these conferences, progressive NGOs now found themselves not only blocked at every turn, but also fighting to hold their ground. The swiftness of this reverse stunned many.[10]

Women's rights activists at the Beijing Conference in 1995 had sung: "We're going to keep on moving forward ... Never turning back, never turning back."[11] Five years later, feminist activists found it hard to move forward, and feared the clock might even be turned back. Wedded to the consensus-building process used both by the U.N. and by feminist leadership models, some feminist leaders struggled over their next move: should they try to include the new activists, or throw them out of the caucuses? Some leaders, in an effort to honor diversity, tried inclusion and found their caucuses paralyzed with nonstop debate and an inability to reach common ground. Other women's movement leaders held the caucuses in undisclosed locations to prevent the outsiders from attending.[12]

Unified by their opposition to a common enemy and by their shared outsider status, Christian Right leaders relentlessly pursued their goals. Embracing his outsider status, Austin Ruse told supporters why they should be proud of what they had done: "We are what they are calling the unholy alliance. Here's my message – you can beat them too. You can build your own coalitions, you can wreck their consensus, we are all so far behind that all you have to do to make the place better is to show up, and you must show up because if you don't stop them, no one else will."[13] Reflecting on the changed political climate since 2000, Charlotte Bunch, the executive director of the Center for Women's Global Leadership, one of the leading NGOs in the global women's movement, put it this way: "they've succeeded in halting the progress. We are now defending past gains rather than going forward with what is next."[14]

Progressive NGOs, while they enjoyed some debate and dissent, for the most part had shared a similar worldview. The global women's movement had succeeded in developing a common agenda – across lines of region and culture – and advancing it by lobbing U.N. member states.[15] Now there was a coalition of NGOs that disagreed with fundamental concepts that defined the global women's movement agenda, in particular gender equality, women's rights and reproductive rights. While this new NGO coalition was still a minority, they were able to exert considerable pressure by building a persistent voting bloc that could disrupt efforts to build consensus during U.N. negotiations. By encouraging and giving moral and technical support to a number of socially conservative member states, this new group of NGOs was able to stall efforts to introduce new reproductive and sexual rights in particular. Even those issues that were less controversial to conservatives, such as poverty and violence against women, were pushed aside by the polarizations defined by this new culture war.[16]

Stage 2: Insiders (2001–Present) – The "New Sheriff in Town" Comes to the Commission on the Status of Women

With only a minority of NGOs and governments of Beijing+5, the Christian Right could stall the work of others, but not advance its own agenda. What's more, its "strange bedfellows" coalition of governments pulled less weight than governments of the industrialized world which generally supported (at least on the surface) many of the objectives of the global women's movement. When George W. Bush became president of the United States in 2001, the Christian Right's influence dramatically increased in Washington and at the U.N. Now the Christian Right had influence over the leading player at the U.N. – and it was anxious to flex its muscle.

The Bush Administration, responding quickly to Christian Right lobbying, appointed social conservatives to key embassy positions. In 2001 Ellen Sauerbrey was appointed U.S. Ambassador to the U.N. Commission on the Status of Women (CSW) and for family concerns. She also served as a U.S. Ambassador to the U.N. Human Rights Commission in Geneva. Sauerbrey, a two-time Republican candidate for governor of Maryland who chaired the Maryland presidential campaign of President George W. Bush,[17] dedicated her work to the "pro-family" cause. She traveled widely seeking to build strong alliances, particularly in Latin America. She attended the 2004 World Congress of Families and made trips to Honduras, Nicaragua and Costa Rica. Her speeches echoed the rhetoric of Christian Right NGOs when she called for socially conservative governments to resist pressure from socially liberal ones. Speaking to Latin American leaders she remarked:

> Too often, member states at the U.N. come under extreme pressure to join consensus with their region, which means taking positions on social issues that are in direct conflict with the policies of their government and even their national constitutions. Countries that are about marriage, parenthood and the family should resist such pressure. They should band together when issues of importance to the family are debated at the U.N.[18]

The U.N. monitors the implementation of the Beijing Conference through five-year reviews and through the U.N. Commission on the Status of Women, which meets annually in March. With the Bush Administration under the Christian Right's influence, subsequent CSW meetings were heavily affected by the polarity of the American culture wars. Christian Right NGOs played a key role in drawing the U.S. into the "pro-family" bloc of nations originally forged by the Holy See. By sponsoring events and nurturing relationships with government delegates, they encouraged this conservative bloc to maintain a stronger conservative stance and not bend to pressure from more progressive U.N. member states.[19]

The 2003 CSW, which was to focus on violence against women, underscored how the culture war could engulf and disrupt these annual forums. The CSW's emphasis on the theme of violence against women was critical to the global women's movement because the international community did not identify violence against women as a major issue until the 1995 Beijing Conference. The Beijing Platform for Action lays out a number of forms of widespread violence and strategies to address this pervasive problem. Feminists hoped that the 2003 CSW would help draw more attention to this concern. Controversy erupted however when feminists attempted to draw attention to religiously motivated violence against women. They cited the Taliban in Afghanistan, honor killings in Pakistan, and religious justifications for domestic violence as some of the examples of religiously sanctioned violence.

Conservatives viewed the proposed language as religion bashing – yet another confirmation of feminism's animosity toward religion. They called for governments to oppose the amendment. Feminist NGOs that had fought for the rights of women during wartime also wanted to insert language that echoed the newly established International Criminal Court Statute, a statute vehemently opposed by the Bush Administration. The CSW document therefore called for the prosecution of those "responsible for violence against women committed in situations of armed conflict and post-conflict situations, such as murder, rape, including systematic rape, sexual slavery and forced pregnancy."[20] In calling attention to "forced pregnancy," feminists were trying to address situations like the civil war in former Yugoslavia in which Serbs forcibly impregnated Croat women prisoners – an act designed to destroy another race. Conservatives viewed efforts to hold the rapists accountable as a stealth effort to make abortion a human right. Explaining how she thought such a phrase might be misused, a Mormon NGO alleged: "To some, a forced pregnancy is any pregnancy wanted or unwanted, which a woman was 'forced to continue' because of the unavailability or illegality of abortion. By legitimizing the term 'forced pregnancy,' feminists hope to establish abortion as a human right for women."[21] Ultimately, the CSW was unable to adopt any agreed conclusions on the theme of violence against women. It was a major diplomatic failure – the first CSW in recent memory to end with no governmental agreement.[22]

Dismayed that governments failed to reach consensus, the European Women's Lobby (EWL – a coalition of 3,000 women's organizations in Europe) called upon U.N. Secretary General Kofi Annan to do something to stop what they perceived as a religious backlash against women's human rights. In their view, activists were undermining women's rights in the name of religion: "It is our view that women's human rights have been undermined by representatives of governments with a fundamentalist agenda under the guise of upholding 'cultural and religious values.'"[23] The EWL warned that the groundbreaking decisions of the 1990s (Beijing and Cairo) "are now being challenged by powerful well funded coalitions made up of government representatives with traditional beliefs and fundamentalist religious leaders."[24]

Option I: Compromise Helps Both Sides (2003)

If the 2003 CSW demonstrated the paralysis caused by the polarization of the culture wars, the 2004 CSW may represent the potential creative synergy that could develop under adept facilitation. The 2004 CSW focused on two issues: the role of men and boys in achieving gender equality, and women's role in conflict prevention and peace building. Thanks to strong leadership on the part of the Canadian Chair of the proceedings, the CSW reached agreement despite conflict between feminists and the Christian Right over the topic of men and boys. Mindful of the previous year's impasse, government delegates and NGOs strove to find consensus and to avoid another breakdown in negotiations.[25]

The definition of fatherhood is another politically loaded concept in the U.S. culture wars.[26] In the view of social conservatives in the U.S., feminism and other modern developments have undermined men's roles in the family[27] and have initiated several initiatives that emphasize fatherhood. Promise Keepers, one of the best known of these, made a name for itself when one of its leaders called men to get on their knees and apologize to their wives for not exercising lordship over the family. Much of the movement is perceived by progressives as trying to reassert a superior position for the father as the head of the family, with authority over women and children. On their part, conservatives assert that feminism has turned women against men and minimized the importance of fathers in the upbringing of children.[28]

Christian Right NGOs working through the U.S. sought to insert language emphasizing the importance of men's roles as fathers. Feminists believed this was an effort to narrow the definition of family (excluding single-parent, extended families as well as lesbian-headed families) as well as to assert a dominant role for fathers. Christian Right NGOs sought to correct what they viewed as feminist efforts to usurp or denigrate the roles of fathers, devalue marriage and encourage single-parent households.

Conference flyers circulated by Mormon NGOs emphasized the biological differences between "females" and "males," promoted the benefits of marriage, and touted research findings about the need for a father in the home.[29] Concerned Women for America hosted a briefing called "The Daddy Difference: What a Father Means in a Child's Life."[30] In an article on their website, CWA reported:

> NGO representatives reacted harshly to a positive portrayal of fatherhood. At a U.S. briefing to NGOs, one exclaimed to Ambassador Ellen Sauerbrey that if the document mentions fathers, it should address fathers who abuse children, because "it's fathers who are raping girls." This met with applause from other NGOs. Ambassador Sauerbrey responded that "responsibility" goes with everything, including fatherhood.[31]

In the end, the CSW actually reached consensus around fatherhood that conceded ground to both sides. The topic of fathers was introduced and progressive concerns about honoring "many forms of family" and equal roles of men and women were also protected. The consensus around fatherhood provides a small but all-too-infrequent glimmer of possibility that arises in this increasingly global culture war. For Parvina Nadjibulla, who represents the progressive leaning United Methodist Church at the U.N., the Christian Right's efforts to put fatherhood on the agenda actually opened up an interesting debate. In Nadjibulla's view, the polarization between feminists and the Christian Right drain time and energy from "the real issues of the day." In her view, the political polarization often prevented both sides from finding real solutions. At its best, said Nadjibulla, like all conflict and debate, a contentious presence could actually force people to think more carefully and strategically: "The movement was comfortable using lots of language and not having to justify it. Now we have to think twice about it and be more accurate. The positive thing is we have to have clear strategies and clear points to make."[32]

For Nadjibulla, who later became a leader on the Beijing+10 strategy committee, the debate has wider ramifications for the women's movement:

> For the longest time we had the luxury of assuming that this perspective was the only perspective out there. What the religious right reminds us of is that there are people out there who have a different perspective and we need to constructively engage with that perspective. We especially need to connect in a way that engages with those people on the ground. If the religious right articulates it in a more articulate way for them then we have a problem.[33]

While the CSW debate provided an important moment of compromise, and even self-reflection, the more common result of debate has been a stand-off between the two sides.

Option II: A Stand-Off at Beijing+10 Leads to the Women's Movement Treading Water

At the 2003 and 2004 CSW, the leaders of the global women's movement deliberated over what direction the movement should take as the tenth anniversary of the Beijing Conference approached. Most U.N. conference agreements are reviewed every five years. The tenth-year anniversary would open up another opportunity to put new issues on the agenda and draw attention to unfulfilled commitments. Many NGOs were even hoping for another U.N. world conference since such meetings are larger and more influential.[34]

Yet the political climate had clearly changed. One statement by movement leaders said that a fifth World Conference on Women should be held, but the timing should be carefully considered in light of several factors, including "the experience of other review processes such as Cairo+10 [on reproductive health], and the political climate in general."[35] Any reviews in 2005, it said, "should be focused on implementation without any text negotiations." Those who questioned the viability of another world conference observed "the geo-political

climate and backlash that poses a danger of losing ground."[36] Getting
more explicit, a representative of the government of Brazil said "in light
of explicit North American unilateralism and the clear advancement of
various forms of fundamentalism, the possibility of a U.N. Women's
Conference in 2005 could mean great risk of setbacks ... particularly
in the area of sexual and reproductive rights."[37]

Women's rights advocates working with sympathetic government
delegates from the European Union and Latin America tested the
political climate in 2004 by asking the CSW to reaffirm the principles of
the 1995 Beijing Platform for Action. Though it had signed the Beijing
Platform for Action, the U.S., operating under the new directives of the
Bush Administration, opposed the resolution. The U.S. called for a vote
on the issue – a procedural move that is ordinarily avoided to safeguard
diplomatic relations and preserve the preference for consensus building.
The European Union and other voting blocs lobbied hard to prevent
the U.S. and its allies from voting against the measure, asking them
merely to abstain – a measure that often allows a government to voice
dissent diplomatically. As women's movement NGO representatives
waited for the vote to come up on the boards, many felt it was a
moment of truth. Would the international community stand by its
Beijing commitment to the world's women, even though the world's
superpower had broken ranks? If not, how many countries would
break away from the consensus? When the votes were posted on the
U.N. voting board, only one country had voted against it: the United
States. NGO representatives breathed a sigh of relief.[38]

The vote revealed both strength and a weakness in the global
women's movement. The global consensus that emerged from the U.N.
conferences on women had strong support from a wide range of U.N.
member states: it was not dependent on the world's superpower or any
other regional bloc alone. In fact, the more the U.S. acted unilaterally
in this international forum and others (such as pressuring members of
the Security Council to support the Iraq invasion), the more influence
it lost. The U.S. was unable to galvanize even those member states that
had loosely cooperated around a pro-family agenda at the U.N., in
part because of the Iraq War and also its refusal to support economic
proposals of the G-77 voting bloc of developing countries. Despite such
reassurance, the fact remained that the U.N.'s most powerful member
state, influenced by the Christian Right, was willing to pull out all the

stops to oppose the global women's movement's agenda and even prior U.N. agreements. Although the U.S. stood alone on this round, they might find allies in the future.

Lead NGOs in the global women's movement therefore initiated a series of global consultations during the CSW and via the Internet to reach consensus as to what the movement's next steps should be.[39] A committee of U.N. member states aided by the U.N. secretariat determines the goals and procedural rules for each review. NGOs often influence this process, since it sets the parameters for what can be accomplished and even establishes the rules for NGO participation and input. The consultations would inform how the Beijing+10 session would be structured, as well as reexamine some of the assumptions for the entire movement.

While some NGOs enthusiastically promoted the idea of a fifth world conference on women which would break new ground, lead movement strategists realized that opening the Platform for Action up for debate might provide a window of opportunity for conservative forces to reverse prior gains. As the ten-year anniversary of Beijing approached, leaders of the movement advocated with diplomats and U.N. staff that Beijing+10 focus on simply reviewing how governments had implemented the Beijing Platform for Action rather than on drafting new agreements. The only negotiable document would be a brief, general political declaration that would simply affirm the Beijing Platform for Action. Rather than push the international community into new territory, the global women's movement realized it would struggle just to hold its ground. The decision reflected the fragile political climate caused by the presence of new conservative players on the U.N. scene.[40]

At Beijing+10, feminists hoped that the draft declaration would quickly be adopted, leaving time for more substantive talks on advancing women's economic equality and political participation, and reducing violence against women.[41] The U.S. would accept the declaration only if U.N. member states added wording clarifying that the declaration created neither any "new international human right" nor "the right to abortion."[42] U.N. conferences and conventions remain neutral on the legality of abortion. Yet inserting this phrase would have compromised that neutrality, pushing international consensus more in the direction of making abortion illegal. At the last hour, the

U.S. dropped its insistence on adding this phrase and the declaration was adopted unanimously. The leader of the U.S. delegation, Ellen Sauerbrey, said that the debate over the proposed amendment had been helpful in assuring the U.S. delegation that the Beijing documents do not create new human rights and that the terms "reproductive health services" and "reproductive rights" do not include abortion. In her explanation of the U.S. position, Sauerbrey commented, "we have heard no delegation disagree with our interpretation ... This week we heard an international consensus on this point, which is useful to clarifying the intent and purpose of Beijing."[43]

A United Nations press release diplomatically described the conference thus: "A Declaration reaffirming the commitments made ten years ago in Beijing and calling for further action from governments was adopted at the end of the first week. This was the most significant outcome of the meeting ... ."[44] In other words, the governments had held to their old commitments, but they made no specific commitments for the future.

While women's rights activists were appalled by the power of the U.S. to diminish the proceedings, Dr. Farooq Hassan, a former Pakistani ambassador who has worked closely with the Christian Right coalition over the years, found the U.S. position and strategy to be embarrassingly weak. In his opinion, the U.S. might have mounted more of an obstacle. Instead, said Dr. Hassan, the U.S. has so little respect for the U.N. they don't care to put an enormous amount of energy into such reviews. U.S. delegates did not even bother to expend political capital lobbying other "pro-family" governments. Christian Right organizing was also weak, he complained. Pro-family NGOs had not sent trained lawyers who would know how to work the system better. "They were nice people, but amateurs," he said in frustration of the pro-family NGO representatives and the U.S. delegation.[45]

It should also be noted that the success of such meetings is not merely determined by the political outcome. More than 2,600 NGO representatives from all regions of the world attended the meeting to share strategies and innovative projects among themselves and with the 1,800 government delegates from 165 member states that gathered. Christian Right organizing, while it has the potential to slow or delay progress, has a long way to go before it comes close to mustering that sort of political capital.

Feminist Strategy on Addressing the Christian Right: What's Lacking

In the years between Beijing+5 and Beijing+10, the rise of fundamentalism became one of the top concerns of the global women's movement. A feminist strategy paper drafted under the leadership of the Center for Women's Global Leadership in 2003 and 2004 listed four obstacles to "moving forward" with the Beijing Platform for Action: neoliberal globalization, fundamentalisms/extremism, militarism/imperialism and patriarchy.[46] For each obstacle, an alternative vision was recommended. With regards to fundamentalism, the creation of "open secular and spiritual spaces" was recommended as a framework for strategic proposals. It was notable that for an alternative vision, the movement recommended open spiritual spaces in addition to secular ones. Often, liberals and feminists have advocated only strengthening secularization as an antidote to religious conservatism rather than trying to engage religious communities as well as working with religious progressives. Though constantly noted as a major obstacle, surprisingly little of the document proposed strategies for countering fundamentalism, as compared to the other three roadblocks. In fact, it was a glaring oversight. A report of discussions held at the 2004 CSW, written by three leading NGOs in the movement listed 18 goals and 49 strategies, but not one of these proposed ways to address fundamentalism.[47]

The inability of women's leaders to take even basic steps to address fundamentalism is a key weakness in the global women's movement that must be addressed. While many religious women have provided leadership to the U.S. feminist movement, there has often been a suspicion of religion on the part of many feminist leaders.[48] The secularism of the feminist movement is slowly being challenged however. Charlotte Bunch, widely respected for her role in providing strategic leadership for the global women's movement, noted in an interview: "the secular women's movement needs to work more closely with people who identify [themselves] as Christian and with other faiths, so the Christian Right doesn't have the ability to label us as anti-religious."[49] Charlotte Bunch's recommendation suggests that feminist leaders will have to thoroughly reevaluate the implicit, and sometimes explicit, secularism of the movement if they are serious about maximizing its ability to improve women's lives whether they are secular or religious.

Women's rights NGOs have been more willing to engage with cultural and religious issues surrounding Islam than those confronting Christianity. Because progressives view Islam as a religion of the oppressed, they seem more comfortable partnering with Muslim women activists than with Christian activists. Still, challenges remain in this area as well. In a recent article in a publication by AWID (Association of Women in Development), a leading women's rights and development NGO, Eman Ahmed explored the relationship between the feminist movement and religion in Pakistan. In this rare article exploring religion and women's rights, Ahmed observed, "Between the maulvis' [mullahs'] retrogressive and patriarchal brand of Islam and the women's movements' reluctance to enter into a religious discourse, Pakistani women keen on engaging with religion in a progressive manner are alienated." This is counterproductive she suggested, especially in an era in which post 9/11 Islam bashing has in some cases radicalized the Pakistani middle and upper classes. Ahmed makes a critical observation for the women's movement: "Just as the secular ideology of the women's movement is not an attack on religion, a willingness to work within a religious framework does not undermine the principles of women's human rights." She advocated that "to be inclusive and expansive, human rights must work with religion," and specifically that feminists "increase our efforts to support and work with liberal, female Islamic theologians who are feminist."[50] This greater willingness to engage with Islam might broaden the feminist movement's understanding of the importance and potential of religious communities working for cultural, social and legal changes that affect women's rights.

Option III: Political Compromise and Christian Right Activism at the U.N. Special Session on Children

The inauguration of George W. Bush in January 2001 suddenly bolstered the influence of social conservatives at the U.N. Special Session on Children and confirmed the Christian Right's new influence in NGO forums. Even before his inauguration, the preparatory committee ("PrepCom") newsletter reported: "Christian conservatives appear to be making a determined attempt to infiltrate and disrupt key NGO caucus meetings in the hope of imposing their own agenda."[51] Moreover, this particular reporter was baffled by the apparent anomaly of some Muslim and Christian conservative NGOs working closely together. I had also witnessed well-trained Mormon and Muslim youth take over the "youth caucus" at one of the PrepComs and deliver a conservative statement to U.N. member states representing the world's youth. In retrospect, these anomalies could be explained by a broader range of new alliances that were forming. But at the same time these seemed like a series of unusual events. Because we did not see the larger infrastructure behind these events, we were taken by complete surprise by the hard line taken by the U.S. against child rights at the Special Session. As one NGO newsletter reported: "Many had expected the Bush Administration to be lukewarm towards international commitments, but no one expected to hear it so soon, and delivered with such force."[52]

Clearly the 2001 U.N. Special Session on Children would mark a major turning point for the Christian Right, which had made its debut at Beijing in 2000. As the Bush Administration stepped into office Austin Ruse celebrated: "There's a New Sheriff in Town." The Bush Administration rushed to appoint Christian Right leaders to U.S. delegations to the preparatory meetings for the upcoming U.N. Special Session on Children. According to Washington insiders, the White House was directing the State Department's work for the Special Session rather than letting the State Department take the lead. Christian Right leaders appointed to the U.S. delegation during the preparatory meeting for the Special Session included William Saunders of the Family Research Council, Bob Flores of the National Law Center for Children and Families, and Paul Bonicelli, executive director of the National Center for Home Education. Saunders and Bonicelli were joined by Janice Crouse of Concerned Women for America and John Klink, an experienced U.N. negotiator who once worked for the Holy See. The president of Save the Children Federation was the only nongovernmental representative from a moderate NGO.[53]

The goal of the U.N. Special Session on Children was to review progress made on the Plan of Action of the World Summit for Children adopted in 1990 and to focus international attention on emerging issues, including the sexual exploitation and sale of children, the use of child soldiers, and the devastating impact of the AIDS pandemic on youth and children. With final preparatory meetings coming almost immediately after Bush's inauguration, no one suspected that the

Administration would move so fast to appoint lead representatives and invest so much in a U.N. meeting on social issues. The meeting quickly became politicized along the lines of the U.S. culture wars, drawing media attention and energy from the emerging issues governments had expressed interest in addressing.[54] The negotiations during the preparatory meetings for the Special Session were grueling. By the last PrepCom, only 85 per cent of the document had achieved consensus, leaving leaders worried that the Special Session itself would remain mired in debate rather than allowing for a celebration of international consensus. Indeed, when the final Special Session took place in June 2001, the polarized negotiating sessions had to be closed to NGO observers – a rare action for a U.N. meeting on social issues.[55]

Several issues polarized the debate and the U.S. stood at the center of each.[56] The U.S. opposed efforts to make the U.N. Convention on the Rights of the Child (Child Rights treaty) the overarching framework for the outcome document of the Special Session. The U.S. has never ratified the Child Rights treaty, which is the most ratified human rights treaty in history (only one other government – Somalia – has not ratified it). It asserted that it could therefore not endorse an Outcome Document that required U.S. ratification. In addition, Christian Right leaders opposed child rights, alleging that they threatened parental rights. The Christian Right also opposed ratification of the treaty because it remains suspicious of international treaties in general, advocating instead for national sovereignty. Often overlooked yet critical to a complete analysis of U.S. positions is the fact that the Child Rights treaty also calls for economic and social rights, in particular welfare protections for children. To the dismay of progressive activists, in February 2001, U.S. Ambassador Michael Southwick made it clear that the Bush Administration took issue with social and economic rights, which underpin the treaty. The role of government, he asserted, is to create the conditions in which these rights (economic and social) can be realized: "This is not something that states can confer. It is not an entitlement."[57]

In the area of reproductive health and services, the Christian Right and the U.S. had many allies. The U.S., the Holy See and a coalition called "Some Developing Countries (SDC)" opposed the guarantee of sexual and reproductive rights and services for adolescents. The SDC, led by Sudan, included many of the countries that had stymied

Beijing+5 negotiations and that constituted Austin Ruse's "pro-family bloc".[58] Reproductive health NGOs and a few government voting blocs wanted to add reproductive rights to the Child Rights platform. The Like Minded Group (Canada, New Zealand, Australia, Switzerland, Norway, Liechtenstein and Iceland) along with the Rio Group (of Latin American nations) pushed for a progressive stance on reproductive health for adolescents. The AIDS pandemic had made reproductive health and sex education for young adults even more urgent since in many regions they are among the most vulnerable to HIV/AIDS. In many countries adolescent children marry and have children before the age of 18. They therefore have special needs, especially in the area of reproductive health. Reproductive services would include having access to birth control, sex education and in countries where it is legal, abortion, all of which the Christian Right opposed.[59]

In a preparatory meeting for the Special Session, a blunder by a Canadian diplomat fed into the assertions of Christian Right NGOs that liberals were surreptitiously trying to legalize abortion. The diplomat stated during a debate, that the term reproductive "services" did include the right to abortion. In reality international law remains neutral on abortion, calling on governments to make sure it is safe in countries where it is legal. Still, the gaffe over the word "services" gave credence to the Christian Right conviction that U.N. conferences and treaties would seek to stretch legal definitions to include new rights without formal international agreements, and proved useful in legitimizing Christian Right fears to other U.N. member states as well as its U.S. constituency.[60]

The U.S., the Holy See and SDC also opposed the recognition that various forms of the family exist, although this had been agreed at earlier U.N. conferences, including the Beijing conference. The U.S. pressed for defining a family strictly as a union "based on marriage between a man and a woman."[61]

Finally, the U.S. fought with the European Union over European attempts to ban the use of the death penalty for crimes committed before the age of 18.[62] The U.S. is one of a handful of countries that still allows the death penalty for under-18s. (The minimum age for execution is set by each state; most states have an age limit of 18, others have age limits of 17 and 16, while eight states have no minimum age limit.)

A Hollow Victory

In the final hours of the Special Session, the European Union and the U.S. struck a deal, leaving other negotiators with the choice of either accepting the E.U.-U.S. language or for blocking consensus. Angry at what they labeled a backroom deal, some negotiators stormed out of the negotiations in protest, but eventually accepted the document that the E.U. and U.S. had finalized. The E.U. had agreed not to include the words "reproductive services" in the paragraph on adolescent health in return for U.S. support for language calling for elimination of the death penalty in countries that had ratified the Child Rights treaty. While progressive activists were outraged, they took consolation in the fact that the Outcome Document does reaffirm the agreements made at the Beijing conference and the International Conference on Population and Development, or Cairo conference, both of which affirm reproductive services. The compromise was more one of language than substance. In addition to allowing references to the Cairo and Beijing agreements, the U.S. lost its battle to define the family more narrowly. The Outcome Document stated "various forms of the family exist."[63] Conservatives had clearly lost on ultimately barring international commitments to reproductive health services and redefining the family. Interestingly, progressive NGOs expressed frustration and Christian Right NGOs celebrated when the term reproductive health "services" was eliminated in the final agreement.[64] For progressive NGOs, accustomed to expanding on their previous gains on social issues with every U.N. meeting, the Special Session was a disappointment. [65] Said Jo Becker, the spokesperson of the Child Rights Caucus, "Governments squandered an opportunity ... After nearly universal ratification of the Convention on the Rights of the Child, it's a disappointment that the treaty is not the centerpiece of the Outcome Document."[66] For conservative religious NGOs, it was one of the first language battles they had won. They had succeeded in making the words "reproductive services" even more contentious and suspect than ever before.

In the end, the U.S. seemed to have put most of its political capital into weakening the final document's commitment to child rights as defined in the Convention on the Rights of the Child. The debate over "services" appeared to be a straw man – a fabricated issue that drew all the attention and energy but was not actually the main agenda of the U.S. The U.S. used much of its political capital to address issues that were of secondary, but not central, concern to the Christian Right platform. It might be said that the U.S. government even used Christian Right concerns over abortion to cloak its more controversial moves. Less notice was given in the American media to the U.S.'s ardent support for the death penalty and its determination to undermine support for government funding for child welfare.[67] Given the impact of poverty on children in the U.S. and worldwide, the failure to draw attention to this matter is perhaps the greatest loss suffered at the Special Session.

Stage 3: A Proactive Agenda on the Issue of Family

The Christian Right moved from outsiders to insiders with the help of the Bush Administration. As its strategy shifted it began to advance its own policy initiatives rather than merely blocking progressive ones. Under the leadership of Mormon NGOs, for example, the Christian Right leaders used the occasion of the tenth anniversary of the U.N. International Year of the Family to organize an intergovernmental conference and to try to introduce a resolution that would advance conservative "pro-family" policies. The Christian Right was now in the ironic position of using legal structures they opposed to advance an agenda they supported. The activism of these groups now mimicked that of the progressives they opposed. Where once only progressive NGOs pressed member states to host U.N. world conferences that enabled them to advance their causes, so the Christian Right is starting to create venues that might enable it to advance its objectives concerning the family.

The tenth anniversary of the International Year of the Family (IYF+10), celebrated in 2004, provided a clear opportunity for the Christian Right to advance their own platform. In light of the effectiveness with which well-established feminist NGOs had made it difficult for Christian Right NGOs to break into the Beijing and women's rights arena to advance a proactive platform, the U.N.'s work on family provided them the space to advance their own agenda. Aiding the effort was the fact that not many people in either the U.N. or NGO community were interested in the topic or the anniversary. At the time, the U.N. was downsizing the New York City offices that addressed the family. Moreover, few progressive NGOs were even interested in the topic.

The few interested NGOs were members of the NGO Committee on the Family, which is affiliated with CONGO (the Conference of NGOs) and officially acknowledged by the U.N. Department for Economic and Social Affairs. The NGO representatives that joined this committee tended to be progressive leaning, professionally trained social workers and psychologists. David Roth, co-chair of the committee, described the committee's views in an interview: "they agree that the nuclear family is the appropriate ideal choice to form the fundamental unit of society, but they also believe in being realistic about this world, and feel the need to endorse views that go beyond the traditional understandings and definitions of the family."[68]

Christian Right NGOs in 2004 opted out of this official body and formed their own NGO committee called the International Year of the Family+10 (IYF+10) Committee. Though new and not officially affiliated with the U.N., the committee quickly established a high profile and launched proactive initiatives to change U.N. policy. The NGO coalition enjoyed strong support from several U.N. missions, including the United States, Qatar, Benin and Nigeria.[69]

On the International Day of the Family, celebrated on May 13, 2004, the IYF+10 Committee demonstrated the seriousness with which it had moved into this new field of activity. While the official NGO Committee on the Family held an event in the Church Center across the street from the U.N., the conservative IYF+10 obtained government sponsorship to hold a meeting at the U.N. itself. Its event was announced in the U.N. *Daily Journal* and attended by a number of diplomats. While the progressive NGO Committee on the Family drew around forty participants, mostly older adults, the conservative IYF+10 Committee drew a larger crowd of all ages, including a number of young people.[70]

The Doha International Conference on the Family

Throughout 2003, the IYF+10 Committee led by Mormon NGOs worked with the government of Qatar to host a conference in celebration of the tenth anniversary of the International Year of the Family. According to Dr. Wilkins at the Mormon World Family Policy Center (WFPC), the center's summer symposiums for delegates had drawn the attention of Ambassador Al-Nassar of Qatar. The ambassador approached the WFPC with the idea of co-sponsoring an event to celebrate the tenth-year anniversary of the International Year of the Family. Significantly, Al-Nassar at that time was head of the G-77, a U.N. negotiating bloc of 177 countries largely from the developing world. This was an auspicious coincidence, given the Christian Right's interest in the developing world as a potential ally. Qatar worked through the General Assembly to get the body to recognize the Doha conference as a celebration of the International Year.[71] Christian Right organizations at times stretched the General Assembly statement, describing the celebratory event as a policy making conference on par with a U.N. world conference (which can shape international policy). C-FAM suggested that "'The Doha Declaration' could set the global agenda for international family policy for the next decade."[72]

The IYF+10 coalition worked closely with several governments, including the U.S. The U.S. often played a quiet role supporting the initiatives of smaller governments. Ellen Sauerbrey, U.S. Ambassador on the Family indicated in a speech at a United Families Intenational (UFI) gathering that the U.S. was working with Qatar on a resolution supporting the Doha event.[73] The Doha International Conference for the Family slated for November 2004 was preceded by two regional dialogues intended to build consensus among "pro-family" advocates. The first was held in Geneva, Switzerland August 23–25, and the second in Kuala Lumpur, Malaysia October 11–14, 2004.[74]

One of the stated goals of the conference was to build a body of scholarship on the family. Toward that end, the planning committee invited a number of prominent U.S. scholars who have underscored the connection between a healthy society and the stability of individual families, conclusions that resonated with Christian Right arguments. Most notably among them was Dr. Gary Becker, a professor of economics at the University of Chicago who was Nobel Laureate for Economics in 1992. Others included sociologists Dr. David Popenoe from Rutgers University, Dr. Steven Nock of the University of Virginia, Dr. Norval Glenn of the University of Texas, Austin, and Dr. W. Bradford Wilcox of the University of Virginia. While the Christian Right NGOs clearly found value in these professors' academic work, this did not mean that these academics were necessarily supporters of their agenda.[75]

A list of the nationalities of the political leaders in attendance sheds light on the degree to which the G-77 is potentially interested in the "pro-family" agenda, although it must be said that alliances at the U.N. are always fluid. Even when a NGO coalition has the support of a government official, other branches of government might overrule that individual's support, and changes and leadership can lead to different commitments. Other than Qatar, political leaders from the Arab League were from Algeria, the United Arab Emirates (UAE), Bahrain, Kuwait, Oman, Jordan, Lebanon and Tunisia. Many were clearly Gulf States and U.S. allies (partners in the war on terror). Malaysia also sent several representatives. The Organization of Islamic Conference and the Gulf Cooperation Council sent official representatives. While it's not clear whether they were represented at the conference, Indonesia, the world's largest Muslim nation and Iran at the General Assembly endorsed the Declaration, specifically mentioning its content on the definition of the family. There was a much smaller presence from Africa – representatives from Nigeria and Ghana attended. Two government representatives from Latin America came: El Salvador's U.N. ambassador who was also the vice-chairman of the Third Committee, which oversees issues of the family and Costa Rica's ambassador. The president of the Pontifical Council for the Family, His Eminence Alfonso Lopez Trujillo, represented the Holy See.[76]

The Doha Declaration

At first glance, the Doha Declaration may appear to be uncontroversial. Yet what is striking, remarked David Roth, co-chair of the progressive NGO Committee on the Family, is what it does not say: "There is no mention of sexual or reproductive health services, abortion, planned parenthood and the right of parents to determine the number and spacing of their children." U.N. resolutions and declarations usually acknowledge other major related conference agreements to build on past gains. The Declaration, said Roth, did not reference the Millennium Development Goals to halve poverty by 2010, or the Convention on the Rights of the Child.[77]

Rather than reaffirm prior entire U.N. treaties and conferences on women and children, the Doha Declaration references mere phrases and articles from international law. The Doha Declaration does affirm the Universal Declaration of Human Rights (1945) because Christian Right groups believe this declaration laid out a positive framework from which successive treaties unfortunately departed. In an introductory section called "Reaffirmation of Commitments to the Family" the Doha Declaration cites portions of the Children's and Women's Convention that it can agree with such as "Motherhood and children are entitled to special care and assistance," and "Everyone has the right to life, liberty and security of person." In a section called "Call for Action," the declaration calls upon governments to take action in the areas of cultural, religious and social values, human dignity, family, marriage, parents and children. These sections echo other "pro-family" concerns around the definition of marriage, a defense of religious values against secularization, a critique of population policies, and an emphasis on human dignity rather than human rights. The declaration makes two references to American concerns about home schooling – a surprise given this international context. The declaration calls for governments to "Reaffirm and respect the liberty of parents ... to choose for their children schools, other than those established by the public authorities ... and to ensure the religious and moral education of their children in conformity with their own convictions."[78]

Several issues that do not often get a lot of mention by the Christian Right were included in the Doha Declaration and perhaps reflect the influence of its international partners. The preamble mentions the impact of globalization on families and the section on family calls for governments to "strengthen policies and programs that will enable family to break the cycle of poverty." The same section calls for governments to support families "in addressing the scourge of HIV/AIDS and other pandemics including malaria and tuberculosis." It also calls for "effective measures to support the family in times of peace and war." The section on marriage surprisingly calls attention to the problem of violence within marriage and the family. A final section calls for the promotion of "equal political, economic, social and educational opportunities for women."[79]

Who Won on the Doha Debate?

On December 6, 2004 the U.N. passed a resolution celebrating the tenth anniversary of the International Year of the Family. The resolution noted the conference held by Qatar as one of many events celebrating this particular International Year. The General Assembly did not adopt the Doha Declaration as Christian Right organizations had hoped. However Christian Right NGOs celebrated as though the declaration had become international law. The World Family Policy Center stated:

> The United Nations General Assembly adopted a consensus resolution on Monday, December 6, 2004, welcoming the Doha International Conference for the Family and noting its outcomes – including the Doha Declaration. As a result of this action, the Doha Declaration takes its place in the formal canon of legal documents comprising the growing body of international law.[80]

Christian Right NGOs declared an enormous victory over their enemies – in particular the liberal European Union and Brazil (who allegedly threw UFI representatives out of their office). Slater later wrote, "The anti-family delegations were determined to defeat [the Doha Declaration] but were unprepared for the battle." The Mormon *Meridian Magazine* had called on their subscribers to email U.N. missions in support of the declaration. These emails, said Susan Slater of WFPC, made the difference. "Opposing governments felt pressured into silence and country after country made formal statements in favor of the Doha Declaration."[81]

Not all "pro-family" coalition members agreed with the analysis of the WFPC, UFI and C-FAM. Dr. Farooq Hassan, a Pakistani lawyer and former U.N. ambassador who works closely with UFI and other Mormon NGOs, cautioned his partners. "Nothing is gained, in my view, by an exaggerated and belabored construction of its place as a U.N. document or not," he commented in an interview with Islam Online, a Qatar-based Internet forum for Muslims and one of the largest websites designed for the Muslim world.[82] Dr Hassan explained, "the GA [UN General Assembly] text does not refer to the Doha Declaration at all but merely to the outcome of the Benin and Doha conferences. Secondly, it does not endorse it as such but simply 'notes' it." In legal terms, said Hassan, the word "notes" legally does not imply the U.N. has taken on obligations or new juridical commitments. In addition, another celebration of the International Year held in Beijing promoted liberal policies on the family. According to Hassan, General Assembly endorsement of the declaration was not essential to their success. The importance of the declaration lies in the fact that it was supported by other U.N. member states and that it "might well lead to newer and more clear interpretations of international law on the subject."[83]

In fact, Dr. Hassan had other concerns about the Doha Conference outcome. In his view, the declaration failed to address "many serious problems that are at the center of international debates on marriage and family issues." Hassan observed that the conference did little to assess international legal issues rather than making assertions about morality.[84]

Hassan also critiqued the declaration as not recognizing the contribution of Muslim states. The declaration itself "essentially aims to address Western problems."[85] The conference speakers largely drew on statistics and problems in the U.S. and Europe: "The problems and the situations in the West and North America are different from the ones that exist in Asia, Southeast Asia and Africa. And that kind of a detailed examination, I think, is still to be done by experts and NGOs." Even more striking, Dr Hassan lamented:

> I cannot help but note with sadness that within the United States, generally the right wing that is pro-family is also pro-war. I do not say that the individuals or organizations I met fall into that category ... But I hope that through cooperation on pro-family issues we can learn to understand each other as individuals and also as peoples ... and that over time we might strive together for justice in other arenas.[86]

These concerns are explored further in the final chapter of this book.

Dr. Hassan's analysis of the technical legal outcomes of the General Assembly decision is accurate. However, during the debates over the adoption of the resolution, liberal-minded delegates did express concern that the GA resolution was regressive in their view. In the final minutes of the session, the European Union disassociated themselves from the resolution, asserting that it "brought in non-consensual elements," and didn't build on international consensus. After the resolution was adopted, several member states went on record with their opposition to the resolution: the Netherlands, Canada, Australia, Iceland, Liechtenstein and New Zealand. They expressed concern that prior agreements on respecting the diversity of families and on women's, children's and reproductive rights were not referenced in the resolution. Specifically, New Zealand "regretted that the text and the Doha Declaration only promoted one model of the family at the expense of others," while Liechtenstein alleged that "the process had been flawed and had lacked inclusiveness."[87] Regardless of whether the Doha Declaration had been adopted or not, liberal governments seem to have viewed the GA resolution on the International Year as a potential threat.

Was the Doha Conference and its declaration a success for Christian Right NGOs? The answer to this important question of course depends on how one defines success. In terms of creating a binding legal norm and precedent, they did not. Christian Right activists exaggerated when they implied the conference was on the same level as other conferences.

However, there were just as many reasons that the Christian Right was correct to proclaim the effort a success. It is remarkable that the group was able to develop an alliance with Qatar to host an intergovernmental conference that could also produce a common agenda, an achievement noted to a small degree as reflected in the resolution. Even if the declaration did not have a direct impact on legal norms, the fact that there was any common platform could prove significant in the future as a lobbying tool for future declarations with more legal weight. Even declarations with little legal weight can have significant repercussions in an international system that relies on the majority of states putting pressure on others to conform to international norms. Both legal treatises and media reports on international gatherings, in turn, reinforce these norms. In fact, media coverage of a U.N. event is often almost as important as the event itself in determining outcomes. By exaggerating their Doha victory, Christian Right NGOs could build some enthusiasm around their pro-family platform at the U.N. among both supporters and sympathetic outsiders. Thus the Doha victory did shape public perceptions that they were significant international players. They enjoyed similar success in shaping public perceptions in the U.N. debate over human cloning, an achievement addressed in the final chapter of this book.

The key to future Christian Right successes will hinge on whether they can form a coalition with G-77 governments. As Dr. Hassan has pointed out, the Doha Declaration and conference still reflect more of the concerns of developed rather than developing countries. In their speeches on the tenth anniversary, many of the G-77 governments emphasized poverty, development and rapid globalization as the primary concerns for families.

One advantage that conservatives have in creating such a coalition is their accessible language of family. Conservatives and progressives talk about their goals in very different ways and that influences the way that they talk about family. Liberals view family policies through the analytical lens of the family's various components – women, children, reproduction. They view family as a "cross-cutting" issue, meaning it is important less as an issue in and of itself, and more in terms of how family policy impacts other social issues like women's rights, children's rights, and reproductive health. Delegates from the European Union in their statements to the General Assembly on the family spoke largely about their support for the Beijing Women's conference, the Conference on Population and Development and the Children's and Women's Rights Treaties. In contrast, speakers from the developing nations always spoke of the family as a social category in and of itself. This was a noticeable difference because there were more speakers from the G-77 than from Europe. White American conservatives might be a minority at such events but their language easily connects with the worldviews of delegates from the developing world. By the same token, the delegates do not see support for the family removed from the reality of economic forces. Consequently, both Christian Right and secular Euro-American NGOs will be challenged in their pursuit for the loyalties of the global South. Just as the Christian Right might find itself challenged to address economic inequality to win over the developing world, progressives may need to find a way to articulate a vision for the family that is more sympathetic and moves beyond a simple deconstruction of it into its constitutive parts.

Beyond U.N. Conferences: Playing the Role of U.N. Agency Watchdog

The Christian Right's agenda goes beyond stalling or inserting its agenda into U.N. conferences. To have a greater impact on the U.N.'s work, it must influence not just what governments agree to, but how those agreements are implemented. One of Austin Ruse's main goals is to turn U.N. agencies "back to their proper work … we will convince governments that agencies should return to their original mandates. [The] UNFPA [the U.N. Population Fund] could be cut out of business." U.N. agencies like UNFPA, said Charlotte Bunch in a recent interview, have to be more cautious about speaking out on issues of choice and sexuality. The committee of experts that oversees the implementation of CEDAW (the U.N. Convention on the Elimination of All forms of Discrimination Against Women), the U.N. women's rights treaty adopted in 1979, knows that much of what it says "might be skewed in a column by conservative commentators and therefore has treaded more carefully in recent years."[88] To maintain the political pressure, C-FAM continues to publish "white papers" or exposées on U.N. agencies and human rights bodies including UNICEF (the U.N. Children's Fund) and UNFPA. Under the administration of George W. Bush, C-FAM with Population Research Institute (PRI)-led attacks on UNFPA that continually resulted in the U.S. withholding its $34 million contribution (14 per cent of UNFPA's budget) from the agency.[89]

Security Concerns and Opposing the International Criminal Court

Christian Right NGOs focus largely on social concerns rather than issues of peace and security. However the Christian Right's strong opposition to the International Criminal Court (ICC) may provide a vehicle through which the Christian Right expands its influence from social issues to an agenda that includes international security concerns. Its opposition to the ICC has helped draw it into a stronger alliance with another sector of the New Right: neoconservatives.

The ICC, inspired by the Nuremburg trials that prosecuted Nazi war criminals after World War II, was established in 2002 to try genocide, war crimes and crimes against humanity. The Christian Right has mobilized millions of Americans to oppose the International Criminal Court, lending great support to neoconservative intellectuals and policymakers who have helped the Bush Administration to oppose it.[90]

While not so successful in influencing the Rome Statute, which established and defined the court, the Christian Right has successfully lobbied the Bush Administration and Senate to weaken the court. Under the Bush Administration, the U.S. has not only opposed the court, it has sacrificed a great deal of international good will by actively trying to sabotage the new institution. Why go to such unprecedented lengths to undermine an international treaty that claims such universal support?[91] While a Democratic president may not have pressed for ICC ratification either – President Clinton waited until his final days in office to sign the Rome Statute – no one would have predicted the amount of political capital President George W. Bush would spend undermining the ICC.

John Washburn, the convener of the American NGO Coalition for the ICC (AMICC), a coalition that seeks U.S. support for the ICC, attributes the Bush Administration's aggressiveness to a convergence of interests on the part of neoconservatives and the Christian Right:

> This convergence has made the ICC a huge deal. Otherwise I don't think for example that John Bolton [Undersecretary for Arms Control and International Security in the Bush Administration] would make anywhere as big a deal out of this, nor would he be as successful in this campaign, which is costing the U.S. so much internationally. I don't think the President would care anywhere near as much.[92]

Both the Christian Right and neoconservative organizations like the Federalist Society see international treaties as threatening U.S. sovereignty. Neoconservatives advocate a "unipolar" foreign policy in which the U.S. unabashedly takes advantage of being the world's sole superpower. In the words of one neoconservative policy paper, the U.S. should "take the actions necessary to ensure that our efforts to meet our global security commitments and protect Americans are not impaired by the potential for investigations, inquiry or prosecution by the International Criminal Court, whose jurisdiction does not extend to Americans ... ."[93] The Christian Right has unique concerns: it fears the ICC will be used by liberals to advance liberal social views, just as liberals have used the U.S. judicial system to advance their views on civil rights, abortion, school prayer and gay rights. It views the court as another form of what it calls "judicial activism," using the court system to support liberal social values. Douglas Sylva, C-FAM vice-president, put it this way:

> Many American conservatives believe that whatever happens at the United Nations can be ignored – at least until the black helicopters start flying. But there is a culture war raging at the United Nations, and the winners get to write the laws that will be enforced throughout the world by the new International Criminal Court. Who needs black helicopters for world domination when lawyers are handy?[94]

Richard Wilkins, law professor from Brighton Young University and director of the WFPC, while recognizing the good intentions behind the court, views the ICC as an effort by liberals to advance gay rights and abortion through judicial activism: "The International Criminal Court could well become the mechanism by which the Western innovation of judicially (rather than legislatively) crafted social policy and its accompanying consequences are exported to the rest of the world. Of all revolutions through the centuries, this is the quietest."[95]

Wilkins led a delegation of Christian Right activists in Rome to advocate that the court not become another vehicle for liberal views on homosexuality and abortion. Though supportive of the ICC, John Washburn provided a sympathetic view of the players in the "culture clash" that transpired between Christian Right and feminist NGO leaders at the Rome meeting. Dr. Wilkins "got himself caught squarely in the sights of the Women's caucus for Gender Justice, a tough, vigorous and relentless outfit." The women's caucus was working to make sure that crimes such as the rape of women during wartime were included in the Rome Statute: "They gave him a tough time, and he resented it, but more than resenting it, he became convinced that the court was a vehicle for the worldwide enforcement of extreme forms of left wing feminism."[96]

Washburn is that rare leader that can see the larger picture. An adept coalition builder, he seems to genuinely respect both sides of the debate. He observed:

> ... the women's caucus had an unbelievable opportunity to realize the gender crimes area of the Beijing declaration. And then here comes the Vatican and this "right wing nut" – in their view. And he as a tenured professor of a prestigious university of course didn't appreciate this. I can appreciate how they felt, but I can also commiserate with him. He felt he was discriminated against because of his religious status. It was a mess, mess, mess.[97]

Washburn offered a unique view of this Christian Right leader: "It's too bad, because he was one of the few people with his politics and perspectives that went to Rome. I'm sorry because with a little effort I think we could have made some progress with him." For Washburn, the introduction of different perspectives is of value to the debate. The CICC offered a balance of diverse sectors of civil society while managing to stay focused and organized. This diversity enriched the ICC and made it more effective in Washburn's view. He has been to Salt Lake City twice to talk with the Church of Latter Day Saints leadership about the court. He thinks they may one day be able to find common ground.[98]

The CICC was known for its discipline and for holding NGOs to a mainstream stance. In Washburn's view the negotiating process in Rome worked to temper possible extremes, because all sides were taken into account in the final definitions of controversial words like gender, abortion and genocide. Perhaps because of the culture clash, the lack of trust and the politicization of the issues, Washburn suggests, "It was very difficult for Wilkins to understand that what he was worried about was taken care of, what is good enough for the Vatican should be good enough for him."[99]

Washburn is very reflective about his experience of working with a wide range of religious and non-religious actors shaping the ICC. He has a perspective gained from years of building coalitions. "The elitist groups to which you and I belong" he told me, "are so turned off by evangelicals that they are turned off to their potential. I think it is important that we do what we are in theory committed – and that is to show respect." What will happen if we don't find ways to do that? Washburn without hesitation responded: "One, we won't learn from them – their organization, what they offer people. Two, Christianity in the U.S. will become theirs. Three, if we do not bridge this gap, they will not in turn learn from us."[100]

Watching NGOs, Challenging Global Civil Society

Given this chapter's focus on examining global democracy, it is fitting to conclude with an exploration of the Christian Right's ambivalent views of global civil society. In addition to influencing U.N. policies and agencies, the Christian Right also seeks to monitor and reform NGOs themselves. Just as they demonstrate conflicted views of the U.N., Christian Right NGOs also show ambivalence towards civil society. For instance, Labor Secretary Elaine Chao, speaking on a conservative panel about NGOs both criticized NGOs for being anti-liberty yet urged conservative organizations not to "write off the United Nations and other multilateral international organizations as a waste of our time and resources. Conservatives need to pay attention to these organizations."[101]

In 2003 the American Enterprise Institute and the Federalist Society opened the newest front on the culture war: a program called NGO Watch. The purpose of the program is "to bring clarity and accountability to the burgeoning world of NGOs" which they view as being increasingly powerful yet unregulated.[102] When the International Committee of the Red Cross (ICRC) exposed human rights abuses by Coalition forces in Iraq, an NGO Watch report threw a sliver of doubt into the ruling by alleging that the ICRC was being "highly selective in its allegations of international law violations." When Doctors without Borders (Médecins sans frontières – MSF) withdrew its workers from Afghanistan because the U.S. practice of using humanitarian aid for political gain was endangering aid workers, NGO Watch hinted that the MSF abandoned the vulnerable for political reasons. Such allegations often get picked up in what has been called the echo chamber of conservative radio, Fox News, and the Internet.[103]

This critique of NGOs launched by the Christian Right, neoconservatives and economic conservatives reveals fundamental differences with progressives and moderates over definitions of democracy. Traditionally, political scientists have viewed the presence of NGOs as one measure of the strength of democratic societies. Community leaders and non-profit organizations form the building-blocks of what those who study successful democracies call "civil society." Such organizations help organize the voice of the people, deliver valuable services and help strengthen communities. In fact, a hallmark of undemocratic governments is controlling civil society.

The supporters of NGO Watch however turn this view on its head, accusing NGOs of being by nature undemocratic and unrepresentative because they assume quasi-government roles they were not elected to hold. Austin Ruse put it this way: "These most undemocratic organizations provide democratic cover for a shockingly undemocratic process. International civil society decides it wants something and that's it, out pops the International Criminal Court or Land Mines Treaty, negotiating processes dominated less by governments and more by NGOs."[104]

Christian Right leaders portray NGOs as representing a liberal minority advocating narrow goals. Austin Ruse of C-FAM speaking at a C-SPAN panel on NGOs hosted by the Federalist Society described two types of NGOs: those that engage in service, and those that "campaign" or do advocacy. Many of the latter, he says:

> ... are not so benign. They are radical in that they seek to impose a vision on the world that is shared by few, a vision that is shared mostly by the "wide spectrum" of opinion that is found mostly at the Women's Studies Department at Vassar. These are the sorts that strike a blow against capitalism, the unborn, against the freedoms we enjoy here, against the United States itself.[105]

NGO Watch may be able to put pressure on NGOs by jeopardizing their funding. In August 2004 an exposé on the NGO Watch home page was entitled "Corrupting U.S.AID's mission?" The lead read, "As NGOs become more political, it may no longer be appropriate for U.S.AID to give them funding for development projects."[106] The topic echoes the stance of the Bush Administration, which has sought more stridently than other U.S. administrations to control the policies and activities of organizations that receive funding from its agencies. During the conflicts in Afghanistan and Iraq, for instance, NGOs receiving government contracts to deliver services or requesting access to war zones found the U.S. government demanding that they advertise they are present under the auspices of the U.S. government. Such demands compromise the neutrality of humanitarian organizations in conflict zones. If their workers are identified with occupying powers, they lose their ability to deliver services and to do so safely, not only in Afghanistan or Iraq but throughout the rest of the world as well. If they don't comply with these new policies, humanitarian organizations, whose years of experience in a region are valuable and often unrivaled assets, must abandon those whom they wish to help. Many NGOs rejected government aid or decided to steer clear of working in these countries altogether. These policies not only place humanitarian workers in harm's way, they jeopardize one of the cheapest and best aid delivery systems the U.S. government has at its disposal.[107]

Why is it that conservatives who press for the deregulation of the corporate sector complain that NGOs are "unregulated"? Political scientist Jean Hardisty has suggested that the American Enterprise Institute (AEI), established to defend multinational corporations and the free market from liberal criticism, views government and the free market as the only valid sectors of society. The idea of a third sector or "third force" (especially one that is progressive) threatens that view.

NGOs interfere with the free functioning of the economy because they are not motivated by profit, and often critique free market excesses such as unfair labor or damaging environmental practices. In the AEI's view, society runs smoothly if the economy is left to function freely, guided by the "invisible hand" described in Adam Smith's *Wealth of Nations* (1776). Anything that is not tied up in the freedom-supporting capitalist enterprise smacks of socialism and communism, that is, systems opposed to freedom, democracy and religion. Working with these assumptions allows someone like Jeremy Rabkin, an AEI fellow and Cornell University professor, to conclude that NGOs are a "Stalinist concept."[108]

Ironically, conservative NGOs practice the same type of activism that NGO Watch criticizes. Ruse accuses NGOs of using media and allies in the capitals of U.N. member nations to influence debates, encouraging NGO representatives to sit on government delegations, influencing the hiring and firing of delegations' members, and hectoring lobbyists in what he terms a "dirty process." Truthfully, both sides engage in these types of activities, and when described in less pejorative terms, such activities are merely age-old advocacy tactics: the process whereby one influences the composition of government delegations and their positions, and uses media to frame public debates.

A recent Federalist Society panel that aired on C-SPAN on the topic of NGOs featured speakers from both left and right who explored the successes and failures of the NGO sector.[109] If NGO Watch can provoke dialogue, debate and evenhanded critique of a spectrum of NGOs, rather than just those that disagree with its agenda, then it might have a valuable contribution to make. One can hope (even if naively) that its NGO Watch program will move in such a constructive direction. Austin Ruse complains that the U.N. has excluded conservative NGOs, especially pro-life NGOs. It must be said, however, that these NGOs also chose not to be at the U.N., many of them because they opposed the U.N. itself. Ruse and others have changed the landscape of NGOs at the U.N. in a relatively short time. If this trend continues, the NGO landscape at the U.N. will continue to grow in diversity. Conservative and progressive NGOs will be met with a new challenge. The question is: will they seek to destroy one another, or will they seek to engage in a spirit of creative debate?

The Future of Global Civil Society

For those who remain optimistic about the potential of global civil society to address the world's problems, the authors of the book *Globalizing Family Values* make a disturbing observation: "we reject the idea that an emerging international civil society is inherently democratic and progressive."[110] The Christian Right has heightened the conservative religious voice at the United Nations, thereby demonstrating that not all of global civil society is progressive. Since they have just started, we can only speculate on what their effect on civil society might be. I have heard variations on the following questions: Will their presence make global civil society less democratic because they seek to restrict reproductive rights, women's and children's rights and gay rights (as these concepts are defined by liberals)? Does religious activism at the U.N. threaten to make the U.N. less democratic by compromising the separation of church and state? Does the globalization of the Christian Right portend the rise of global fascism, as some fear?

Labeling Christian Right NGOs and their enormous constituency as fascist writes off the belief system of a large percentage of the world's population, and prevents the dialogue that is the cornerstone of democracy and progressive values. The contribution of both progressive and conservative religious NGOs in shaping civil society and influencing policies is well documented and explored in Chapter 1 of this book. Their participation in civil society should not be restricted any more than other NGOs, all of which operate out of a particular system of belief, whether socialist, humanist, secularist, or human rights-based to name a few.

The literature on global civil society provides a more strategic way of assessing the impact of Christian Right global organizing on global democracy. Political scientists have observed that international NGOs (INGOs) form bridges between the grass roots and global policy elites.[111] The strength of global civil society is dependent on how well NGOs represent their constituencies.

The problem for civil society is not that the Christian Right is present at the U.N. or organizing globally, but that by default it has been the NGO coalition most vocally representing the voice of religion at the U.N. and internationally. As mentioned in the Introduction, some scholars have suggested that the New World Order in the post-

Cold War era will be structured along lines of cultural and religious difference. When it comes to social issues at the U.N., the clash is not between Muslims and Christians (indeed they are allies), but rather a clash between a secular global North and a religious global South, along the lines described in Phillip Jenkins' *The Next Christendom*. The Christian Right is furthering this process by experimenting with new alliances. Tragically, both secular and religious liberals have a hand in fostering this divide between the secular and religious worlds. Secular liberals play into this polarity by failing to tolerate religion; religious liberals exacerbate the divide by allowing religious conservatives to dominate the public arena.

Reinforcing the dynamics of the culture wars allows both sides to ignore the diversity of religious opinion. Religious communities have a wide range of viewpoints on global issues; perspectives that fall along a progressive to conservative continuum. All of these viewpoints should be represented and heard in global civil society. Too often conservative evangelicals are seen monolithically rather than as a diverse constituency with a range of interests. Consider the following examples of religious participation at the U.N.

On October 18, 2004, a hundred representatives of evangelical organizations from around the world gathered at the United Nations for a press conference. Speaking for the World Evangelical Alliance, composed of 3 million churches, Gary Edmonds declared, "Governments are given by God and have a moral responsibility. Christians need to hold their governments responsible."[112] The purpose of the press conference: To endorse the Micah Challenge, a campaign to halve global poverty by 2015 as called for in the U.N. Millennium Development Goals (MDGs). The campaign, representing 267 Christian relief organizations, the Baptist World Alliance and World Evangelical Alliance, plans to rally 25 million Christians to support the MDGs, which include eradicating hunger, reducing child mortality, empowering women, combating AIDS, improving maternal health and ensuring environmental sustainability.[113]

A few brief stories from my own experience, as a religious leader engaged in progressive activism at the U.N., might be helpful to illustrate further how evangelicals cannot be pigeonholed. I recently chaired a panel on religion and women's rights during the Beijing+10 meeting. A Nigerian Pentecostal took me to task – not for the fact that our panel of church leaders spoke about sex education, AIDS, religion and violence and homosexuality, but because we didn't have more resources available for her to take home and no sign-up sheet for her to join our coalition. This exchange illustrated to me how we religious progressives do not think strategically about expanding our networks. The reason we are not strategic is nothing less than tragic: deep down many of us do not take ourselves and our work seriously enough. When you believe in your work and its effect on people, you want to sign up potential allies! And you have extra pamphlets on hand to explain your position!

A Muslim woman from Malaysia working with Mormons and other religious conservatives at Beijing+10 suggested in an interview with me that while she agreed with the values of the pro-family coalition, she wasn't sure how much they were really willing or able to help the women she was working with in Malaysia. "I don't know about all this politics," she confided. I imagined that despite her solid fieldwork, women's rights activists would mostly not support her work because she was against legalized abortion. Yet when progressives discount women like this, they are writing off a large percentage of the world's women. Religious communities are more complex than most people realize – and nothing demonstrates this fact than the surprising new alliances being forged by the Christian Right.

3
Assembling a Pro-Family Alliance

W HEN CHRISTIAN RIGHT ORGANIZATIONS SUCH as Jerry Falwell's Moral Majority formed in the 1970s they united Pentecostals, fundamentalists and evangelicals to fight organizations like the U.N., not reform them from the inside. Many of these groups demonized the U.N. as a playground of the Antichrist and the stomping ground of godless communism. This chapter reveals how a loose coalition of conservative religious NGOs at the U.N. is unified by their opposition to a set of common enemies but inspired by different leaders as well as organized by different agencies. The coalition is made up of socially conservative white evangelicals, Catholics and Mormons, and to a lesser extent Muslims, who have forged an alliance to influence international policy on the turf of an organization whose very existence some of them have opposed.

The leaders of this new coalition have created a compelling "pro-family" rhetoric at the U.N. and around the world. But it is unclear how far their project can go. On the one hand, the Christian Right global project is deeply rooted both in the U.S. political context and its particular culture wars. It is also increasingly tied to the project of American empire as defined by the conservative intellectuals called "neoconservatives." On the other hand, this "pro-family" rhetoric resonates with people from across the world, despite the fact that these same people may disagree with American Christians on many other issues.

My interviews with Christian Right leaders revealed that there were actually three intertwined networks (Catholic, Mormon, and Protestant Evangelical) of leaders and organizations and each network formed from a different initial impetus. While each network is committed to a conservative family agenda, each speaks to a specific religious constituency. Each of the three was galvanized by the leadership of religious figures like John Paul II and religiously inclined politicians like George W. Bush, and each speaks through a different set of NGOs. While initially they had never planned to work together (indeed each did not always know the other had similar networks), their family agendas were similar enough to allow cooperation. Powerful international players in the Vatican, U.S. business, and political elites encouraged the networks to work more closely together. While they can sometimes amplify their influence by cooperating closely, it was never planned that way. Each came to U.N. forums expecting to be a lone voice among opponents. Yet each network found to its surprise allies in other denominations, faiths and countries.

Understanding the main networks helps one navigate through the ever-proliferating list of socially conservative NGOs at the U.N. The new groups have all emerged from one of the following three pro-family networks: the Catholic Church, the Mormon Church, and Evangelical Protestantism. Because each of these networks is tightly connected to a different religious culture, the future success of their work rests on the solid foundations of a growing constituency, elite support, and a culturally specific rhetoric.

From Rome: The Conservative Catholic Network

For those who conceptualize the Christian Right as dominated by conservative evangelicals, it may seem odd to start this chapter with the Papacy. However, Pope John Paul II, whose long tenure and charisma arguably made him one of history's most influential popes, is the best starting point for understanding the Christian Right for two reasons. First, the Vatican's political affairs office, the Holy See, has often provided leadership for a conservative view on family, women's roles in society, and reproductive health policy at the U.N., making it a natural ally of conservative religious NGOs. In fact, many conservative Catholic leaders view their work at the U.N. as a response to Pope John Paul II's call for the faithful to influence international policy on family and reproductive health. Second, Pope John Paul II, through his own vision of inter-religious cooperation and his promotion of a "culture of life," inspired religious conservatives to form inter-religious coalitions to address concerns around family and morality. The Christian Right's work with the Holy See at the United Nations and its coalition building must be viewed in light of this broader context.

The Struggle to Claim the Legacy of Pope John Paul II

The passing of Pope John Paul II afforded an unprecedented opportunity for non-Catholics as well as Catholics to reflect on the leadership of one of the most significant figures of the twentieth century. An examination of how various commentators viewed the Pope's legacy provide us with some interesting insights into how the culture wars are shaping both conservative and progressive cultures. Throughout his papacy and after his death, American conservatives claimed Pope John Paul II as their hero for his defense of what he called a "culture of life" and his moral leadership in the face of communism. Yet a close look at the Pope's leadership on a range of issues would suggest a much more complex picture. He opposed the Iraq War, critiqued capitalism and consumerism, and forged new ground in interfaith relations. One wonders if historians centuries from now might puzzle at the fact that this man was so adamantly labeled a conservative in the culture wars.

That the Pope would come to be viewed as an arch-Conservative demonstrates the power of both conservative and liberal leaders of the culture wars in shaping public perception. While social conservatives, neoconservatives and Wall Street claimed John Paul II as their man, liberals – both secular and religious – tended to disassociate themselves from the Vatican. The fact that the Pope's stance on abortion defined his papacy for American religious liberals and conservatives demonstrates again how culture war issues like abortion and sexuality today serve as the most important litmus test for how a political figure is defined, rather than such pressing issues like poverty or peace.

It's impossible to say what the Pope's legacy might have been, had progressive religious leaders and NGOs fervently claimed the Pope as their own. After all, they could have pointed to his stance against the Iraq War, critique of consumerism, interfaith efforts, opposition to the death penalty, quest for peace in the Middle East and his identification with the common person. Despite his complex record, though, there is no doubt that by the 1990s John Paul II had inspired both conservative

Catholics and evangelicals to consider taking their family agenda to the world community.

The Inspired Leadership: The Pilgrim Pope as a Media and Organizing Figure

John Paul II in many ways modernized and radically reinterpreted the role of the papacy in the modern world. Known affectionately as the "Pilgrim Pope" by his supporters, John Paul II logged more kilometers than all the other popes combined, visiting around two hundred countries. Rather than hold court in Rome like those before him, John Paul II traveled the world reaching out to the faithful and building new partnerships. This represented a profound shift in the papacy: rather than remaining a distant, all-powerful patriarch, John Paul II was viewed as a servant of the people. His first act at every stop was to kneel and kiss the ground, a profound physical symbol of the sacredness of life. His travels and personal warmth made the Pope a highly regarded and well-known international figure.[1]

John Paul II took unprecedented steps to heal and build relationships with evangelicals, Jews and Muslims. American evangelicals, who before this papacy tended to view Catholicism and the Pope with great suspicion, by the end hailed John Paul II as a hero and great spiritual leader. Evangelicals identified with the Pope's opposition to secularism and efforts to lead a spiritual and moral revival around the world. His style of holding large open-air meetings reminded many evangelicals of their own Billy Graham's big tent revivals. Pope John Paul II's invention of the phrase "culture of life" and his opposition to communism resonated deeply in the evangelical world. According to one evangelical leader, as evangelicals became more involved in the public arena "the pope provided a moral impetus that we didn't have internally within our own community."[2]

World-renowned evangelist Billy Graham once praised John Paul II as being the most significant Christian leader in the past hundred years. Another evangelical in reflecting on the Pope's legacy compared John Paul II favorably to two major evangelical church leaders Bill Hybels and Rick Warren:[3]

> In this respect, John Paul II was not all that different from Bill Hybels or Rick Warren. He tried to harness the forms of popular culture to conservative

piety in order to reinvigorate the church. Ironically, while much of American Catholicism has resisted Wojtyla's conservatism, many lapsed American Catholics have fueled the growth of evangelical megachurches such as Willow Creek and Saddleback.

This observation also highlights the major realignment in American, and possibly global, religion: conservative Catholics have more in common with conservative evangelicals than with more liberal Catholics.

According to some, the exchange went both ways: the Pope learned from his travels and exchanges with evangelicals throughout Asia, Africa and Latin America. According to a recent story in the popular conservative evangelical magazine *Christianity Today*, the relationship between Pope John Paul II and evangelicals can be traced as far back as the 1970s in Poland. John Paul II, then Karol Wojtyla, forged a partnership with Billy Graham and the evangelical ministry Campus Crusade for Christ as they sought to establish ministries behind the Iron Curtain to communist Eastern Europe. According to David Scott, who worked for Campus Crusade Poland, Wojtyla helped usher Campus Crusade into Catholic Poland. In fact, claims Scott, on October 16, 1978 when Wojtyla was assuming his new role as Pope John Paul II, the person preaching in his home pulpit in Krakow was none other than Billy Graham.[4]

This pope's flair for drama, his wide travels and adept use of media made him the best-known pope in all of history. His international and interfaith vision, combined with his promotion of a "culture of life" encouraged Catholics, evangelicals and even Muslims to advance their moral concerns at the United Nations.

The Original Impetus for U.N. Action: Objections to the Cairo Conference (1994)

Throughout the summer of 1994, Pope John Paul II gave a series of twelve ten-minute reflections that called faithful Catholics to advocate conservative stances on birth control, abortion and family at the U.N. International Conference on Population and Development in Cairo, Egypt. Well-known Catholic neoconservative and official papal biographer George Weigel, described the Pope's leadership through the summer of 1994 as "the *sine qua non* of the defeat suffered by the international advocates of the sexual revolution."[5] The Pope's weekly messages inspired not just Catholic but also evangelical leaders both to attend the Cairo conference and then to establish bases of activism at the United Nations. C-FAM president and founder Austin Ruse, expressed it this way: "During the lead up to Cairo the Holy Father gave a number of talks to Wednesday audiences. In those days he called people of all faiths to go to Cairo to lobby on behalf of life, faith and family. People of all faiths answered the call, and that was the basis of the movement. That was the beginning."[6]

The Unique Religious Influence of the Holy See at the U.N.

Besides moral suasion, the Vatican actually possesses a measure of real power at the U.N. that gives it a unique religious influence over proceedings. The Vatican through the Holy See has what is technically called "permanent observer" status at the U.N. Although this status technically gives it less authority than a member state, in many respects, the Holy See functions with the full authority of a U.N. member state, particularly at U.N. conferences. Other religious conservatives paid attention when the Holy See proved that religious voices could have a direct impact on a U.N. conference. At the Cairo Conference on Population and Development, for example, the Holy See's alliance with representatives of Muslim nations on the issue of population policy inspired Christian Right NGOs to pursue alliances with Muslim governments and religious leaders. George Weigel viewed the Cairo conference as a "watershed event for anti-abortion advocates who were inspired by the resistance of Islamic, Latin American and some African countries to the libertinism enshrined in the Cairo draft document."[7]

Even today, the Holy See continues to lend legitimacy and support to Christian Right networks. Alfonso Trujillo, the Pope's Pontifical Council on the Family has also focused much of his time and energy on opposing family planning and the legalization of abortion. He has traveled widely to support the anti-abortion efforts of Catholic NGOs. He made a special visit to the Holy See office in New York just prior to the UN Special Session on Children to praise and encourage Christian Right efforts (including Mormon and evangelical NGOs) to oppose reproductive health during the Special Session.[8] In addition to Catholic pro-life NGOs, the meeting included conservative evangelical NGO representatives from the Family Research Council and Concerned

Women for America.[9] Trujillo also participated recently in the
World Congress of Families III in Mexico City as a keynote speaker
representing the Vatican.

The Representative NGO: The Catholic Family and Human Rights Institute (C-FAM)

Although a handful of "pro-life" Catholic organizations held a quiet
presence at the U.N. for years, the Catholic Family and Human Rights
Institute (C-FAM), directed by Austin Ruse and established in 1997,
quickly raised the profile of Catholic family efforts among the U.N.
community. Progressive NGOs found his rhetoric inflammatory. Weeks
prior to the Beijing+5 preparatory meeting he alarmed feminist leaders
with the first of many calls to his constituency to join the battle for
family. In his fax Ruse called for the "children of Abraham" to fight
"one of the most radical and dangerous documents you can imagine."[10]
When three hundred Christian Right activists showed up weeks later,
Ruse's one-man operation enabled Christian Right NGOs to project a
highly visible presence. After this modest success at the Beijing meeting,
Austin Ruse and C-FAM became for many in the U.N. community
what Pat Robertson and the Christian Coalition are to Progressives
in the United States: dangerous religious ideologues. While no single
organization leads this loosely organized coalition and other Christian
Right organizations play a role just as important, C-FAM remains the
most well known of the pro-family groups at the U.N.[11]

Ruse played a major role in outlining the Christian Right's initial
political strategy at the U.N. Inspired by the Holy See's coalition-
building efforts at the Cairo Population Conference in 1994, Ruse at a
1999 meeting of "pro-family" organizations in Geneva proposed that
pro-family forces foster the formation of a bloc of socially conservative
governments to oppose legalizing abortion internationally and to take
a conservative stand on social issues. Ruse feels fairly successful in
that regard. In his view, "the U.N. General Assembly is fine with
our coalition."[12] Even so, he acknowledges that they had only about
thirty countries (out of 196) on their side, keeping them in a largely
defensive posture.[13]

C-FAM also encouraged many Christian Right NGOs to apply for
consultative status, shepherding them through the accreditation process

and showing them around the U.N. system.[14] Most significantly, Ruse played a major hand in encouraging the evangelical behemoth Focus on the Family (described below), to seek consultative status. Ruse continues to encourage other New Right organizations like the Federalist Society and Heritage Foundation to become active at the U.N.[15]

Austin Ruse's flare for stirring controversy and his ability to send out provocative rhetoric via the Web and email technology well reflected his experience in the publishing world (which included some work with *Rolling Stone* magazine). His experience with media helped C-FAM achieve its superstar reputation early on, as did his ability to draw on already existing networks from parent NGOs and an already developed and tightly knit Christian Right infrastructure. With a small staff (just Ruse and an assistant), C-FAM's influence depended on its partnerships with larger organizations and still does today.[16]

C-FAM's work has enjoyed much more success at the U.N. than the older, more specifically pro-life Catholic NGOs with which it works. C-FAM works in close partnership with larger Catholic anti-abortion organizations such as the Population Research Institute and Human Life International. (In fact, Human Life International (HLI) in Canada helped establish C-FAM.) HLI Canada is an affiliate of HLI International, a controversial international Catholic anti-abortion organization. Established in 1972, HLI International's application for U.N. consultative status was turned down in the early 1990s because of the extremist anti-Semitic and anti-Muslim statements of its leader Father Marx and his aggressive language (he has since been removed).[17]

C-FAM represents a new, more sophisticated style of Catholic activism: in addition to its operation in New York a few blocks from the U.N., Ruse has established an office in Washington, DC. While one cannot predict if he will attain sufficient funding, Ruse has big dreams for the future. First, he wants to set up a global network of branch offices in major world capitals. Ruse recognizes that to influence the United Nations, one must ideally be able to influence the capitals of U.N. member states.[18] Second, Ruse wants his organization to tackle an array of policy questions and move beyond the group's present focus on pro-life activities. For now, though, Ruse's immediate goal is to make C-FAM into the premier conservative social policy expert at the U.N. in order to strengthen the involvement of Washington-based conservative organizations in the U.N.[19]

From Salt Lake City, Utah: The Mormon Network

There are many striking parallels between the story of the Catholic network and the forces that created a strong Mormon presence at the U.N. The growing role of Mormon NGOs in the Christian Right, especially at the U.N. is often overlooked, yet substantial. The largest of these are the World Family Policy Center (WFPC) and United Families International (UFI). Their strength and potential, described below, must also be understood in terms of the resources of the Mormon Church, or Church of Jesus Christ of Latter Day Saints (LDS). Like the Vatican, the Mormon Church brings vast resources and a global presence to efforts to build a global "pro-family" movement.[20]

Given the Mormon Church's future prospects, financial resources, growing membership, and close affinity with conservative family values, Mormon NGOs are poised to have a tremendous international impact. The Church of Latter Day Saints is now the richest religion in the United States per capita, with over $25 billion in estimated assets and $5 billion in estimated annual income.[21] Sociologist Rodney Stark projects that during the coming century Mormonism will become the most important world religion to emerge since the rise of Islam some 14 centuries ago. With over 10 million members worldwide, the LDS Church is poised to surpass the Church of God in Christ and the Evangelical Lutheran Church in America and become the fifth largest denomination behind Roman Catholics, Southern Baptists, United Methodists and National Baptists. A generation ago, Mormons were concentrated in the U.S., but now less than half live in the U.S. and Canada and over a third live in Latin America.[22]

Mormon views on the family easily lend themselves to the traditional family values of conservative evangelicals and Catholics. The Mormon faith in fact emphasizes a direct link between the family and salvation. The family takes on a spiritual dimension not seen in most Protestant and Catholic theology. [23] Exaltation, the process by which men become gods, is available only within family units. Women obtain spiritual reward in the hereafter only through marriage since the priesthood, available to all men, is not open to women. During the nineteenth century, Utah church authorities were under pressure to produce large families (as well as practice polygamy) since elite status in heaven had much to do with family size. Although polygamy is prohibited by the church today, a good Mormon's spiritual duty includes having large families so that they can provide earthly tabernacles for souls-in-waiting. Not surprisingly, concludes one expert, "LDS authorities consider [family] among their most sacred trust and do everything in their power to protect it."[24]

It is also not surprising that current LDS leadership views gays and lesbians, abortion and feminism as major threats to Mormon beliefs about the family. In 1993, Boyd Packer, the LDS hierarchy's chief theological watchdog and a contender for the church presidency after the current president Gordon Hinckley, warned that three "dangers [of an] intensity and seriousness that we have not faced before [had made] major invasions into the membership of the church." These were the gay and lesbian movement, the feminist movement and "the ever present challenge from so-called scholars or intellectuals."[25]

The Inspired Leader: Hinckley Charts a More Public and Conservative Course

There are striking similarities between the conservative and transformative leadership styles of Mormon President Gordon Hinckley and Pope John Paul II. Since the time he became the president of the Church of Jesus Christ of Latter Day Saints in 1995, Hinckley has taken an already conservative institution further to the right on theological and family issues. He has operated as a conservative influence on the church since becoming a national leader in 1981, only two years after the inauguration of John Paul II's papacy.[26] Just like John Paul II, Hinckley as president also has raised the LDS's public profile, broadened its global vision, and explored how to build interfaith alliances around moral concerns. In fact, he is the church's most-traveled president ever and organized the effort to build an unprecedented number of temples in places such as Hong Kong, Alaska, Mexico, Spain, England, Colombia, Canada, Hawaii and Bolivia.[27] When the Winter Olympics were held in Salt Lake City in 2002, a once-marginal culture announced its global credentials.[28]

Hinckley's conservative activism dates back to his effort to stop the proposed Equal Rights Amendment (ERA) from being ratified by the Utah state legislature. [29] The defeat of the ERA in Utah helped doom the amendment. The anti-ERA effort was the first time people from traditional Christian churches had worked with members of the Mormon Church. Phyllis Schlafly, a Catholic who spearheaded a successful national anti-ERA campaign just before the amendment was poised to be ratified, worked alongside Mormons to ensure its defeat. She recalled the initial difficulty in getting social conservatives to work together: "I'd say, 'Now, the person sitting next to you might not be "saved" but we're all going to work together to stop ERA.' Getting the Baptists and the Catholics together, and getting *them* all to work with the Mormons – this was something! I made them do it!"[30] All would ultimately cooperate because they wanted to defeat the ERA. As a *Boston Globe* headline at the time read, "It's Do or Die for the ERA: Mormon Power is the Key."[31]

The Original Impetus for U.N. Action: Objections to the Beijing Conference (1995)

With the elevation of Hinckley to president of the church in 1995, the official LDS Church leadership and its flagship educational institution, Brigham Young University (30,000 students), began to emphasize more emphatically traditional Mormon teaching on the family and sought new ways to strengthen the traditional family through public policy initiatives. Soon after the 1995 U.N. Conference on Women in Beijing, the Hinckley First Presidency and the Twelve Apostles issued a proclamation called "The Family: Proclamation to the World." The proclamation challenges the feminist assertion that gender is a social construct and emphasizes traditional gender roles and families: "gender is an essential characteristic of individual pre-mortal, mortal and eternal identity and purpose."[32] Fathers are to "preside over their families in love and righteousness and are to provide the necessities of life and protection for their families. Mothers are primarily responsible for the nurture of their children." The proclamation is apocalyptic in tone when it contemplates changes in family structure: "Further, we warn that the disintegration of the family will bring upon individuals, communities, and nations the calamities foretold by ancient and modern prophets." It calls the LDS Church to action: "We call upon responsible citizens and officers of government everywhere to promote those measures designed to maintain and strengthen the family as the fundamental unit of society."[33]

Faithful support of the proclamation has become an important litmus test for Mormon institutions like Brigham Young University (BYU). The university administration tries to enforce the proclamation's views in all areas of university life, everything from shaping curriculum and censoring student newspapers, to using it as a basis for hiring and firing faculty. In fact the American Association of University Professors (AAUP) in 1998 censured BYU for limiting academic freedom.[34] BYU ignored the censure, saying that the AAUP had a long-standing bias against institutions with religious owners or missions.

The LDS and Brigham Young University have supported efforts to promote the traditional family at the U.N. but they apparently have not given direct financial aid. In my interview with Richard Wilkins of the WFPC, he indicated that the LDS hierarchy was neither directly involved in any Christian Right coalition nor had the WFPC received money from the church. Nevertheless, the extent to which either the official church or BYU backs or initiates Mormon NGOs operating at the U.N. also has much to bear on their success. As the history of the rightward shift of the church indicates, the Mormon presence at the U.N. is part of a more general thrust in the Salt Lake City church to promote the traditional family in public policy forums.

The Representative NGOs: United Families International

The persistent "pro-family" activism of Susan Roylance, founder of United Families International (UFI), paved the way for Mormons to participate at the U.N. Her journey to the U.N. began in the 1970s when she participated in the 1977 National Women's Conferences, first in Washington State and then in Houston. The conference, which drew 20,000 participants and 2,000 delegates, was funded with federal dollars. Delegates ratified a National Plan of Action that dealt with topics as wide-ranging as the ERA, civil rights and disarmament. Roylance was appalled by what she saw: "it was not just about ERA, it was about abortion and gay rights – it was a lesbian conference."[35] At the conference she went toe to toe with the vocal feminist activist and New York Congresswoman Bella Abzug, who had secured federal funding for the conference. The experience so frustrated her she decided to run for Congress from Washington State. Her bid failed but she helped form United Families of America which maintained an office in Washington, DC for several years.[36]

Roylance's activism took a new turn in 1995 when she attended preparatory meetings for the U.N. Fourth World Conference on Women in Beijing; again she ran into her nemesis Bella Abzug. Roylance was shocked: "I thought she had faded into the woodwork after losing her congressional [seat], but here she was doing through the U.N. what she couldn't do in Congress."[37] Since the last time Roylance had seen Abzug, she had established WEDO (Women's Environment and Development Organization) which became an important player in the global women's movement. When Roylance introduced herself during a strategy meeting at the Bejing forum, the participants laughed and jeered at the name of her organization. "It was a shocking experience for me, realizing the word family was a distasteful thing for these women."[38] The final insult was when conference leaders marginalized a Nigerian speaker who planned to critique the official position of the women's movement on family life. Roylance remembered that Carol Ugochukwu was slated to give a "speech that said feminists [had] got it wrong on families, so they put her in a corner."[39] Perhaps the only thing she held in common with the majority of the 40,000 women who attended the Bejing conference was a renewed dedication to take her message to the world at large. Roylance found that Hinckley's Proclamation on the Family inspired others to join the "pro-family cause." With the backing of her organization, Roylance has participated in twenty U.N. meetings since the Bejing conference.

UFI's Susan Roylance Recruits Dr. Richard Wilkins of WFPC at BYU

In contrast to the activist UFI, the WFPC is more of a think tank on family issues. While the center is part of the BYU system, the WFPC's president Dr. Richard Wilkins says that only a small part of WFPC's funding comes through the university. And while it is located on the BYU campus, he says it has only a loose administrative connection. As an academic center, the WFPC is governed by an advisory board. This board is made up of both BYU faculty and experts from outside the university. The faculty members meet weekly to better coordinate the WFPC's work with the BYU's J. Reuben Clark School of Law, School of Social Work, School of Family Life and the David M. Kennedy Center for International Studies.[40]

Roylance played an important role in convincing Dr. Wilkins to work beyond the ivory tower. She first met him while lobbying on abortion legislation. He was defending the State of Utah in a court case regarding abortion, that had been brought by the American Civil Liberties Union (ACLU). Roylance sought Wilkin's legal expertise to find out whether the Beijing Platform for Action really could have an impact on domestic law. She had to be persistent: "He was and is a very busy man, so I waited for him outside the courtroom."[41] Wilkins was at first reluctant to get involved with this international project. His anti-abortion advocacy in the U.S. had already left him frustrated. After spending years fighting *Roe* v. *Wade*, he had come to the conclusion that "The people's moral sense is numb. We are a society that can no longer think about fundamental values and it doesn't do any good to talk about fundamental values."[42] Despite his initial hesitation, Wilkins finally agreed to at least write a chapter for Roylance's book *The Traditional Family in Peril*. It was writing this paper that eventually piqued his interest in studying the impact that international law had on U.S. domestic policies: "I became somewhat troubled. It seemed the U.N. was beginning to make decisions that were best made at the local level."[43]

He received further confirmation that he should get involved once he attended the Second U.N. Conference on Habitats (1996). At first, he had no interest in attending. During the eight months prior to the U.N. Conference on Habitats (Habitat Conference) Roylance kept asking Dr. Wilkins to help her project. "You've got to be kidding," he thought, "no one wants to pay attention [to morals]."[44] Yet he kept waking up in the middle of the night. Finally, he pulled himself back together enough to get "back in the saddle" as he puts it and participate in a political event. As he left Salt Lake City for Istanbul he was hardly optimistic that he could have an impact on the proceedings. He had drafted a paper to deliver at the NGO forum and brought proposed amendments to the Habitat Agenda to give to delegates. At most he thought his work might cause some decision maker to exercise caution before "further undermining traditional social values."[45]

Wilkins came to the Istanbul conference with 35 UFI lobbyists; they hoped to lobby for amendments to the agenda that emphasized a traditional view of the family and opposed reproductive health services.[46] As Wilkins describes it, during the course of the conference, Johnson Mwaura, a member of the conference's coordinating committee, stopped by their information booth. Although no one was there at first, Mwaura came back repeatedly until he was able to talk with Wilkins. Mwaura invited him to put his name on the list of NGO speakers to address the government plenary. In a turn of events that demonstrates the power of globalizing religion and culture, Wilkins discovered Mwaura was an LDS elders' quorum president from Nairobi, Kenya.[47]

Opposition to Mwaura's choice for speaker was intense, says Wilkins.[48] He almost didn't get the floor, but at the last minute an Algerian delegate protested that there was no diversity among the speakers. The delegate's motion to hear another perspective was seconded and Wilkins was able to give a hastily written speech based on the LDS Proclamation on the Family. Evidently the speech had made an impact because two days later, Arab delegates at the conference issued a statement saying they would not sign the Habitat Agenda if it failed to recognize religion and family as the basic unit of society and to define marriage as a relationship between a man and a woman. A day later, the G-77 nations (a voting block of African, Asian and Pacific Rim countries and China) made a similar statement. Both groups also refused to sign an agreement obligating nations to provide abortion services. By the time the conference was adjourned, the Habitat Agenda was a pro-family document, says Wilkins. According to Cory Leonard, "People were dumbfounded. Developing countries, Islamic countries, Latin American countries all approached him and asked how to move forward."[49] At the time, Leonard served as director of student programs at BYU's David M. Kennedy Center for International Studies. Leonard and the Kennedy Center joined Wilkins and the BYU Law School in starting an organization that would come to be called the World Family Policy Center. "I thought no one was listening," Wilkins concludes, "What I realize now is that both sides weren't being presented."[50]

The WFPC, which Wilkins describes as an academic center focused on building intergovernmental dialogue and networking, holds summer symposiums for government delegates and scholars from all over the world who are interested in the "pro-family" movement. Wilkins estimates that between seventy and a hundred of the U.N. diplomatic corps, largely from Catholic and Muslim countries, come to these meetings each year.[51] The programs feature speakers like Mr. S. Shahid Husain, a senior adviser to the Organization of the Islamic Conference, and Mr. Esko Aho, a former prime minister of Finland. Some participants are assisted financially, though not all. Through these meetings the WFPC established a relationship with Ambassador Al-Nassar of Qatar. Al-Nassar approached the WFPC with the idea of hosting an intergovernmental meeting during the International Year of the Family to provide a "fresh perspective" on the concept of the family at the U.N. (see Chapter 2).[52]

The WFPC Collaborates with the Howard Center

Dr. Wilkins of the WFPC has worked closely with Dr. Allan Carlson, the president of the Howard Center in Rockford, Illinois. Together they have sponsored a series of global conferences on the family that bring political leaders and intellectuals from around the world to discuss the breakdown of the family. The original idea for the World Congress of Families came up by chance when in 1995 Allan Carlson, a Lutheran, was invited by two sociology professors to speak at Moscow University.[53] The professors were enthusiastic readers of Carlson's book *Family Questions: Reflections on the American Social Crisis* (1988). The professors and Carlson, joined by a lay leader in the Russian Orthodox Church, came to the conclusion that what they needed was to bring together scholars and leaders from "newly free Europe and Russia" to meet with leaders from the West.[54]

U.N. meetings in Cairo, Beijing and Istanbul weighed heavily on the minds of these leaders, says Carlson, because they believed the Orthodox and more conservative position "were not represented by national governments by and large."[55] The first World Congress of Families, held in Prague in 1997, unexpectedly drew over seven hundred people. Inspired, he thought they could do even more in the future: "We decided we needed something bigger and broader. We needed a gathering representing religious orthodoxies, particularly in three Abrahamic faiths."[56]

By coincidence, Dr. Wilkins had decided to attend the Prague conference and met Carlson. At the time, Wilkins was already forming the WFPC. As they flew back from the conference together, they laid the groundwork for what would become the World Congress of Families II in Geneva, Switzerland. Their relationship was helped by the fact that elite Mormons already sat on the Howard Center's board. The Center's founder and a principal financier, John Howard, was good friends with Dallin Oaks, one of the Twelve Apostles of the Mormon Church. When Oaks had been university president in the 1970s, BYU had opposed implementation of Title IX (a federal law which required colleges to spend money equally on women's and men's sports teams) as well as the Equal Rights Amendment.

Brigham Young University offered to cover half of the expenses of the congress, and U.N. missions secured a room on the U.N. grounds in Geneva. Inspired by the Holy See's efforts to build alliances with the Organization of Islamic Conferences, Carlson planned to "extend a hand to Muslims and Orthodox Jews." Carlson sensed that "there is a hunger in the Islamic world for these kinds of relationships, because Islamic nations are going through difficult changes, particularly those casting their lot with modernity. They see this as an alliance with parts of the West that are not destabilizing. They are trying to develop alliances and communication with good elements."[57] The Geneva meeting drew around a thousand participants.

The terrorist attacks of September 11, 2001 derailed plans to host a conference with the government of Dubai, according to Carlson. But in the spring of 2003 a group of lay Catholic businessmen from Mexico, inspired by the Geneva meeting to start a pro-family, pro-life network called Red Familia (Family Network), came to Carlson with the idea of putting together a World Congress of Families in Mexico City. Carlson, who seems to be more comfortable in the world of ideas than with his role as a global organizer confessed, "To be honest, I didn't know Red Familia existed."[58] The Mexican leaders of Red Familia took the lead organizing the logistics and financing for the conference.[59] Carlson claims the Mexico WCF drew around three thousand participants (see Chapter 5 for more on Red Familia).[60]

Allan Carlson, a Lutheran who has written prolifically on family and public policy, strikes one as more of an academic than a global organizer. The success and growing diversity of the World Congress of

Families events surprises and pleases him, but he is hardly the crusader one might expect from one who is fostering an unlikely partnership of Catholic, Mormon, evangelical, Muslim and a few Jewish scholars and activists. He is also a utopian dreamer who speaks admiringly of the Amish as the "masters of modernity" because they "have managed to tame modernity and make technology their servants rather than their masters." He believes that a Baptist experiment in communitarian living called Heritage Homestead in Texas can provide a model for a better world. Heritage Homestead has inspired 5,000 other self-sufficient, family-centered agrarian communities. When I asked whether such idealistic models can inform modern national policy decisions he responded, "I don't know. The folks at Heritage Homestead have managed to do it. We can learn some things, not all. Maybe we'll home school, and be self-sufficient in vegetable growing. We will do it not because it's efficient, but because it's pro-family."[61]

One might wonder how such community-centered sentiments might sound to the corporate internationalists and others in the New Right coalition. Carlson's solution to the problems caused by industrialization appears to be to return to a pre-industrial era, an idea explored in depth in his book *The New Agrarian.*[62] Is there a disconnection between Carlson and corporate sectors of the New Right? When I asked him this question he responded in the affirmative: "I think there is." Although he spent eight months as a fellow at the American Enterprise Institute at one point in his career, the Howard Center fought the AEI's position on the marriage penalty tax-relief proposal because it still encouraged a two-wage earner family structure. The AEI's version of the policy won out. "The current alliance between pro-family conservatives and corporate America is unstable," he acknowledges, "just as are some of the alliances on the Left."[63]

Carlson's career path in some ways echoes that of Richard John Neuhaus, a well-known Catholic neoconservative, who like Carlson once held a position in the Howard Center's parent organization, the controversial Rockford Institute. Neuhaus was literally thrown out of the Rockford Institute in the 1960s for confronting its leadership for their anti-Semitic views.[64] In the late 1990s, the Rockford Institute moved even further right as its board began to support a neoconfederate organization called League of the South. The year the Rockford Center cemented its relationship with League of the South, the Howard Center obtained an "amicable divorce." Carlson left Rockford and took the helm of the Howard Center: "We were doing things that did not make sense under the same umbrella. Different folks wanted to do different things." When asked whether he agrees with Neuhaus' characterization of Rockford, Carlson says that he feels it is inappropriate to talk about former colleagues but in speaking of the "divorce" confesses: "We were working internationally. *Chronicles*, the Rockford Magazine, is meant to be a controversial opinion magazine."[65]

From the American Heartland: Conservative Evangelicals

Conservative white evangelical Christian Right NGOs came to the U.N. more reluctantly than did Catholics and Mormons who traditionally have not displayed the suspicion that evangelicals hold towards the U.N. The task of involving conservative evangelicals in the U.N. project is therefore the most difficult, but, given their political clout, quite powerful. If Catholics bring to the coalition strong relationships with the Holy See, conservative evangelicals bring the world's superpower through their connections with President George W. Bush.

Three of the five key players in the Christian Right in the United States are active in the Christian Right at the U.N.: Focus on the Family, the Family Research Council and Concerned Women for America. These have harnessed largely conservative evangelicals, but also growing numbers of Catholics and Mormons, for the causes championed by their leaders. Their involvement shows that while average conservative evangelicals may be wary of any involvement at the U.N., their leaders actually have a significant commitment to influencing U.N. policy.

The Inspired Leadership: George W. Bush as President of Good and Evil[66]

President George W. Bush, like Pope John Paul II, has inspired religious conservatives to engage in international activism and to embrace new partners. President Bush has compensated the Christian Right for its loyalty more than any other president before him. The U.N. has been one of many arenas where he has provided them with clear victories on issues they care about. Bush's use of religious images and moral absolutes in the War on Terror contributes to widening evangelical interest in foreign affairs and suspicion for the United Nations. Finally, the president's sympathy for these NGOs has opened up funding streams that will help these NGOs establish or expand some of their international operations.[67]

George W. Bush is the culmination of a series of presidents that have inspired conservative Protestants to political action. President Jimmy Carter awakened conservative evangelicals to the possibilities of political power; Ronald Reagan whetted their appetites, and George W. Bush embraced them as insiders. If Reagan supported the church like a flying buttress, from the outside, Bush, a born-again Methodist, is more a pillar in the nave, say authors of *Right Nation*. "When G.W. meets with Evangelical Christians, they know within minutes he's one of theirs," says Doug Wead, an evangelical who worked with both Bush presidents.[68]

When George W. Bush during the 2000 election debates was asked to name his favorite philosopher, he responded without hesitation or explanation, "Jesus." The moderator of the debate paused for a moment, seemingly taken aback, then asked Bush to elaborate. He simply responded, "because he changed my heart." Bush's answer floored liberal Americans. But to millions it was an answer that resonated – they may have cheered at the answer or uttered a reverent "Amen!" To at least a third of the population, George W. Bush was speaking to their souls.[69]

Most popular American presidents have evoked religious language in their speeches to some degree, but Bush has done so in a manner more provocative than even President Ronald Reagan. Princeton ethicist Peter Singer, who analyzed Bush's public statements, says that "No other president in living memory has spoken so often about good and evil, right and wrong."[70] He has spoken about evil in 30 per cent of all the speeches he gave between the time he took office and June 16, 2003. His speeches use "evil" as a noun far more than as an adjective (914 to 182). The most striking example was his use of the language of "crusades" and the "axis of evil" after the September 11 terrorist attacks, echoing Reagan's labeling of the Soviet Union as the Evil Empire. The U.S. is framed unabashedly as a "moral nation" fighting not to advance its own interests, but to spread American values.[71]

His opponents deridingly suggest that his is the first "faith-based Presidency," because of his willingness to make decisions based not on fact and rationality but on faith.[72] Scientists have accused the administration of manipulating science to fit its policy goals, including questioning nominees to scientific advisory panels about whether they had voted for President Bush.[73] Bush's faith is one that leads him to see the world in black and white, in simple truths – a quality his supporters love but his detractors fear, because it oversimplifies complex global concerns.[74]

Bush's Connection to White Evangelicals

President Bush's basis for appealing to conservative Christian faith is personal, but it is also political. Religious conservatives constituted 40 per cent of Bush's vote in 2004.[75] Religiosity is just as much a partisan predictor for Republicans as race is for Democrats. Nine out of ten African Americans voted for Al Gore in 2000. Nearly nine in ten "high-commitment evangelicals" voted for George W. Bush. A study in the magazine *Campaigns and Elections* revealed that Christian conservatives now exercise either a "strong" or "moderate" influence in 44 Republican state committees, compared with 31 in 1994.[76] They are weak only in six states, all of them in the Northeast.

The conservative religious vote helped win Bush's reelection. Both Democrats and Republicans often rely on church leaders to get out the vote. Candidates in both parties have been known to speak in churches while on the campaign trail. What is striking about Bush's strategy is that congregations were directly contacted by the Bush campaign rather than by a special interest group. The 2004 Bush campaign enlisted thousands of religious congregations around the country to distribute campaign information and register voters; an effort that many, conservatives and liberals alike, feared might compromise churches' tax-exempt status. The outreach effort was conducted on an unprecedented scale: in just one state 1600 congregations were involved.[77]

Like the Pope, Bush and his campaign advisers have pushed harder than any other conservative president to reach out to other faiths. Bush has made a successful effort to chip away at the Democratic Party's Catholic support. He won the votes of a majority of religiously active Catholics in 2000, the best showing among them by a Republican presidential candidate since 1984.[78]

He invited a Muslim imam to the launch of his faith-based initiative program, appointed a staff person to work on Arab-Muslim outreach, and refers to 'mosques' in speeches about religious institutions. Bush's autobiography pointedly tells how on his first trip to Israel he was part of a delegation that included a Methodist, two Catholics, a Mormon and several Jewish-American friends. "It is important for any leader to respect the faith of others," he writes. The chapter on his born-again experience concludes with the story of how two members of that delegation, a "gentile" and a Jew, had snuck away from the group to go down to the Sea of Galilee and pray together underwater.[79]

The Original Impetus for U.N. Action: The Invitation of George W. Bush (2000)

Christian Right leaders often complained that under Reagan and the first President Bush their success at turning out the vote for the Republican Party did not translate to clear gains for their own objectives. In contrast, George W. Bush has appointed more Christian Right leaders to his administration than his father or Ronald Reagan. Bush's receptivity to the Christian Right's concerns has meant unprecedented access for them in governmental affairs. For his cabinet, Bush chose former Senator John Ashcroft as U.S. Attorney General. Since the Justice Department handles issues such as abortion, the selection of judges, the death penalty, and civil rights, Ashcroft's new position was a major victory for the Christian Right.[80] Demonstrating the importance of its relationships with Christian Right leaders, the White House even appointed an official, Tim Goeglein, to do "Christian outreach."[81]

White Evangelical conservatives became more involved at the U.N. when Bush appointed them to serve as government officials and NGO delegates at U.N. conferences. For example, the Bush Administration appointed Wade Horn to serve as the U.S. mission's liason with Christian Right NGOs. Wade Horn, the Assistant Secretary for the Administration of Children, Youth and Families, is a proponent of abstinence education, marriage promotion and national fatherhood initiatives. He served on the U.S. delegation to the U.N. Special Session on Children and speaks frequently at Christian Right conferences related to the U.N.[82]

The NGO Representative: Focus on the Family

Dr. James Dobson's Focus on the Family (known as Focus) is quite possibly the largest, most influential evangelical political and cultural influence in the United States today.[83] Dobson's books have sold more than 12 million copies and the Focus on the Family newsletter reaches more than 3 million donors, a number comparable to the circulation of *Newsweek*.[84] The heart of Dobson's ministry, a radio program called *Focus on the Family*, reaches an audience estimated to exceed 5 million listeners a week. Only the conservative radio talk show host Rush Limbaugh, and Paul Harvey, speak to more Americans weekly. Moreover, Dobson's radio programs broadcast to 120 nations in 17 different languages.[85]

For thirty years his programs, which combine psychology and conservative biblical principles, have provided a forum in which Dobson could worry aloud about abortion, divorce, gay rights and contraception. These programs found a ready audience in the United States. Dobson first knew he had identified a deep unmet need when he wrote his first book while earning his doctorate in child development at the University of Southern California. *Dare to Discipline* became a bestseller. Journalist Steve Rabey once characterized the popular work as a blend of "biblical principles, Christian psychology, common sense, a nostalgia for the 1950s, and a conservative reaction to trends like the sexual revolution, youth rebellion, psychedelic experimentation, and the women's movement."[86] Although Focus is a largely Christian ministry, not an advocacy organization (only 5 per cent of its resources go towards public policy advocacy), Dobson has given voice to the concerns and values of millions of Americans who hearken to his wisdom on family matters. Until the 2004 Presidential campaign, when gay marriage became a major issue, Dobson has not been directly and openly engaged in partisan politics and rarely agrees to interviews with secular media.[87]

It took some time for Focus to become active at the U.N., said Austin Ruse, because they had such a negative reaction to the Beijing conference.[88] Thomas Jacobson, Focus's U.N. representative confirms that Focus originally had no interest in the body: "This was never something Focus envisioned we would be doing when we started 27 years ago."[89] The U.N. Conference on Women in Bejiing pushed the group into the U.N. arena: "Tom Minnery, the VP of Public policy and a few others went to Beijing 'just to find out what was going on.'" They were "astounded at what they saw: the atmosphere was decidedly feminist." "Focus is not anti-women," Jacobson clarifies, "but we were concerned about the tone there. It was anti-family and anti-life."[90]

Jacobson explained that Minnery felt that nations from regions like Latin America who want to voice a more traditional conservative position were being prevented from stating their position. Minnery and other "pro-life, pro-family" forces began to speak to diplomats and found that some of the Latin American diplomats "came to be more courageous and demanded to be heard. They were able to have some input, but strongly [were] resisted."[91] Once again, the fact that the Christian Right message resonated with other people came as a pleasant surprise to conservative activists.

For years after the Beijing conference, Focus had only tangential involvement in any U.N. meetings. But in 2001 Jacobson was brought on to work full time at the U.N. Of the fifty Focus staff that address policy issues (only 5 per cent of Focus work is policy oriented), he is the only staff person focused specifically on the U.N. However the resources of Focus – its marketing, mailing, events planning office, and most of all, its international division – are at his disposal.[92]

Austin Ruse proudly told of getting Focus on the Family to obtain U.N. Economic and Social Council (ECOSOC) status. For Ruse, Focus was "the big one" because it is one of the largest conservative evangelical ministries in the world: "Now [their] work at high levels with governments ... would shock you."[93] Focus already has the kind of infrastructure Ruse dreams about: it has ministries in twenty countries around the world, all of which are run by nationals who sign a licensing agreement to use the Focus on the Family label. Focus on the Family (USA) provides support for marketing and product development. Through affiliates, Focus can indirectly influence the capitals of U.N. member states. In a recent dramatic example of this capacity, Focus on the Family (Costa Rica) successfully advocated that their government respond to a draft U.N. resolution to ban human cloning. Costa Rica submitted a draft that would seek a total ban on all forms of cloning – including therapeutic cloning. This eventually resulted in a partial victory for the Christian Right and Bush Administration (this effort is covered in detail in Chapter 5).[94]

One of Focus's greatest challenges is to explain its U.N. involvement to its constituency. Dobson and Focus promoted Timothy LaHaye's popular *Left Behind* series, which features a fictional U.N. Secretary General as the Antichrist. In addition, many conservative evangelicals would oppose collaborating with Mormons and Muslims. U.N. representative Jacobson shared that there has been no effort to interpret his office's activities in the Focus monthly newsletters, although it is discussed in *Family News in Focus*, a more limited circulation newsletter circulated to those interested in public policy.[95] Jacobson in fact has a more pragramatic view of the U.N. than someone like LaHaye: "I believe having an institution, a world institution, is inevitable in our day and age. Once you had international communications and travel, then from that point forward you have people either talking or fighting. I think it's much better to have them talking to one another."[96]

While Focus on the Family follows more of a ministry model, its modest work at the U.N. is enhanced by working with two more advocacy organizations: the Family Research Council (FRC) and Concerned Women for America (CWA). Two decades ago Dobson established the FRC as a separate organization to advocate conservative social policies in Washington without jeopardizing Focus on the Family's tax-exempt status or Dobson's reputation as a spiritual leader. Gary Bauer, who ran in the Republican Party presidential primaries four years ago, was the FRC's first director. The FRC in 1998 boasted a membership of 450,000 and a budget of $14 million.[97]

The involvement of Concerned Women for America – like Focus on the Family and the Family Research Council – indicates that the U.N. is not the concern of just a few small Christian Right NGOs. CWA, the largest conservative evangelical women's organization, was founded by Beverly LaHaye in the early 1980s to "protect the family through prayer and action." Beverly LaHaye is the wife of Tim LaHaye, a co-founder of the Moral Majority (and the best-selling author of the *Left Behind* series). Founding members of the CWA's advisory council include the wives of Jerry Falwell, Senator Jesse Helms and television evangelist Jimmy Swaggart. Its revenue in 1992 was $8.2 million.[98] The executive vice-president of the CWA, Wendy Wright, regularly writes for the CWA website on U.N. issues and is a high-profile spokesperson for conservative women in her own right.[99]

Conclusion

For decades progressive activists dominated NGO activism at the U.N., partly because there was little competition from conservative organizations. That era has now passed. Every year more conservative NGOs form and seek accredidation at the U.N. It is hard to keep track of all the smaller ones. "Right-to-life" groups include: Couple to Couple League, CARE (based in the UK), the American Life League and International Right to Life Federation (accredited in 2000) and the Campaign Life Coalition (accredited in 1999). Conservative women's groups include the Eagle Forum, Endeavor Forum, Real Women of Canada, Worldwide Organization for Women (accredited in 1999) and World Movement of Mothers. Latin American organizations seeking consultative status include: the Latin-American Alliance for the Family (ALAFA), Family Action Council International (FACI), Family + Foundation, Red Familia, Social Sector Forum (Argentina), and the Spanish Family Forum. The numbers of conservative religious NGOs and their international connections continues to increase annually.

Besides being the first ones at the U.N., progressive NGOs understood the promise of the U.N. as a unique world political forum. Because the U.N. was a relatively new institution, and a relatively small number of activists were present, a handful of sharp, effective NGO leaders could make a significant difference in particular arenas, especially social issues. The ability of progressive NGOs to quickly score major victories now becomes harder as the field becomes more crowded. Just as other global NGO movements emerged over concerns such as the environment and human rights, so now Christian Right NGOs are addressing the state of the world's families (including fears about homosexuality, feminism and reproductive health technologies).

In the U.S., many American political leaders acknowledge that conservative activists have out-maneuvered the political Left.[100] While progressives lost their connections with their grass roots, conservatives, especially Christian conservatives, have maintained and increased their networks and infrastructure. After years of complaining that liberal elites controlled American culture, conservative leaders launched their own media empire and network of think tanks to shift the ground of debate in the United States effectively to the right. In many ways, they caught progressives by surprise. Few realized the growing strength of the Christian Right and New Right until they had been out-organized. A few still deny the political savvy of their opponents.

While the U.N. presence of these groups remains modest, their connections with growing religious communities and elite leaders gives groups like C-FAM, United Families International, the WFPC and Focus a solid foundation for future success. Their vitality stands in stark contrast with the aging cadre of progressive NGO leaders and faltering agencies. Only one obstacle remains to achieve the Christian Right goal of creating an effective global network with a massive constituency on par with that of the global women's movement. That is the still ambivalent relationship between Muslims and American-based Christian conservatives. How this story plays out will tell us how much this new movement's influence can grow. The next chapter evaluates the opportunities and challenges that Christian Right NGOs face in building this kind of global movement.

4
A Global Religious Right?
The Prospects and Challenges of
International Interfaith Alliances

W HEN CHRISTIAN RIGHT NGOS SHOWED up at Beijing+5, they stood out for their homogeneity – an island of white Americans in a sea of racial and ethnic diversity. Despite coming from the world's superpower, however, they claimed they had the developing world's best interest at heart. Specifically they claimed that they were at the conference to protect the God-fearing families of the developing world from the onslaught of secular Western feminists. A Christian Right flyer distributed at the Beijing+5 gathering exclaimed, "The West is promoting: Forcing the homosexual agenda and widespread abortion on other countries through 'rights' language. This won't help women. DON'T LET THEM DO IT TO YOUR COUNTRY!"[1]

Moreover, Concerned Women for America's newsletter after Beijing+5 complained to constituents that the conference "tried to denigrate the concept of motherhood. But developing countries at the U.N., whose cultures revolve around families – in partnership with pro-family activists – showed that valuing motherhood is essential to preserving civilization."[2]

Long-time NGO leaders wondered what to make of Christian Right claims that they wanted to protect the developing world: did they really believe their agenda helped families in the developing world, or were they cynically making a claim to strategically build an alliance with delegates from the developing world? Whether the conservatives believed their arguments or not, feminists and other progressives greeted the claims with derision. Leaders in feminist NGOs speculated that anyone with connections to the U.S. Religious Right, a movement giving strong support for American military superiority and typically supportive of missionary activities, could hardly show the cultural sensitivity and diplomatic savvy to create multicultural, interracial, and international coalition with other NGOs and non-Western governments.

By and large, the conventional wisdom about these groups was soon refuted by their obvious success. True, these Christian Right activists did experience problems building enduring alliances with Muslims, but in other ways they did accomplish their goals. Why did the conventional wisdom get it so wrong? People had made their judgments on the basis of second-hand caricatures and stereotypes to begin with and not first-hand experiences with these people. The traditional lack of interest in religious developments among progressives set them up for a failure to understand, let alone respond in the face of, these groups' potential.

Since 2000, in fact, the Christian Right has defied the conventional wisdom and actually has made impressive strides in developing partnerships with groups outside North America. This is particularly true of their efforts with Latin American social conservatives. Forming partnerships with Muslims has proved to be much more problematic, but some inroads have been made. Protecting motherhood has emerged as a much more powerful rallying cry than anybody thought it would.

Christian Right NGOs understand what all experienced NGOs know: to have real political influence a group must have a more comprehensive strategy than just lobbying the delegates who briefly attend U.N. conferences. They must directly lobby governments in capitals. C-FAM's Austin Ruse planned to eventually have an international network in key world capitals, while groups like Focus on the Family already have an extensive network with twenty national affiliates.

The Christian Right's coalition building extends beyond reaching out to an international group of NGOs. At the same time, they are building partnerships with other groups, including neoconservatives and young people. One of the reasons it is important to understand the Christian Right's alliances with neoconservatives is that they complicate their other alliances. For example, conservative evangelical and Catholic partnerships with neoconservatives – an influential group of intellectuals who have played a strong role in shaping American security strategy – both strengthens and complicates the Christian Right's capacity to build an alliance with Muslims. Once we understand the larger picture of Christian Right alliances, we can compare the trajectory of these NGOs to the past growth of other progressive NGOs, for example, feminist ones.

Moreover, these NGOs have cultivated a strong relationship with young people. One also can say something about the future of the Christian Right through its ability to attract younger generations of activists and train new leaders. The current ability of Christian Right organizers to create global networks of young leaders starkly contrasts with the disinterest of the aging cohorts of feminists and other liberal activists in reaching youth. Whether considered individually or together as a whole, the Christian Right outreach projects represent an ambitious play for global influence.

Attack of the Clones: The Potential of Christian Right Global Partnerships

The United Nations debate on human cloning offers a striking example of how the development of Christian Right networks outside the United States – in this case Costa Rica and Germany – might influence U.N. policy in decades ahead. Christian Right NGOs have strategically identified the U.N. General Assembly as their preferred lobbying forum (the General Assembly is the largest U.N. organ, made up of all U.N. member and observer states) because these representatives answer most directly to the pressure of traditionalists in socially conservative countries. In a recent interview Austin Ruse explained, "There are many at the U.N. that don't want us there. But there are several 'U.N.s' [and the] General Assembly [one] is fine with our coalition."[3] While they can't influence the majority of U.N. member states, Ruse claims they have around thirty solid member-state allies. In some cases, that brings them close enough to being able to influence important U.N. debates. This was certainly true in the cloning debate. Despite showing the Christian Right's potential influence, the debate also exposed the political minefields leaders will need to negotiate to build an international coalition. While the Christian Right made a major push for the measure by working through the U.S., they found their effort stymied by Muslim states angry over U.S. unilateralism.

The Debate over Therapeutic Cloning

The ethical debate on human cloning is a complex subject. In addition to the Christian Right, many other sectors of civil society watched the debate closely, including scientists, corporations and human rights NGOs. The complexity of the debate stems partly from the fact that there are two kinds of cloning at issue, reproductive and therapeutic. In its most basic form, cloning involves inserting animal or human DNA into an unfertilized egg whose own nucleus has been removed. The most controversial form of cloning is called reproductive cloning and it raises a host of more vexing ethical dilemmas than the other form. In reproductive cloning the altered embryo is then placed in a surrogate mother and develops into an exact physical replica of the DNA donor. Many governments, scientists and ethicists are opposed to reproductive cloning.

The second kind of cloning, therapeutic cloning, produces and then destroys embryos that are only a few days old in order to reap their stem cells, which scientists believe can eventually be used to treat grave diseases such as Parkinson's and Alzheimer's as well as spinal injuries and strokes. They might even be used to reproduce defective organs. In contrast to the near-universal opposition to reproductive cloning, the international community is sharply divided over the ethics of therapeutic cloning. On the one hand, those who oppose therapeutic cloning believe that destroying an embryo at any stage of development is the destruction of human life. They assert that human stem cells, harvested from adult stem cells, are sufficient for research and therapeutic purposes. On the other hand, supporters say that therapeutic cloning offers unrivalled promise for the treatment of many diseases. Creating an embryo from a patient's own cells would create tissue that is a perfect match for the transplant, resolving the problem of organ rejection.

The arguments for and against human cloning, similar to the debates over abortion, hinge on the deeper issue of when life begins.

The central question is whether a human life is being taken when stem cells are harvested. Worldwide, conservative religious believers come down on different sides of the issue, not to mention the fact that many conservative believers and scientists disagree. The Roman Catholic Church and conservative evangelical leaders say that therapeutic cloning involves the taking of a life. Many scientists argue that the embryo in its earliest stages of development cannot be called an individual human being and point out that therapeutic cloning research will save lives. Caught in the middle, Muslims are still debating the issue.[4]

To build a case against therapeutic cloning, Christian Right groups made two arguments that surprisingly invoked the logic of progressive arguments. Besides the older claim that therapeutic cloning would involve the taking of human life, they went on to argue that money would better be spent on addressing HIV/AIDS, tuberculosis and malaria, issues which are of greater concern to developing nations.[5] Moreover, conservative women argued that women from the developing world would in particular be exploited as greedy governments and businesses sought to harvest women's eggs, placing their health in jeopardy. In covering the story for their network, for instance, CARE, based in Britain, claimed, "developing countries feared their women being turned into 'egg farms.'"[6]

Concerned Women for America (CWA) argued for a total ban on human cloning to protect women's rights. Wendy Wright, speaking about the U.N. debates to a constituency of conservative evangelicals and Catholics explained:

> Pro-life organizations provided information showing how cloning exploits women ... Massive numbers of women's eggs would be needed to produce clones. It would require 80 million women to supply enough eggs to clone stem cells just for the United States' 16 million diabetes patients. To produce the eggs, women have to undergo hyper-ovulation through injections of potent drugs and surgery to extract the eggs.

She concluded, "It is likely that poor and vulnerable women will be the targets for supplying eggs – those least likely to be in good health or have access to basic medical care."[7] Interestingly, the CWA argument is similar to one made by the women's health organization, Our Bodies Ourselves (OBOS). In fact, it is possible that the CWA borrowed the argument from this pioneer in the field of women's health. OBOS has long warned that the cloning industry could turn women's eggs and wombs into commodities and create the infrastructure for a new eugenics movement.[8]

These kinds of arguments and fears baffled scientists who complained that the debate had been railroaded by "extremists."[9] Arthur Caplan, director of the Center for Bioethics at the University of Pennsylvania in Philadelphia and, in 2003, chair of an U.N. advisory panel on the ethics of cloning claimed partisans freely circulated misinformation. The notion that women would be exploited "is just silly," he said. "It makes it sound as if you've got women treated as egg-laying hens."[10] Gregory Stock, director of the Medicine, Technology and Society Program at the University of California spoke for a number of frustrated bioethicists saying, "This is about a religious issue that is not resolvable by logical discussion."[11] Despite the reaction of the scientists, the fact that even liberal Western European governments wanted to ban certain cloning procedures suggests that it was not just a few extremists who worried about the potential abuse inherent in such procedures.

A Christian Right Victory

In 2001, when an Italian scientist announced that he planned to clone a human being, France and Germany proposed that the U.N. develop an international convention against the reproductive cloning of human beings.[12] Representing populations generally opposed to all forms of cloning, the two governments were concerned that those seeking to clone a human being would engage in venue shopping, searching for a nation that had no ban on human cloning.[13] In December 2001, France and Germany introduced what they thought would be a fairly uncontroversial General Assembly resolution to ban reproductive human cloning, while not taking a position on the therapeutic version.

Thanks in part to Christian Right lobbying, the resolution sparked a heated four-year debate on cloning. Rather than accept a partial ban, Christian Right NGOs working with government allies in Washington, Latin America and Eastern Europe, reasoned that there should be a total ban on both forms of cloning or no ban at all. Many wondered why the Christian Right had taken this all-or-nothing approach: why not accept a resolution on reproductive cloning first and then later seek one on therapeutic cloning (which promised to be more difficult)? For its part, Concerned Women for America took the position that once a ban on reproductive cloning was adopted, "the world would most likely lose interest in the issue of therapeutic cloning."[14] The CWA expressed suspicion regarding Germany's politically pragmatic position as a rationalization for human rights violations. Germany had suggested a two-step process: since some countries were already engaged in therapeutic cloning, the U.N. should not seek a ban on the process until there was an international consensus. After years of debate, Larry Goldstein, a stem cell researcher at the University of California, San Diego, complained, "Rather than ban the thing we all agree on, we end up with no ban, because the extremists refuse to compromise."[15]

By the fall of 2003, representatives from the U.S, the Vatican and Costa Rica emerged as leaders in the fight for a total ban, outlawing not just reproductive cloning, but therapeutic cloning as well. According to Thomas Jacobson, Focus on the Family's representative at the U.N., Sixto Porras of Focus on the Family (Costa Rica) helped convince the president and foreign minister to take leadership on sponsoring a U.N. resolution to ban therapeutic cloning as well as reproductive cloning.[16] The resolution was quietly supported by the U.S. Administration, which had been backing legislation in the U.S. Congress that would criminalize therapeutic cloning.[17]

The Costa Rican resolution if adopted would have urged states to "prohibit any research, experiment, development or application in their territories or areas under their jurisdiction or control of any technique aimed at human cloning, pending the adoption of an international convention against human cloning."[18] In a clear appeal to the sensibilities of less developed nations, the resolution strongly encouraged "States and other entities to direct funds that might have been used for human cloning technologies to pressing global issues in developing countries, such as famine, desertification, infant mortality and diseases ... ."[19]

Christian Right NGOs helped build support for the Costa Rican resolution by holding events and lobbying delegates. Christian Right organizations also worked in various capitals around the world to pressure governments to accept the resolution. C-FAM's Vice-President

Douglas Sylva claims that a minister in the German Bundestag had received a copy of C-FAM'S Friday Fax criticizing Germany for supporting therapeutic cloning.[20] The minister brought the issue up in the Bundestag, launching a debate that, according to Sylva, made Germany retreat from its leadership in the cloning debate. Germany had banned all research on human embryos in 1990. Yet earlier in the year, Chancellor Gerhard Schröder had suggested that German biotechnology companies were falling behind because of the ban. His remarks provoked a heated controversy among Germans who are more conservative on the cloning issue in large part because they wish to avoid any actions that would give the slightest appearance of repeating the eugenic experiments of the Nazis.[21] Though difficult to prove, it's possible that Christian Right organizations were able to exploit Schröder's vulnerability on this emotionally fraught issue. In any case, Belgium later took the lead on the resolution.[22]

Despite such successes, however, Christian Right NGOs were not able to garner the support of a frequent ally: the Organization of the Islamic Conference (OIC). Surprisingly the OIC failed to support the Costa Rican resolution. In November 2003, the delegation of Iran, on behalf of the member states of the Organization of the Islamic Conference, moved to adjourn the debate until the sixtieth session of the General Assembly to be held in September 2005.[23] The motion to adjourn passed by just one vote: 80 were in favor, 79 against and there were 15 abstentions. Had this motion not passed, claimed U.S. Deputy Ambassador James Cunningham, a total ban would have passed with 100 votes.[24] In contrast, one journalist saw the hand of the U.S. government in the stalemate: "some observers are suggesting that the United States has been tactically maneuvering the discussions into a deadlock so as to appease both its religious right and U.S. industries that are already researching therapeutic cloning."[25]

The OIC's actions angered some Christian Right leaders who had expected the Muslim community to support the Costa Rican resolution. Thomas Jacobson of Focus on the Family complained that the delay was an attempt to wait out the Bush Administration, which was seeking a ban on all forms of cloning.[26] Jeanne Head, the representative for the International Right to Life Federation suggested that the OIC compromise position did not represent the beliefs of its own member states. She observed bitterly that though the chair of the

OIC claimed the action was a consensus decision by the OIC, 16 of the 57 OIC members were co-sponsors of the Costa Rican resolution (U.N. official records confirm this observation). The OIC includes members from several regional groupings that often have competing interests. Revealing some of the possible geopolitical tensions inherent in Christian Right NGO alliances with Muslim governments and NGOs, Head pointedly observed "All but two of the Arab OIC members voted for the non-action."[27] Dr. Farooq Hassan, a former Pakistani ambassador to the U.N. who has worked closely with pro-family NGOs saw this as being indicative of the fact that the issue of cloning has not been the subject of debate in Islamic society. The OIC member states preferred not to commit themselves to either position to retain room to maneuver in the future. An article in the *New York Times* likewise speculated that the OIC position was based on the fact that Islam does not teach that life begins at conception.[28] According to the Hastings Center, the success of the OIC resolution moved the group to the center of the U.N. cloning debate. The OIC delegates had reviewed a new fatwa, or official religious ruling by an Islamic legal scholar, issued in January 2003 that may have weakened support for a total ban. In the fatwa, Ahmad Al-Tayyeb of Al-Azhar University in Cairo ruled that the blastocysts created through nuclear transfer should not be treated as human subjects, but rather they were the bearers of potentially beneficial cells.[29]

The effort to agree to a legally binding resolution banning reproductive cloning ultimately failed because conservatives blocked it. While conservatives could have supported such a ban, they stood firm in their resistance to any partial measure. In the end, Britain summarized the frustrations of its allies, saying that the Assembly had missed an opportunity to adopt a convention prohibiting reproductive cloning because of the intransigence of the other side.[30] Two years later when the U.N. General Assembly was again to take up the issue, the U.S., its government allies and the Christian Right had a new strategy in place. They would campaign for a declaration.

A U.N. Declaration on Human Cloning

Although the U.N. General Assembly could not agree on a resolution against human cloning, a declaration against human cloning slipped through the Assembly in the winter of 2005. A declaration, unlike a resolution, is not legally binding. At most, it carries some weight as a reflection of the will of the international community and was used in this instance with great effect by the Christian Right and its allies. The U.N. Declaration on Human Cloning calls on U.N. member states to "prohibit all forms of human cloning in as much as they are incompatible with human dignity and the protection of human life."[31] In addition, the declaration specifically appeals to women's rights and the needs of the developing world. It reminds the international community to be "mindful of the need to prevent the exploitation of women" and calls on nations to take into account "pressing global issues such as HIV/AIDS, tuberculosis and malaria, which affect in particular the developing countries."[32] The U.N. General Assembly on March 8, 2005 approved the declaration 84 in favor to 34 against – with 37 abstentions – after a contentious vote in the U.N. Legal Committee.[33] In fact, the debate generated controversy in a number of quarters. Belgium went so far as to claim the controversy and divided vote had weakened the force of the declaration.

Though non-binding, the passage of the declaration has had an impact in other parts of the world. Just a few days later, on March 10, 2005, the European Parliament passed a resolution that called for a ban on the trade in human egg cells. The legislation was adopted following media reports alleging that British fertility centers, to overcome a shortage of egg cells were paying large amounts of money for the egg cells of Romanian women. A statement released by the European Parliament declared: "The House condemns any trafficking in the human body and its parts. The House wishes to see egg cell donation, like organ donation as a whole, strictly regulated in order to protect both donors and recipients, and to tackle all forms of human exploitation."[34]

Clearly Christian Right NGOs hope the declaration may have an impact in the U.S. as well. Family Research Council President Tony Perkins stated, "Surprisingly the U.N. is showing the leadership that we hoped the U.S. Senate would provide. The Senate needs to take a firm moral stand and pass a total ban on human cloning as was stated by President Bush."[35] After years of complaining that American liberals were using international law to get around the U.S.

government, ironically, the Christian Right had found a way to do the same.

Building Global Partnerships: From Mexico to the Muslim World

To influence international law, an NGO movement must have a strong, well-coordinated international network that can work domestically in each national political context. In achieving a measure of victory against human cloning, for example, Christian Right strengths were demonstrated by the ability of Focus on the Family to work through its networks in Central America. However, Christian Right weakness lay in the fact that they lacked a strong influence with the members of the Organization of the Islamic Conference, a bloc which the Christian Right clearly believed they had a chance to win over.

The Christian Right faces a unique set of resources and challenges in developing an international NGO network like other big NGOs. Its greatest strength lies in established Catholic institutions and in the new evangelical revivals mushrooming across the globe. The Christian Right has the capacity to capitalize on an infrastructure of churches, missionary organizations and humanitarian projects that already spans the globe. This potential is best illustrated by the Christian Right's successes in Latin America. While the Christian Right has made modest gains in the Muslim world, the Christian Right's affinity for an aggressive American foreign policy and neoliberal economic agenda has strained its alliances with the Muslim world. Perhaps even more important, according to their Muslim NGO allies, Christian Right leaders still lack the cultural sensitivity and focus required to develop long-term relationships with cross-cultural partners. Their largely American-focused agenda blinds these key leaders to the ways they could address the real concerns about family integrity held by many in the developing world.

Building a Latin American Connection: The Red Familia, Mexico

The story behind the rise of the Mexican-based Red Familia (translated in English as the Coalition for the Family) underscores how Christian Right networks can reasonably hope to keep expanding their global network. According to Allan Carlson of the Howard Center, the most promising prospects for Christian Right global networking appear to lie in Latin America due to its proximity, its tradition of conservative Catholicism, and its burgeoning evangelical population.

With the backing of wealthy Catholic businessmen, Red Familia quickly became a national umbrella organization, bringing together 150 domestic and international organizations. The story behind its organization echoes in surprising ways the history of U.S.-based pro-family groups. First, there is the same focus on the state of the family. The word "family" is incorporated in the title of the organization, just like Focus on the Family and the Family Research Council. Along with the focus on the family, the group has a similar list of complaints (divorce, mothers not spending enough time with children, sexuality on TV) that they believe threaten home life. Second, the fact that they focus on traditional values allows them to attract an interfaith coalition of religious conservatives. Although the group is led and funded mostly by Catholics, the group is reaching out to Protestants also. Third, they cooperate with Mexican President Vincente Fox, who bears some resemblance with George W. Bush in his public support of religious conservatives. These similarities indicate that the Christian Right might continue to globalize not only because of U.S. initiatives but because global economic and social trends are creating the same conditions in many countries that the Christian Right first addressed in the U.S. In the case of Mexico, both developments came together to create an indigenous pro-family alliance.

The story of Red Familia begins with the positive experience of a number of Mexican Catholics participating in the World Congress of Families in Geneva in 1999. As discussed in Chapter 3, Christian NGOs held a yearly congress between 1999 and 2004. Inspired by the 1999 event, the Mexicans decided to establish Red Familia. They started modestly: the network sent a letter to each of the three Mexican Presidential candidates urging them to strengthen the family. According to Jesus Hernandez, a Red Familia founder, only one of the three candidates responded: Vincente Fox.[36] This proved more than a coincidence.

In fact, there are a number of striking parallels between how Fox established a rapport with Mexican Catholic conservatives and how Bush did the same with America's evangelical conservatives. Although the close relationship between Fox and Bush is famous, the Mexican leader also has a similar background and political base to Bush: he established a reputation as a businessman, led the conservative party in his nation's politics, and knew how to connect with religious conservatives. This was a winning combination for Fox as it was for Bush. In fact, both pursued similar strategies in their 2000 campaigns. A businessman who was once the CEO of Coca-Cola's Mexican branch, Fox led the National Action Party (PAN) to victory in July 2000. The victory by PAN, which was founded by a group of pro-business conservative Catholics in 1939, ended the 71-year rule by the socialist-inspired Institutional Revolutionary Party (PRI).[37]

Like Bush, Fox knew how to mobilize Mexico's religious conservatives. Fox generated positive publicity among religious conservatives when, early in the campaign, his campaign paraded a banner with the Virgin of Guadalupe – a symbol of both popular nationalism and the Catholic far Right. One can argue that this was a similar gesture to Bush claiming in a Republican debate in 2000 that Jesus was his favorite political philosopher. In any case, Fox later abandoned the symbol in response to objections, but he had made his point to religious conservatives. There were other ways he communicated his sympathy for the religion of conservatives. For example, he spoke in favor of the teaching of religious values in public schools, but later backtracked. On another occasion, he said he was opposed to abortion but said he would sign a law allowing it if the majority wanted it. Fox executed a successful campaign against the tired PRI machine. In the end, Fox won the support of many leftist intellectuals as well as a majority of Mexico's base Christian Community movement, a group that emphasizes liberation theology and tends to be more progressive. Just as Bush rewarded his religious base by promoting their views and representatives in U.N. forums, Fox as president gave symbolic support to conservative family forums.

In the spring of 2003, Hernandez and his colleague Fernando Milanes first began building international partnerships on family issues by flying to Illinois and presenting a proposal to Allan Carlson at the Howard Center. The two men wanted to host the World Congress of Families in Mexico and said they could raise the necessary support. Surprised and delighted, Carlson met the two Mexican leaders who would soon contribute a new energy and resources to planning future congresses.[38] The Mexican leaders proved adept and strategic in their fundraising and planning. Without their help, says Carlson, the Howard Center would not have planned a third World Congress for 2004.

The planning process for the conference illustrated a productive partnership between Mexican and U.S. NGOs. The Howard Center suggested speakers – many of them the usual suspects from past events or, as one pro-choice group said, the "who's who of the pro-family, anti-choice movement." Yet the speakers list also included powerful Mexican Catholic businessmen, and Martha Fox, the wife of Mexican President Vincente Fox. The ideas articulated by speakers chosen by the Howard Center and the principles shaped at the Geneva conference clearly resonated with the domestic "pro-family, pro-life" networks already operating in Mexico. The main issues of concern were homosexual marriage, abortion, population control, anti-family media, parental rights and the U.N.'s "anti-family" agenda.[39] Conference leaders eventually hailed the event as forging "an international pro-family alliance transcending national borders, cultures and faith traditions."[40] The Red Familia in fact adopted the Geneva Declaration as the Red Familia's organizational principles. When I interviewed him in the summer of 2004, Hernandez was busy finalizing the final declaration of the World Congress. He hoped that the declaration would inform the outcome of the upcoming Doha conference.

The financial support of Catholic businessmen and political support by the Fox Administration made the conference a resounding success. To reach businessmen, Red Familia developed a conference brochure that emphasized the importance of stable families in creating a stable economy. According to Hernandez, their corporate supporters are concerned about the impact of family stability and morality on the economic development of the country.[41] Grupo Bimbo, one of the world's largest bakeries, generously contributed to the meeting. Its founder, Lorenzo Servitje, a long-time PAN supporter, spoke at the conference. Servitje describes himself as a strong proponent of Catholic social doctrine and often voices what he sees as the links between his Catholic values and his business practices. He is also an outspoken conservative cultural critic who has tried to leverage business pressure to influence Mexican television.[42] At the conference, Servitje spoke of the role of business in strengthening the family and the importance of strong families in maintaining the social fabric. In a speech that would clearly resonate with American social conservatives, he warned that the family and society were being undermined by several factors: poor education at home, unstable marriages, mothers (as the backbone of the family) who worked outside the home, sexual immorality and a media that promoted irresponsible behavior as well as contraceptives.[43] Speaking of the role of business in supporting family life, he also said that corporations ought to create work conditions necessary to support mothers with children.

Besides Grupo Bimbo, Red Familia also received financing from some of Mexico's most powerful corporations, including Pemex, the national oil company; Cementos Mexicanos (CEMEX), the world's fourth largest cement company; Gigante, the ubiquitous superstore of Mexico; Grupo Televisa, the world's largest Spanish-language television program producer, and even Grupo Azteca, Mexico's number two television station.[44] The Fox Administration also did its share to support the meeting through the contributions of the Division for Family Services (DIF) and the Division for Social Services. Demonstrating the president's personal support for the project, Martha Fox participated in the event.

Mexican women's rights and sexual rights groups monitoring the conference criticized the organizers and speakers for not honoring the diversity of family structures and the secular nature of the country's public square. These critics feared that economic and political elites wanted the conference to support the privatization of education, a development which would give the Catholic Church a monopoly over Mexican intellectual life.[45] In fact, the World Congress of Families III was critiqued daily by progressive Mexican NGOs who monitored the proceedings carefully. They were appalled by the conference's call to protect the "natural family." "These people have gone too far," said Jose Maria Covarrubias, leader of the Mexican Circulo Gay. "Their positions ignore history and the signed international treaties that support sexual diversity and the commitments to respect it."[46] Mario Arteago, president of the Mexico Pride committee which campaigns for gay rights said that the definition of family was unrealistic and intolerant: "That structure of dad, mom, son, daughter, dog and cat no longer reflects the reality of the bulk of the population."[47]

Hernandez and others worked to make sure Mexico's World Congress went beyond allowing NGOs to share ideas, but actually influenced policymakers. The Red Familia recruited regional leaders and U.N. diplomats to attend. Jesus Hernandez and Fernando Milanes flew to New York City nearly every month leading up to the conference to meet with U.N. diplomats and encourage them to attend. He managed to convince 26 U.N. delegates to make the trip to Mexico for the World Congress of Families. The Red Familia also sought to build its Latin American networks by getting representatives of the family services divisions of ten Latin American countries to attend the conference – an impressive turnout by any measure. In all, he says there were 58 different countries represented and 3,100 participants and delegates.[48]

The 37 members of the World Congress planning team offer a window into the movement's global connections. The planning team included religious leaders, civil society leaders and politicians from Australia, Cameroon, Czech Republic, India, Germany, Kenya, Mexico, Morocco, Nicaragua, Pakistan, the Philippines, Russia, the United States and Venezuela. The highest-ranking members of the committee were Moktar Lamani, the head of the Organization of the Islamic Conference, Martha Fox, and Francisco Tatad, former majority leader of the Philippines Senate (1992–2001). President Bush sent a letter praising the conference, while two members of his administration represented the U.S. government: Wade Horn and Ellen Sauerbrey.

Many members of the planning committee for this World Congress already fell into one of three categories: they either ran pro-family, pro-life networks, held national office, or served in Catholic Church programs. In other words, they did not come simply as interested individuals. For example, Senator Tatad in 1997 directed the International Right to Life Federation (Asia Pacific).[49] In Australia, Peter Westmore is president of the National Civic Council of Australia and the publisher for *News Weekly*, and Babette Francis is the coordinator of the Endeavor Forum. The Countess Christine de Vollmer is the founder and president of the Latin American Alliance for the Family (ALAFA) and Provida de Venezuela (Provive). Married to a millionaire who served as Venezuela's ambassador to the Vatican/Holy See, she herself is highly connected with the Vatican, serving as a consultant to the Pontifical Council on the Family.[50] Gwendolyn Landolt is the vice-president of Real Women of Canada. Michaela Freiova is director of the Family Values Program at the Civic Institute of the Czech Republic.

To this day, Red Familia continues to build its regional network and influence. In the wake of the World Congress, says Hernandez, the Red Familia has opened offices in twelve Mexican cities, including Mexico, Puebla, Guadalajara, Chihuahua, Leon, Cuernavaca and Merida. Though himself a Catholic, Hernandez expresses the same openness to inter-religious collaboration as other Christian Right leaders. The network is diverse he says, including Protestants, Catholics, Mormons and some Pentecostals and Jews.[51]

The network has been working on domestic policy initiatives as well. Red Familia's literature claims the network has successfully helped establish the right to life since conception as a constitutional right in Mexico, influenced the position of Mexico in the U.N. Special Session on Children and the U.N. debates on human cloning, preserved the dignity of marriage by preventing the state from making legal comparisons between heterosexual marriage and homosexual unions, and reoriented the "gender feminism agenda" in the Women's Parliament. Red Familia's future agenda is ambitious. They hope to pull together sympathetic civil servants, politicians and political party officials to continue to influence policy. Moreover, they want to open more offices until they have a presence in all federal states and train NGO activists in how to successfully lobby government agencies.

Christian-Muslim Partnerships and Tensions

Forging partnerships with Muslim NGOs, as one might expect, has been more difficult for Christian Right organizations than reaching out to Latin American allies. On the one hand, Christian Right NGOs have made significant advances in forging alliances with Muslim governments and some NGOs. Interestingly, Mormon NGOs, principally the World Family Policy Center led by Dr. Wilkins, have been the most successful. As described in Chapter 3, the WFPC, working with Muslim governments (most notably Qatar), led Christian Right efforts to advance conservative international policies on the family. In 2004, "pro-family" organizations held regional meetings on the family in Geneva, Switzerland (August 23–25) and Kuala Lumpur, Malaysia (October 11–13). These culminated in a conference in Qatar (November 29–30).[52]

On the other hand, as observed in an earlier chapter, Christian Right leaders greatly exaggerated the effect of the Doha Declaration, claiming the U.N. General Assembly had adopted it and that it would now "take its place in the formal canon of legal documents comprising the growing body of international law."[53] In reality, the U.N. had merely noted that the conference took place. While Chapter 3 explored how effective "pro-family" forces had been in influencing international policy, it is also important to explore whether or not they have been successful in building alliances with Muslim NGOs.

Surprisingly, a key Muslim ally publicly rejected the Christian Right assertion that the Doha Declaration had become international law. Dr. Farooq Hassan, a long-time ally of Christian Right NGOs, respectfully but forcefully accused the WFPC and others of overstating their victory. In Dr. Hassan's view, the WFPC's claim reflected an ignorance of international law at best. It also prevented his allies from arriving at a realistic assessment of their strengths and weaknesses. In a personal interview, he shared with me that unlike the World Congress of Families meeting in Mexico, the conference in Doha, Qatar failed to really engage the concerns of Muslim nations.[54] Dr. Hassan was so frustrated at the conference that he had felt compelled to speak from the floor to assert that the Doha Declaration had failed to reflect Islamic concerns. He further claimed that the declaration was written by two Western NGOs: the WFPC and CARE, a small "pro-family" organization based in Britain (not to be confused with the better-known international humanitarian organization by the same name). He continues to publicly denounce the WFPC's claim of victory in the wake of the conference, posting many of his observations on Islam Online. In one essay he reflected that the "topics and themes were those that conceivably may have been presented to a non-Muslim audience in an American city. Topics and addresses that could [have been] meaningful to the wider Islamic base of the family movement were just ignored."[55]

Dr. Hassan's relationship to Christian Right NGOs reveals the tensions that are bound to exist in Christian Right-Muslim NGO alliances. Though a close ally of Christian Right NGOs, he has recently begun to critique their organizing strategies and limited understanding of Muslim views on the family. Dr. Hassan met leaders of the pro-family NGOs in 1997 while serving as the Pakistani Ambassador to the Commission for Human Rights in Geneva and during the drafting of the Rome Statute for the International Criminal Court.[56] He joined the board of United Families International and served as their Ambassador for the Family. He bridges two worlds, teaching at the Center for International Affairs at Harvard University and at the David M. Kennedy Center at Brigham Young University. His affinity for the "pro-family" Christian Right coalition seems to have been forged largely over opposition to homosexuality as well as their focus on family issues, a topic on which Dr. Hassan has written extensively.

Dr. Hassan's critique of the Doha conference has turned into a wider critique of the pro-family movement. He believes "pro-family" NGOs will fail in their objectives if they do not truly engage their Muslim and developing world partners. Christian Right NGOs focus on a narrow platform of issues that are primary for their constituency in the U.S., but not for people in the developing world. "Gay issues are important," he told me, "but not the most important."[57] For Hassan, poverty and child rights – especially child labor laws – should top the list of pro-family concerns. Hassan, who has written editorials in Pakistani papers holding the government accountable for violence against women, also wants to promote women's rights.[58] He opposes polygamy and the "treatment of women as chattel."[59] When I pointed out that in this regard, Hassan seemed to have more in common with progressive NGOs and even feminist NGOs, he agreed, but said that he did not "subscribe to homosexual issues" which progressive NGOs support or tolerate.[60]

In addition, he has critiqued Christian Right leaders as lacking a clear understanding of international law and for being too removed from U.N. procedure. He says he warned Christian Right leaders that they needed to attend U.N. conferences on the family in Sanya, China and two in Islamabad – one on reproductive health and Islam (May 4–6, 2005) and the other on violence against children. While the latter conferences explored issues that Christian Right organizations oppose, participants and themes reflected regional and religious diversity. The International Ulama Conference on Population and

Development, led by Pakistan and supported by the U.N. Population Fund, drew ninety delegates from almost every school of Islamic thought.[61] They therefore carried greater legitimacy in Hassan's view.[62] Hassan contrasted the conference with the one in Doha, which featured American academics. He also asserted that because they failed to participate in the proceedings of these other conferences, Christian Right NGOs could not participate in their debates. He also complains that Christian Right lobbying failed to reach policymakers of real stature in capitals around the world. The conference in Qatar, he claims, was merely the result of Dr. Wilkins' personal connection with the ruling family rather than the commitment of the government or the Muslim world in general.

Dr. Hassan still sees glimmers of hope for a diverse pro-family movement in the World Congress of Families held in Mexico, and in a preparatory conference for Doha, which was held in Kuala Lumpur, Malaysia. Yet when I spoke to him in the summer of 2005, Dr. Hassan seemed on the verge of giving up on the Christian Right pro-family effort. While expressing respect and admiration for the WFPC, Dr. Wilkins and others, he quipped cynically that the letter "U" in UDHR (the Universal Declaration on Human Rights) "stood for Utah, not Universal."[63] He said he would try to work with his long-time allies, but that he now felt they were "not really progressive in the sense that they are not open to input outside their culture."[64]

International Islamic Committee for Woman and Child (IICWC)

Journalist Aelfwine Mischler of Islam Online, a popular Qatar-based website run by a well-known Islamic scholar Sheikh Yusuf al-Qaradawi,[65] has written about other tensions that will prevent an easy working relationship between U.S. Christians and Middle Eastern Muslims. Islam Online covered the Doha conference with articles, papers and blog discussions on the issues it took up. The majority of material is in Arabic, though a few articles are in English. In the course of her journalistic work on the Doha conference and her work with the International Islamic Committee for Woman and Child (IICWC), Mischler encountered Sharon Slater and Susan Roylance with United Families International, and staff from the World Family Policy Center. She was "very impressed with their work"[66] and attracted by the UFI's

Defend Marriage Petition. She published a series of stirring interviews with Dr. Hassan. Despite the obvious interest from the Muslim community in the pro-family cause, writes Mischler, Muslims are still fearful of Christian missions to Muslim areas, the more general culture gap between Muslims and Westerners, and deep differences over U.S. foreign policy in the Middle East (in particular, the Israeli–Palestinian conflict). Moreover, Muslim and Catholic leaders disagree on the use of birth control (Muslims support its use). These tensions will not be easily resolved, especially since the Christian Right are partners with other American conservatives that have reinforced their political positions on the Middle East.

Neoconservatives and Evangelicals: Towards a Moralist Foreign Policy

There will continue to be tensions between Christian Right and Muslim NGOs as along as the former maintain their close ties with neoconservative intellectuals. While this relationship offers definite benefits for the Christian Right, there are definite drawbacks as well, especially as they attempt to create global alliances. The extensive cultural and institutional connections between the two underscores how the larger growth and creativity of the American conservative movement in domestic politics right now is helping to fuel the Christian Right's successes in U.N. forums and confirms that such successes are not the results of a few isolated groups. In both indirect and direct ways, neoconservatives have provided both a broader ideological justification and a supportive institutional framework for Christian Right efforts in U.N. forums. While Christian Right leaders were initially driven to the U.N. by concerns that the international body was making decisions that would impact American law, neoconservative intellectuals invite religious conservatives to view their movement for conservative family values not as a defensive move, but nothing less than as an integral component of a process of American empire-building that will help America save and democratize the world.

To understand the broader implications of the Christian Right-neoconservative alliance, one must understand the neoconservative movement itself; its history, philosophy, and its influence on American foreign policy. "Neoconservative" is a controversial term – it has undergone many changes since it was coined in the 1970s; indeed, its meaning is still being debated.[67] Most would, however, agree that neoconservatives were the architects of the Iraq War. "Neocons" believe that the U.S. should not be ashamed to take advantage of its role as the world's only superpower to aggressively promote American-style values around the world. Some even speak supportively of the need for America to have its own empire.[68] Drawing a parallel to the Pax Romana during which the Roman Empire is said to have maintained peace through military strength, an influential neoconservative policy paper put it this way: "If an *American peace* [italics mine] is to be maintained, and expanded, it must have a secure foundation on unquestioned U.S. military preeminence."[69] In a nostalgic reference to the British Empire, neoconservative *Wall Street Journal* editorialist Max Boot argued in 2001 that "Afghanistan and other troubled lands today cry out for the sort of enlightened foreign administration once provided by self-confident Englishmen in jodhpurs and pith helmets."[70]

Project for a New American Century (PNAC), a neoconservative think tank established by *Weekly Standard* editors William Kristol and Robert Kagan, galvanized lead conservatives around an aggressive foreign policy strategy contained in the work *Rebuilding America: Strategy, Forces and Resources for a New Century* (1997). Throughout the 1990s, neocons found little reception for their ideas by the first President Bush or President Clinton. While they shared with other conservatives their general skepticism for the United Nations, neocons deplored conservative isolationism and the desire to involve entanglements overseas. To their dismay, President George W. Bush also campaigned on a promise of maintaining this traditional conservative policy of disengagement.

The September 11, 2001 terrorist attacks in the U.S. created a political climate that was more receptive to the PNAC's way of thinking.[71] *Rebuilding America* became the basis for the President's National Security Strategy written in September 2002. The dominant theme of the security strategy echoes the classic neoconservative view that a "unipolar" world[72] puts before the U.S. both opportunities and responsibilities: "The United States possesses unprecedented and unequaled strength and influence in the world ... This position comes with unparalleled responsibilities, obligations and opportunity. The great strength of this nation must be used to promote a balance of power that favors freedom."[73]

Rebuilding America urged the U.S. not to downsize its military in the wake of the end of the Cold War, but rather to expand its military advantage. The report calls for the U.S. to develop a new family of nuclear weapons; add $15 to $20 billion annually to defense spending, and dominate the new common spaces of outer space and cyberspace. Similarly, the National Security Strategy asserts, "we must build and maintain our defenses beyond challenge." Embracing the neoconservative skepticism for international cooperation, the security policy warned, "We will not hesitate to act alone, if necessary, to exercise our right of self defense by acting preemptively against such terrorists ... The best defense is a good offense."

Among the signers of *Rebuilding America* were Christian Right leaders Gary Bauer, founding president of the Family Research Council and William Bennett, a social conservative well respected by the Christian Right. How did Christian Right figures like Gary Bauer, usually seen as social critics, develop an interest in national security strategy? "Since the 1970s," write researchers Tom Barry and Jim Lobe, "neoconservatives have been exploring the global-local links of the 'culture war.'"[74] Barry and Lobe suggest that the growing alliance between neoconservative and Christian Right leaders is more forged than organic. At the same time it is clear that many neocon tenets naturally resonate with the Christian Right.

A virulent opposition to communism has shaped both Christian Right and neoconservative foreign policy concerns. Early neoconservative leaders were liberals who drifted to the right because they believed the U.S. needed to take a harder line on communism. Many neocons also grew skeptical over the progress of liberal values and social policies in the 1960s and rejected the type of liberal activism demonstrated on college campuses like Berkeley and Columbia. Like Christian conservatives, neoconservatives criticized the social revolutions of the 1960s and 1970s and welfare and affirmative action policies as having undermined the moral fiber and social structure of the nation.[75]

While not always religious themselves, many neocons adamantly support religion or moralism as an antidote to what they call the "nihilism" of secularism and modernity. How and why they would do so is illuminated in the work of Leo Strauss, a University of Chicago professor some view as one of the founders of neoconservative thinking. The intellectual Strauss first fled Nazi Germany in the 1930s and eventually began teaching in the United States. In the 1960s and 1970s he mentored the first generation of the movement that came to be known as neoconservatives. His experience of Nazi Germany convinced him that the moral permissiveness and political weaknesses of the Weimar Republic had allowed Adolf Hitler to come to power. To Strauss, liberal democracy's emphasis on individual freedom was particularly dangerous because, like the Weimar Republic, it would eventually give way to disorder. He believed that Enlightenment values on which modern democracies were built emphasized reason to the detriment of faith and tradition. This undermined religious values and myths that provided the societal glue for holding people together and stabilizing society. The resultant nihilism, a belief in nothing or in no authoritative truth, led to social and moral chaos. Strauss feared the U.S. would eventually give way to the same dynamics he encountered in Nazi Germany. In his view, the Nazis had rejected God and moral order and therefore were able to do the unthinkable. Strauss stressed the importance of concepts such as good and evil, virtue and morality, over and against what he viewed as the blurry moral thinking of liberals.[76]

This preference for moral absolutes and an emphasis on moral clarity has inspired both religious conservatives and neocons to exercise a missionary-like zeal in advancing their claims. U.S. foreign policy expert Walter Russell Mead describes the neocon missionary spirit as hearkening back to an older, non-institutional and values-based Wilsonianism.[77] Says Mead, "the sort of basic values that they are promoting are very much the sort of Protestant, Christian values that were dominant in 19th-century America."[78]

This moralist worldview allows for a synergy or "fusionism," in the words of Joseph Bottum, between neoconservative intellectuals and conservative Judeo-Christian thought. Bottum describes this new fusionism in *First Things* (a journal sympathetic to neoconservatism), offering the following observation:

> The opponents of abortion and euthanasia insist there are truths about human life and dignity that must not be compromised in domestic politics. The opponents of Islamofascism and rule by terror insist there are truths

about human life and dignity that must not be compromised in international politics. Why shouldn't they grow toward each other?[79]

Similarly William Kristol and Robert Kagan wrote in a 1996 article in *Foreign Affairs*:

> The remoralization of America at home ultimately requires the remoralization of American foreign policy, for both follow from America's belief that the principles of the Declaration of Independence are not merely the choices of a particular culture but are universal, enduring, 'self-evident' truths. That has been, after all, the main point of the conservatives' war against a relativistic multiculturalism.[80]

Not all neocons have been happy with this new fusionism. In a recent article in *The Nation*, Michael Lind, a former neocon, stated that he departed company with neocons when "the Protestant ayatollahs of the Bible Belt" inspired "Irving Kristol, William Kristol and Norman Podhoretz [to open] their magazines to religious-right tirades against abortion rights, gay rights, gun control and – my personal favorite – 'Darwinism.'"[81]

Lind also decried the neoconservative alliance with the conservative Israeli Likud party, an ally embraced by the Christian Right as well. Says Lind, "We [neocons] thought we had joined an antitotalitarian liberal movement, not an alliance of American Likudniks and born-again Baptist creationists brought together to support the colonization of 'Samaria' and 'Judea' by right-wing Jewish settlers."[82]

Neoconservatives view Israel as a launching pad for American-style democracy in the region and as essential for maintaining a U.S military presence in the region. Transforming the authoritarian governments of this oil-producing region into capitalist democracies supportive of the U.S. has been the dream of many neoconservatives. Many conservative evangelicals believe that Christ will return when the state of Israel is restored. They therefore embrace the hard-right Likud policies as promising to restore the full territory of Israel, eliminating Palestinian territories, and thus bringing about the return of Christ. Despite the anti-Judaism implicit in these beliefs (conservative evangelicals believe Jews must convert or be condemned during this Second Coming of Christ), many conservative Protestants in the U.S. raise money to support a hard-right pro-Israeli policy. This has made for one of the strangest political alliances in modern America.

Finally, their tendency to see the world in moral absolutes and dualisms seems to draw both neocons and religious conservatives into an apocalyptic worldview that characterizes world events in terms of cosmic struggles between good and evil. During the Cold War, the Soviet Union was the representative of "cosmic diabolical forces that must be defeated in every corner of the globe" says political scientist and neoconservative critic Shadia Drury. According to Drury, neocon foreign policy is guided not by practical concerns of national security, but by a vision of America's destiny as the biblical Zion that will light up the world, in the words of neocon Harry Jaffa.[83]

The apocalyptic fiction popular among Christian conservatives often lends itself to a black-and-white view of foreign policy. The immense popularity of Dr. Timothy LaHaye's best-selling *Left Behind* series of novels bears testimony to the Christian Right's fascination with the end-times. The series has rivaled the Harry Potter series as the biggest surprise success of the last decade in the book business, even overtaking John Grisham's novels in sales.[84] Apocalyptic fiction is not only immensely popular among both devout Christians and non-church goers, it has in recent decades helped develop and garner support for New Right policies and the Reagan revolution. While apocalypticism is not inherently conservative (the South African anti-apartheid movement drew on such themes), recent popular works integrate apocalyptic biblical texts with a conservative treatise.[85] LaHaye's novels were not the first to use apocalyptic themes in the service of the New Right. Hal Lindsey's *The 1980s: Countdown to Armageddon* contains what one critic called "the veritable blueprint for Reaganism."[86] Not all conservative evangelicals are happy with such politicization of the book of Revelation. Conservative Christian writer Timothy Weber wrote that Lindsey's "observations and remedies come out of right-wing political ideology and have nothing to do with premillennialism per se ... ." Weber analyzed Lindsey's footnotes and concluded that Lindsey's understanding of America's current political, social and military condition "comes almost exclusively from Barry Goldwater's *With No Apologies* (1979) and the conservative Coalition for Peace through Strength ... ." Weber accused Jerry Falwell of the same.[87]

Such themes resonate in general with an American culture already steeped in apocalyptic interpretations of history. A Gallup poll in 1980 showed that 62 per cent of Americans had "no doubts" that Jesus would come again.[88] Drawing on this popularity, Presidents Ronald Reagan and George W. Bush both used apocalyptic images in speeches to a degree unprecedented by other American presidents. Reagan's branding of the Soviet Union as the "Evil Empire" is one example. George W. Bush similarly branded his enemies the "Axis of Evil."[89]

Growing Organizational Alliances with Neoconservatives

Having identified shared values and a potential alliance with religious conservatives, neoconservative intellectuals established think tanks that have institutionalized the search for a common social, economic and foreign policy agenda. This has given Christian NGOs at the U.N. a supportive institutional framework to pursue new initiatives. The solid support that Christian Right NGOs receive from the larger conservative movement contrasts dramatically with the meager support that progressive religious NGOs receive from the larger progressive movement. The institutions that may lend a hand include the Ethics and Public Policy Center, the Institute on Religion and Democracy, and the Institute on Religion and Public Life. Other think tanks help nurture these connections less directly: the Project for a New American Century, the Federalist Society, Heritage Foundation, American Enterprise Institute, Hudson Institute, Free Congress Foundation and Empower America. All of these think tanks are tightly knit, sharing staff, fellows, board members and funding sources.[90]

By opening an office in Washington, Austin Ruse of C-FAM has been able to form nascent partnerships with neoconservative institutions. C-FAM, which has now merged with the Culture of Life Foundation, held an expert-level meeting in Rome with the Federalist Society, Ave Maria Law School and the National Interest (the nation's oldest neoconservative journal established by Irving Kristol) to discuss international standards and their impact on American jurisprudence.[91] One of C-FAM's and Culture of Life's board members, Robert George is also a board member of the Ethics and Public Policy Center (EPPC), established in 1976 to "clarify and reinforce the bond between the Judeo-Christian moral tradition and public debate over domestic and foreign policy issues." EPPC has programs on Jewish, Catholic, evangelical and Islamic studies.

The Federalist Society

As discussed in Chapters 2 and 3, C-FAM has identified organizations like the Federalist Society as potential allies at the U.N. Ruse's mission – to point out how international law influences national laws – "parallels the Federalist Society's opposition to U.S. Federal courts overriding state courts." WFPC president Dr. Richard Wilkins has also been active in the Federalist Society. At a November 2003 Federalist Society conference on international law, he gave two presentations: one on international law and family, and one on the International Criminal Court.

Established in 1982 to move the U.S. judiciary to the right, the Federalist Society mission, as expressed on its website, is to reorder the "priorities within the legal system to place a premium on individual liberty, traditional values, and the rule of law." Interestingly, in 2003, the Federalist Society expanded its activism to include international legal issues by establishing a special project on International Law and National Sovereignty.

The Federalist Society was started by then University of Chicago Law School students David McIntosh and Lee Liberman with neoconservative *Weekly Standard* editor Irving Kristol, whose son Bill Kristol, was a friend of McIntosh's.[92] Chicago law professors taught that liberal judges were inventing rights not found in the U.S. Constitution – chief among them the right to privacy, which provided the underpinning of the 1973 *Roe* v. *Wade* Supreme Court decision on abortion.[93] In the view of the Federalist Society, "Law schools and the legal profession are currently strongly dominated by a form of orthodox liberal ideology which advocates a centralized and uniform society" and liberal ideology is "taught simultaneously with (and indeed as if they were) the law."[94] Therefore, the Federalist Society "has created a conservative and libertarian intellectual network that extends to all levels of the legal community."

Conservatives quickly saw the potential of this student-led organization.[95] Today it is one of the most powerful legal associations in the United States and has chapters at many of the country's universities and law schools to recruit conservative students. Its student division has more than 5,000 law students at 145 law schools. Its lawyer's division has 25,000 legal professionals; 60 metropolitan lawyers' chapters and 15 nationwide practice groups and a new faculty division.[96]

Europe's Problem

A final subject neoconservatives and the Christian Right agree on is the "problem" of Europe. The relationship between two old allies – Europe and America – became the subject of hot debate as the prospect of war with Iraq loomed on the horizon. Progressives cheered France and Germany for challenging American bellicosity and advocating for international cooperation; conservatives chided Europe for being out of touch with reality or worse, protecting a dictator. Defense Department Secretary Donald Rumsfeld turned the phrase "old Europe" into a pejorative term, and contrasted the European countries that resisted the U.S. invasion ("old Europe") with those former Soviet bloc countries newly admitted to the European Union ("new Europe").[97] Rumsfield's point was to suggest that countries like Germany and France were decrepit and out of touch with international realities. Pundits heatedly discussed the origins of the chasm that had deepened between Jacque Chirac's "Old Europe" and George W. Bush's America. The debate touched the everyday life of Americans who started calling French fries "freedom" fries and stopped buying French wine. This rift had deeper significance for Christian conservatives and neoconservatives who have been long concerned with what has been called "Europe's problem."

Robert Kagan in his book *Of Paradise and Power*, which was published after America's rift with Europe over the Iraq War, described the growing gulf between America and Europe in political terms. For religious conservatives, the more important gap is spiritual and moral. The essays of Catholic neoconservative George Weigel have expressed how religious and moral concerns have fused with foreign policy concerns. In one essay, Weigel drew a parallel between the fate of St. Paul's Cathedral in London and western Europe. Weigel described a famous photograph of the nocturnal silhouette of St. Paul's Cathedral against the smoke and fire of London burning after a Nazi aerial blitz during World War II. For Weigel, this photograph poignantly captured the struggle of Western civilization against the overwhelming force of Nazi barbarism. Two generations after the photograph was taken, reported Weigel, Gorbachev visited St. Paul's and said to one of the cathedral officials, "A most interesting building. What is it used for today?" In a dramatic reply to this man who represented to conservatives godless communism, the official replied, "In order, sir, to worship God." Only a decade later, wrote Weigel, he was in London and visited the famous cathedral, only to discover it had been turned into a museum.

For Weigel and other neocons, and religious conservatives in particular, this dramatic turn of events captures the fear and disappointment they see in Europe's secularism. Such images capture the animus behind conservative Christian passion for evangelizing Europe and influencing the European Union. Before the Iraq War the European Union alarmed the conservative Christian community when it voted for its constitution for Europe to avoid reference to the Christian heritage of Europe. To conservative Christians, this represented a rejection not only of religion in the public square, but a denial of Europe's very identity.

Europe's secularity is a threat to the United States for three reasons, according to Weigel. First, Americans owe it to Europe to show concern because of the European foundations for much of American culture. Second, Europe's moral failure, which will no doubt lead to its political failure, is a type of cancer that could spread to the U.S. and to the rest of the world through the European Union. Like the U.N., the European Union threatens to become a super-government through which nihilist values are spread. Third, Europe is experiencing "demographic suicide," wrote Weigel, a demographic meltdown – a vacuum into which a sea of radicalized Islamic populations and North Africans is flowing.[98]

In stark contrast to most of Europe stands Poland, a culture informed by what Weigel approvingly calls the "Slavic view of history," a view both religious and transformational. Poland maintained its religious identity and hence its national identity in the wake of the Third Polish Partition which lasted 123 years (1795–1918), and later in the face of Nazism and communism. More recently, Poles formed the Solidarity labor movement that eventually undermined a communist government. Supported by then President Reagan and Pope John Paul II, Solidarity's resistance to the Polish communist government eventually inspired other movements in East Central Europe and resulted in the so-called Revolution of 1989. Christian conservatives find a historical lesson in Poland's central place in the transformation of Europe in the 1980s and its support of American leadership. How could this country manage to survive and eventually transform all of eastern Europe? Poland fought the death of its identity and its nationhood through its culture, says Weigel, a culture shaped by its unique language and literature but most of all by the intensity of its Catholic faith.

In contrast to Poland, most of Europe strayed from the Christian faith during the nineteenth century when secularization triumphed. This "crisis of civilizational morale" led to World Wars I and II, the Holocaust and the rise of fascism. It also explains why Europeans insist on believing in what Weigel terms "certain fictions in world politics." These include such things as European support for Palestinian rights, and the Kyoto Protocol, and their confidence in such concepts as "international community" or multilateral approaches like the U.N.

Interestingly Weigel urges conservatives to redeem Europe through philanthropy that seeks to rebuild its moral fiber, to fund the war of ideas in Europe, and to support new democracies in East Central Europe. "Europe, in other words, needs something like a Great Awakening," says Weigel referring to the great American religious revivals of the mid-eighteenth century that revitalized American religiosity. Several Christian Right organizations are already engaged in this project.

Take, for example, the following stories that come from Sweden. Sweden, known for its secularity and its progressive social policy, is the last place in the world one would expect to find an organized Christian Right presence. Yet in the fall of 2003 a member of the Swedish Parliament, Mikael Oscarsson, drafted a motion calling for Sweden's National Board of Health and Welfare to examine the connection between breast cancer and abortion.[99] Pro-choice advocates were surprised to find that the argument for the motion paralleled arguments made by the U.S. Christian Right. That same year, another MP wrote a personal motion demanding that the Swedish government stop funding for the U.N. Population Fund (UNFPA). Quoting information disseminated by the Population Research Institute (an organization that helped lead successful efforts to block U.S. funding of UNFPA), it alleged that the U.N. agency was supporting forced sterilizations in China. A group called the Parliamentary Forum for Family and Human Values organizes Sweden's MPs to promote Christian values and work for the inviolability of human life. In the spring of 2004, the Parliamentary Forum organized a seminar for the Parliament called "The Abortion Issue from a Female Perspective."[100] To the surprise of pro-choice advocates, the main speaker was Dr. Wanda Franz from the U.S.-based National Right to Life Committee, a member of the Christian Right coalition at the U.N. For one of the program officers at the Swedish Association for Sexuality Education, this signaled a new phase of opposition organizing. In an email news report, the officer concluded dismally, "Just wanted to let you know that what we have heard will come is now here."[101]

World Youth Alliance – Winning the Next Generation

If Religious Right NGOs are attempting to reframe the political debate in Sweden, NGOs like the World Youth Alliance (WYA) are working toward Weigel's goal of a Great Awakening. Anna Halpine, a young Canadian Catholic in her twenties started the WYA while studying piano in New York City. She got involved at the U.N. by responding to a call to action issued by C-FAM's Austin Ruse for youth to organize at a 1999 Cairo+5 session (the fifth-year review of the Cairo Conference on Population and Development). At Cairo+5 she found reproductive health organizations had organized youth caucuses that claimed to represent the voice of the world's youth. She challenged that assumption by talking to government delegates. When she did, she claims, "For two hours the conference stalled and in that time the world divided."[102] Halpine says developing nations in particular thanked her for her work.

When Halpine started the WYA in 1999, its mission was "to fight against the dehumanizing, anti-life, anti-family trends of an increasingly decadent Western culture."[103] Weigel is a patron of the WYA, while Richard John Neuhaus, a close colleague, is on its board of directors.[104] The organization now claims 1 million members. Like other Catholic conservatives, Halpine sees her marching orders as coming from Pope John Paul II. According to one account, when George Weigel asked Halpine in the summer of 2001, "Why are you doing this on a wing and a prayer," she responded: "Pope John Paul II has told my generation to build a culture of life. Those are our orders. We're just following them."[105]

The WYA has regional offices in Nairobi, Mexico City, Brussels, Manila and New York. The office in Europe appears to be one of the most active. Its European office is especially interested in eastern Europe, "in helping to reorient them after totalitarianism which disregards the dignity of life," said regional director Dr. Gudron Lang who is herself an Austrian Catholic. While its mission is expressed in Catholic terms and its leadership appears largely Catholic, the WYA seeks to come across not as inter-religious but as a not religiously affiliated and non-political organization. "We are completely independent of religious or political groups. We represent all who agree with our position on the dignity of human life," Dr. Lang insisted. The WYA's stated goal is to influence culture, and to attract as many youth as possible into its culture of life program, regardless of religious and even political affiliation. In the words of the WYA's international director, Anna Halpine, "every day young people are drawn to the WYA who are not in agreement with the principles that we are presenting. Still, they are drawn to these principles and drawn to the energy and joy of the other young people working with us ... So I'm in the amazing position of watching the culture of life come alive for young people every day."[106]

Such a nonpartisan approach may be strategic, especially given the fact that other regions of the world are not polarized along religio-political lines as in the U.S. and are not primed for the American-based culture wars. Dr. Lang claims that the WYA even works alongside members of the Green Party. The WYA hosts conferences, book clubs and bicycle rides to promote human dignity and a culture of life. North American director Mark de Young remarked, "We are not about force, but persuasion ... Our goal is to make a cultural transformation."[107]

In other ways, however, the WYA's work promotes a conservative political agenda: "The World Youth Alliance trains hundreds of young people each year in the use of diplomacy and negotiation, message development and grass-roots activities, as well as providing information for our youth to talk about the dignity of the person in different sectors of society."[108] The WYA says it trained 600 youth in 2004 and provided in-depth training to 14 interns from ten countries.

Its priority in terms of U.N. policy has been the human cloning and bioethics debate. Participants in U.N. conferences on women and children have witnessed first hand the sharp organizing capacity of many of these trainees.

In Toronto, Cananda, at the 2002 World Youth Day (a biennial Catholic Church event in which the Pope addresses Catholic youth), the WYA planned a high-level event featuring George Weigel, economist Robert Sirico and U.S. Ambassador to the Vatican Jim Nicholson. "How does a group of twenty-somethings command such names for its program?"[109] marveled a pro-life journalist. The journalist pointed out that the WYA had clearly earned great international respect. Yet it also reveals a commitment from senior leaders of religious conservatism to connect with and promote young activists.

Challenges Ahead

The Christian Right NGOs involved at the U.N. have successfully built partnerships with civil society leaders in particular regions (Latin America) and countries (Mexico), especially cultures with deep Catholic roots. But challenges to their goals remain. It seems likely that the Christian Right will continue to be strongest in Catholic countries and regions, in particular Mexico, Latin America, Poland and eastern Europe. In his interview, Carlson speculated that the next World Congress of Families might be in the U.S., since they have not yet held one there, or Poland or Brazil where there seems to be some interest. (It will be held in Poland.[110]) He and other Christian Right leaders speak enthusiastically about Latin America as the region with the greatest potential. Though conservative social issues would resonate with many African religious leaders, Africa was low on the list as a site for an international gathering – Carlson said the costs and logistics were overwhelming.

Building a true interfaith alliance of Christians and Muslims remains the greatest challenge for Christian Right networks. While it has won over individual Muslims, those Muslims still come from the ranks of U.N. delegates. They have not been able to win over many NGO leaders. Yet we cannot ignore that its Muslim allies express admiration and respect for much of what Christian Right leaders aspire to, even while expressing frustration with certain aspects of the Christian Right NGO platform and failure to allow conservative Muslim ideas to shape the issues.

Muslim alliances also lead to international tensions within Christian Right leadership and its constituency. Dr. Lang of the World Youth Alliance in Europe expressed the sense that Muslims in Europe would not be likely partners, even if the U.N. work involves coalition building with Muslim governments.[111] Her background in philosophy and law led her to believe that the Muslim tradition doesn't share "our idea of human dignity," but she did relish the idea of giving a "speech to thousand Muslims on how human life shouldn't be instrumentalized."[112] Lang said, in contrast, that the WYA does develop alliances with the Green Party and socialists.

Current geopolitics, while sometimes a liability for Christian Right bridge-building with Muslims, can also be an asset. Some nations seeking to build alliances with the U.S. may view support for the Christian Right as one way to strengthen their alliance with the United States. Both Dubai and Qatar are open to hosting "pro-family" conferences and are oil-rich, pro-U.S. governments eagerly seeking to build their connections with the world's superpower and its president's allies. In fact, Qatar's hosting of an interfaith conference in May 2004 was noted favorably in recent neoconservative commentary on U.S. foreign policy in the Middle East. The commentary urged the U.S. to bring stability to the Middle East by building its alliances with the smaller countries – what Fareed Zakaria and others call the "trickle-up" approach to democracy.[113]

Because of the obvious tensions between Christian Right coalition partners, many of the interviewees for this book emphasized that the coalition was a loose one. In the words of Dr. Wilkins, the coalition was a "very loose one of many good friends who are convinced I am going to burn in hell."[114] Despite these groups' conflicting beliefs, he surmised, the coalition could happen because "the joint threat [to all of us religious and family-oriented people] got great enough." After three decades of emphasizing their shared values in the American culture wars, this alliance among Catholics, conservative evangelicals and Mormons will no doubt continue to strengthen.

Perhaps one of the most obvious limitations of the alliance's future growth is its lack of many local networks in the developing world. The most successful NGOs in the U.N. arena are often those who bring

first-hand experience and expertise in the field to bear in their efforts
to influence international policy. Yet only two of the major Christian
Right NGOs operative at the U.N. are engaged at the grass roots in the
developing world. Focus on the Family has indigenously run affiliates
in other countries focused on family ministry. These affiliates receive
resources from Focus, but are independently run. The other is United
Families International, which has established an abstinence-based
AIDS prevention program in several countries in Africa. Roylance,
now retired as the UFI president, says she prefers now to work on
the ground meeting the needs of real people.[115] She introduced the
UFI's AIDS program in 2001 and says it reached 350,000 children
mainly in Kenya, Ghana, Mozambique and Uganda. Roylance has
been struck by the connection between AIDS and poverty, one of
the aspects of the pandemic most emphasized by U.N. agencies.
The UFI is applying for funding from USAID (the U.S. Agency for
International Development). The agency's funding guidelines, set by
the Bush Administration, prioritize abstinence-based programs and
may therefore help strengthen the presence of grass-roots Christian
Right operations around the world.

Conclusion

One way of predicting the future of the Christian Right global NGO
organizing might be to compare it to its nemesis: the global women's
movement. The first U.N. world conference on the advancement of
women took place in Mexico City in 1975. Although the International
Women's Year (IWY) Conference was a meeting of U.N. member states,
feminist organizers found their way to Mexico to put pressure on
the governments. Around 2,000 women, largely from North America
and Europe, launched what would over the next two decades become
a powerful and diverse global women's movement. Two decades later,
at the Beijing Conference on Women in 1995, 40,000 NGO leaders
from all over the world attended the NGO Forum, which met in a
parallel meeting to the official government gathering. It was the largest
NGO gathering in history. The global women's movement succeeded
in mainstreaming women's issues and gender analysis on the map of
nearly every international issue – from AIDS to global security. The
International Year of the Family celebration in Doha, Qatar drew

over 700 NGO leaders, and the Mexico City World Congress of Family drew almost 2,000. Could the International Year of the Family become the vehicle for a global "pro-family" movement the way the International Women's Year inspired a global women's movement?

For some progressives, a global Christian Right "pro-family" movement is unfathomable, largely because they view the Christian Right as innately parochial and Anglo-centric. They suspect that their lack of cultural sensitivity might alienate potential partners suspicious of Western cultural imperialism. Yet the women's movement, today a global and diverse movement, encountered and still struggles with the same barriers today. Progressives also anticipated that conservative views on patriotism and capitalism would impede their alliances in other parts of the world. Yet such differences are in some ways no greater than the uneasy alliance between Western and developing world women's rights leaders when the former place a higher priority on issues concerning sexuality and sexual rights than economic ones.

One factor the Christian Right clearly has on its side is centuries of history and an existing infrastructure established by overseas missionary enterprises. Yet these organizations are not necessarily tied to a concrete political agenda; political conservatives will still need to convince them to enter the political sphere. In contrast, the feminist revolution has had to battle hundreds of years of tradition to make governments address basic rights such as culturally justified violence against women, access to education and economic means, and power to make choices about family planning. It has by no means accomplished all that its leaders hoped that it would, but in two short decades it has launched a seismic shift in how the world's leaders address women's issues. Much of this has been accomplished through international pressure from industrialized nations, and to a lesser extent from the key leadership from some developing nations. The progress is fragile – it is based on the setting of global norms to which some governments conform mainly because they get something concrete in return, such as recognition, development aid, loans from the World Bank. If the world's superpower reverses its stance on these issues, might things slowly swing in another direction? Given that the U.S. is now the world's only superpower, what happens in Washington, DC echoes louder than ever before throughout the world.

The global women's movement has not just taken place in the halls of government leaders, however. Much of its success is evidenced at the grass roots. Women's networks led by indigenous leaders exist in every part of the world. These have been fostered and empowered by international networking, global partnerships with other NGOs, and government and foundation funding streams opened by the pressure of the movement itself. This grass roots-to-global infrastructure is the strongest aspect of the women's movement.

To become a global movement, the Christian Right will most likely have to expand some of its platform on family issues to more concerns of the developing world. If it is able to do this, it will become both a more powerful movement, and potentially a movement with an expanded platform. The growing focus on global poverty among conservative evangelicals in the U.S. may facilitate such a shift. Conservative Christian NGOs, as illustrated in Chapter 1, have opened themselves to an agenda larger than social issues like abortion and homosexuality to address poverty and AIDS. Many NGOs emerge radically changed by their encounter with globalization and global organizing, even as they seek to change the world. Certainly the Christian Right will continue to find itself changed even as it seeks to change others.

Conclusion: Six Strengths of the Christian Right's Organizing Methods

THE CHRISTIAN RIGHT'S MANY SUCCESSES at the U.N. were not accidents of fortune, as many of us would like to believe, but rested on a solid foundation of creative, strategic organizing as well as the crucial support of many powerful elites, both in and outside the U.S. These elites helped the Christian Right to re-imagine their role on the world scene. As they perform their new role, their power is aided by a global revitalization of religion, making religious institutions among the largest civic associations in the world. These religious communities have thrived and maintained their unity because of, not in spite of, elite efforts to secularize society. Riding a wave of religious expansion, this international Christian Right movement is destined to change the face of global civil society over the course of the next ten years. While progressives are accustomed to academic works and newspaper articles implicitly dismissing these kinds of movements as extremist, or "outside the mainstream," it is more important for progressives to take a step back and take note why they will change civil society. While an out-of-hand dismissal of these movements might confirm to us that all is right with the world, and thus is an easy fantasy to indulge in, it does not encourage the necessary standard of self-reflection to which we should hold ourselves as organizers.

There are several basic reasons why they will end up changing civil society. First, the Christian Right's organizing strategies have outpaced both Christian progressives and the larger political Left represented at the U.N. Second, the Christian Right message appeals to a great number of people in the global South, particularly because it embraces two values that progressive leaders often ignore or reject: religion and the family. Third, these conservatives already have a global infrastructure to deliver their message in the form of growing religious communities (Catholic, evangelical and Mormon).

While this book described the dramatic entrance of Christian Right lobbyists in arenas I personally am familiar with and have some expertise, the Christian Right is involved in other equally important U.N. arenas, including the U.N. Commission on Human Rights and the International Conference on Population and Development. More research is needed to understand how the U.N. system will be challenged by the growing importance of these activists. And while the final chapter of this book explored some of the Christian Right's lobbying efforts in other regions of the world, for example, a complete account of those local Christian Right efforts outside the U.S. has yet to be written. Such an account would require both knowledge of U.S. religion and politics as well as the politics of the country in which the Christian Right is expanding. It would fill a gap in the scholarship on domestic and international politics and answer the growing number of questions in this area. I have been surprised at the number of times I received emails and phone calls from researchers and diplomats from secular areas like Canada and Europe who wanted to better understand this phenomenon and its possible impact on their own countries. Moreover, another researcher will have to pick up where I left off and document the full range of Christian Right NGOs currently taking form and entering U.N. fora. For example, Ph.D. student Kirstin Isgro has given the expanding networks of Concerned Women for America the research time and analysis that these groups rarely receive despite their influence. Unfortunately, we tend to focus on people we agree with rather than those we need to understand. Finally, the problematic relationships between Christian Right members and Muslims in NGO circles needs to be studied further because they represent a possible new level of influence.

Because of the size of its constituency (if it can reach Muslims), the Christian Right might rival easily the influence of the global women's movement. Despite the tortured history between feminists and religious conservatives since the 1960s, the development of their respective movements share some interesting parallels that suggest the future direction of the latter. At its beginning in the 1960s, feminists appealed to the world's women; today, the Christian Right reaches out to the world's religious conservatives. Both have sought to put issues on the international agenda that were once not considered worthy of international attention. Feminists called for the U.N. to take seriously women's strengths and experiences, pressuring the nations of the world to address violence against women, rape in wartime, or the right to bodily integrity and to choose the number and spacing of the children they bore. Feminists argued that by nature of the fact that "women hold up half the sky," by respecting women's rights, the world could better reach the principles expressed in the U.N. charter – to end the scourge of war and to promote security, economic and social development. Religious conservatives argue for another paradigm shift, one that puts the experience of family and religion at the center of international diplomacy. To understand Christian Right concerns, progressives will have to think about how the factors of family and religion as well as gender, race and class shape our lives.

The Christian Right's success will depend on how well they grapple with an issue that feminists themselves still encounter: to build a truly global movement, one must be open to expanding the agenda to include priorities of people coming from different parts of the world. Elite white feminists from North America and Europe are forever being challenged and educated by women from the global South who have different strengths and priorities than women from the global North. The women's movement constantly struggles to identify priorities and make sure all voices have an opportunity to be heard. Often, though, voices from North America still dominate. In the same way, the Christian Right is being challenged on how it establishes its priorities, especially as they relate to the economic foundations of family life. Can the Christian Right's agenda, shaped largely by U.S. politics, be opened to the experiences of conservative Muslims in countries as diverse as Indonesia, Malaysia, Egypt and Qatar? These are the questions raised by Dr. Farooq Hassan and how they are answered will ultimately determine the outer boundaries of this new international movement.

After studying the Christian Right's organizing, I found myself as much a student of their strategies as a critic of their positions on social issues. My driving question moved from, "what are they up to?" to "why is the Christian Right so successful?" Like many others,

I often assumed that the Christian Right was inherently "extremist" and "fundamentalist," and therefore ultimately moribund. I could easily dismiss their long-term prospects at the U.N. There was only one problem with this analysis: it didn't fit the facts. My theory was incapable of explaining why the Christian Right continued to gain ground. As I cast about for a new theory, I came to the conclusion (which seems obvious to me now) that progressives were dismissing a powerful social movement with potential global ramifications. Ultimately, I came to an even more disturbing conclusion about my own circle: progressives were actually the ones who pursued outdated organizing strategies. This was an illuminating and painful realization for me, but a necessary one if I was to see why the Christian Right seemed to be making progress.

I arrived at my next insight into progressive culture as I received the same reaction from all my colleagues to my research. As I shared my research with colleagues, I was disappointed when I found them interested more in exposing the right, than learning how to organize their own progressive efforts more effectively. I found little desire on the progressive side to be self-reflective about our use of language, our priorities, and our organizing strategies. Just as the community organizer in me could recognize the fact that the Christian Right thought strategically and got concrete results, the same part of me could see that I had stumbled upon one of the persistent reasons progressives (with notable exceptions) often cannot get traction: our organizing culture reflects a bygone era and, even more damning, we do not want to change. But change we must. The Christian Right and other conservative groups have in essence raised the bar for any future organizing effort; progressives of all stripes have to adjust their program accordingly, conducting the painful process of realistic self-evaluation from top to bottom if we are to get anything done. The alternative is to always be on the defensive, always responding to the initiatives coming from more focused conservative groups.

As I observed and wrote about the Christian Right, my interest in this movement shifted from understanding their strategies to understanding why progressive organizing, in both its secular and religious forms, had become so stubbornly unresponsive to the changing political climate. The excuse of ignorance (I never met people like this before!) and surprise (I was not expecting them to show up!)

can only work so many times. In fact, the challenges are now coming from every direction and not only in U.N. fora. The fact that these challenges are taking place in a number of arenas underscores the pervasive nature of the problem progressives face. From where I sat at the United Nations advocating progressive social policies, it appeared to me that progressive values were being gravely contested in every arena in which I operated (politically, religiously, socially), yet there was no systematic attempt among progressives to take stock, regroup, reorganize and try new ideas and strategies.

For starters, nationally progressive political candidates were being picked off one by one by their better-organized conservative foes. When progressive political candidates in the U.S. repeatedly lost state and national elections, I could see immediate results on U.S. positions at the U.N. and hence the international community. In my religious world, I saw progressive leaders besieged, but no one could offer a way out of the malaise. The mainline Protestant church leaders with whom I worked found their position in the U.S. culture weakened by a declining membership base and undercut by predictable conflicts between conservatives and progressives. Nationally and internationally, the voice of progressive religion grows weaker, yet neither secular nor religious leaders seem to appreciate the significance of this development for the future of human rights advocacy. As a feminist, I found parallel problems in women's circles. Western feminists recognized that family is a powerful symbol for Third World women as is their call for an economically centered feminist agenda, yet they were wedded to a platform that prioritized sexuality issues.

It would be a simplification to judge the Christian Right both nationally and globally as a success propelled by the results of its own efforts: it has achieved a measure of success from its own efforts and the weak state of progressive organizing. One can see that the Christian Right is successful in six areas of organizing while progressives are weak in these same areas. These six strengths of Christian Right organizing enable them to extend their influence. To better highlight the significance of these areas, I have contrasted them with the actions of progressives.

Whatever one thinks of Christian Right aims, it would be difficult to deny that the movement is one of the great community organizing success stories of the late twentieth century and will continue to be so in the twenty-first. Any experienced organizer knows that he or she must excel in the following areas to succeed: an openness to building new kinds of strategic alliances, openness to new organizing techniques, openness to changing funding priorities, and openness to new kinds of rhetorical strategies.

1 Openness to New Strategic Alliances: Secular Conservatives Reached Out to Religious Communities, While Secular Progressives Ignored Them

While the New Right in the U.S. sought to strengthen ties with religious communities, in particular white evangelicals, that was not true of progressives. Progressives and the Democratic Party lost touch, or all but severed relations with religious communities; this resulted in losing their traditional Catholic base.[1] Progressive activists tended to see religion as suspect, rather than as a valuable resource that provides accessible symbols of community, altruism and charity for a popular audience. This distrust flourishes despite the fact that many reforms of the original Progressive Era (1890–1917) and even modern-day progressive agendas were first inspired in large part by religious organizing and values. After God was pronounced "dead" in the 1960s, the political Left in the U.S. gradually divorced itself from those roots. Aside from a few powerful exceptions, most importantly the civil rights movement, liberal elites remained largely suspicious of religion. While religious leaders were occasionally asked to lend a moral voice to a progressive cause, their voice was largely marginalized. White progressive religious leaders themselves often bought into that worldview, allowing their voice to be at the periphery rather than the center. To many progressives, the doctrine of separation of church and state, explicitly or implicitly came to mean that religion should not have a voice in the public sphere. This interpretation of the First Amendment proved dangerous for democracy because it failed to promote a diversity of religious voices in the public square. We are now seeing the results of this self-defeating idea: only conservatives talk about religion. Progressive movements that fail to engage religious leaders and values respectfully will continue to be gravely hampered.

Moreover, we may see the religious–secular divide highlighted by the American culture wars exported through U.N. agencies.

2 Openness to New Organizing Techniques: The Contrast Between Conservative Innovation and Progressive Passivity

In the 1960s and 1970s, progressives dominated the field of organizing and activism. Today, unfortunately, their tactics remain rooted in a bygone era. Progressives, accustomed to winning, and comforted by a progressive view of history – that societies were always progressing (as defined by progressives) – failed to adjust when the effectiveness of the right's infrastructure overtook theirs. The Christian Right and New Right learned from what the political Left did well and tried new strategies. For decades, progressive activists had the upper hand in America. Yet millions of Americans remained discontent with the direction of the nation after the social revolutions of the 1960s and 1970s. New Right activists, as Jean Hardisty puts it, mobilized this discontent.

The results were organizing tactics that fit new circumstances. Where they could not influence existing institutions, they created their own. Christian conservatives can now choose to live in an alternative universe. Hundreds of thousands of conservative evangelicals escape public school "indoctrination" by home-schooling their children, and they participate in national movements that support them in their decisions. Conservative think tanks spin out easy-to-read policy ideas, which are in turn picked up by a vast alternative conservative media empire.[2] Millions get their news from talk radio stations or Christian cable stations or Fox News, which gleefully coined the War on Christmas[3] and captivated Americans who felt their Christian faith besieged by secularism. Millions join listservs and receive newsletters portraying alternative versions of the news from a conservative perspective.

Many progressive activists and religious leaders still operate in a media climate established decades ago, unaware until very recently that their hold on America was being quickly undermined by this growing alternative universe. Progressive leaders, many of them residing in the more secular Northeast, live in their own bubble and have allowed it to drifted farther and farther away from the rest of the U.S.

3 Openness to New Technology

When I first began researching the Christian Right's activities at the U.N., I was struck by how they had established a World Wide Web presence, one that outpaced that of their opponents. I worked for a national church office that served 2.5 million members with hundreds of national staff, but found co-workers hampered, literally for years, by the many bureaucratic obstacles to creating an effective web presence. Not valuing the Internet is partly the result of not taking its potential seriously. Early on, small Christian Right organizations projected an enormous presence by taking advantage of web and email advocacy. Although often considered to be "backwards" by liberal opponents, the Christian Right far outstripped progressives in its ability to use modern technology to broadcast its message.

The Christian Right also benefited from New Right inventions like direct mail. Conservative leader Richard Viguerie borrowed the direct mail advertising technique from the business world and applied it to political organizing in the 1960s. At the time, no one shared mailing lists. Viguerie collected lists by establishing client contracts that entitled him and the client access to the names. His "common market of conservative names" thereby expanded the "conservative universe."[4] Jerry Falwell, the Southern Baptist preacher who founded the new Christian Right, began by harnessing alternative media – buying television and radio time, and later deploying the fax machine and direct mail. Ron Godwin, the Moral Majority's national director said "At our height we were probably the largest religious direct mailer in the country. We had some 500 employees involved, from the mailing house to the cash receiving and the data processing."[5] Falwell harnessed church networks to spread his message. He faxed his *Falwell Confidential Report* to almost 300,000 people, 200,000 of whom were pastors who preached on the issues Falwell raised. Godwin reveals that when Falwell first took on the issue of school prayer, the networks were lukewarm on the issue. Falwell began educating his networks through direct mail and five months later donations started rolling in.

Direct mail not only produced revenue to finance New Right activities, but for the first time enabled them to cultivate a network of like-minded Americans and keep them informed of political activities and perspectives that New Right leaders could not communicate through the national media or Republican Party apparatus. Similar to the Internet today, direct mail helped the New Right to get past institutional gate-keepers on both the Left and the old Right (which it viewed as too moderate) in a cost-effective manner.

Conservative Christians, inspired by their evangelical zeal, have for decades used television and radio to spread the Gospel. In the U.S. there are two hundred Christian television channels and fifteen hundred Christian radio stations.[6] This technology became an effective organizing tool for the Christian Right and New Right. In the 1980s the advent of Talk Radio was made possible by the Supreme Court's ruling that the Federal Communications Commission (FCC) had to give up the "equal time" doctrine that had mandated radio stations to give equal time to different perspectives. The New Right took advantage of this opening and by the 1990s dominated the airwaves. The opening of cable networks enabled conservative media tycoon Rupert Murdoch to start a news station for conservatives, Fox News. Using a populist approach that saw the potential entertainment value in news and, capitalizing on the successes of talk radio, Fox News quickly replaced the once-dominant voice of CNN.[7]

4 Openness to Young People: Conservatives Mentor New Leaders, While Progressives Have Interns

While watching the Christian Right take over NGO caucuses at the U.N., I was struck by the youth of their senior leadership as compared to the older people running progressive NGOs. Their leaders were in their thirties to fifties. Progressive leadership was at least a decade or two older. While progressives had interns, the Christian Right brought in scores of highly trained youth to the U.N., put them on boards and at the head of organizations. The World Youth Alliance, led by a young adult, provided this training on an ongoing basis. Like the youth training programs of the New Right, these youths were trained how to win. This in itself meant that conservative young people were trained to accomplish different goals than their progressive counterparts. Progressive youths are not trained to win. Progressive young adults are taught about the complexity of issues and how to deconstruct society based on gender and race analysis. In contrast, conservative youth at the U.N. knew parliamentary procedure inside and out. They knew how to approach U.N. delegates and draft language for documents. On the progressive side, even many senior advocates had few skills in these areas, preferring to network with other NGO leaders rather than lobby delegates.

In contrast, progressive leadership is dominated by the "Baby Boomer" generation that launched the social revolutions of the 1960s and 1970s. The leadership on the Left is in a collective sense of denial about its age – a much joked about characteristic of this generation. Give me a flyer announcing the themes of a progressive event and I can tell you who the speaker is – for they have spoken for the past few decades to this same topic. My friends in business used to laugh at me when I said I was still "young" in my profession. Any NGO advocate under fifty years of age in progressive circles is considered youthful. While it might seem nice to be viewed as eternally young, it would be far nicer still if progressive leaders would ensure that their values were carried forward to a new generation by opening doors and pushing new leaders up that ladder. To do that requires sharing the door keys and making way on the ladder, and few progressive leaders are yet ready to share the limelight with a new generation. Who are the Ralph Reeds and Anne Coulters of the Left? Anybody who works in progressive circles is familiar with the older generations complaining about the failings of the new generation. Progressive leaders have sometimes suggested that this shows a lack of commitment on the part of young people to progressive values. Tragically, I have to ask: how would they know? They haven't tried to train and organize young leaders. There is a glimmer of hope however. At least two progressive organizations have started large-scale training programs for college students in the past two years: the Center for American Progress, and People for the American Way.

The Christian Right and New Right, realizing the importance of youth recruitment and leadership development, have raised the effectiveness of the political mobilization of the young to new heights. New Right and Christian Right leaders view themselves as training foot soldiers for what they call a culture war, an attitude that leads them to very intentionally develop cadres of leaders to change college campuses, churches and political party structures. To change culture, one must change its supporting institutions; to change these institutions, one needs committed activists. As home-schooling advocate Michael Farris puts it, the conservative movement needs Christian men and women "who will lead our nation and shape our culture with timeless biblical values."[8] Ralph Reed is the epitome of a Christian Right leader: only 29 when he took the helm of the Christian Coalition, Reed is a brilliant organizer who worked his way up through a combination of raw talent and the capacity of senior New Right conservatives to recognize that talent. Reed brought the energy and skill of a new generation to the Christian Coalition; Pat Robertson brought connections, name recognition, mailing lists and start-up funding. Consequently, Reed institutionalized the Religious Right's presence on the U.S. political landscape.

Religious progressives have let their campus infrastructures wither and die. The result is that few among the younger generation are being trained. In contrast, conservative evangelical organizations such as Intervarsity and Campus Crusade for Christ exist on almost every college campus in the United States with little or no competition from moderate or liberal religious institutions. In fact, the mainline response to a declining number of members and the rising median age of those remaining members has been to cut funding to campus ministries.

Nearly every major Christian Right think tank cultivates a next generation of leadership – not just through making internships available but also by intentionally training young activists and intellectuals. The Family Research Council's Witherspoon Fellowship envisages by the year 2025 a "legion of 3,000 leaders serving in public life for the renewal of American culture."[9] Patrick Henry College, the first college primarily for evangelical Christian home-schoolers provides a pipeline into conservative politics.[10] Of the nearly hundred interns working at the White House this semester, seven are from Patrick Henry's roughly 240 students. The 51-year-old Intercollegiate Studies Institute administers a network of eighty conservative college newspapers. The Leadership Institute, whose alumni include Ralph Reed and anti-tax crusader Grover Norquist, claims to have taught nearly 40,000 conservative students since its inception in 1979. "The school is not a series of lectures on political theory and philosophy," says its founder Morton Blackwell. "It is a crash course on how to win." The school trains young people in skills such as election organizing, public relations, starting student publications, writing, direct mail, public speaking and the Internet. Its success has led one liberal to remark, "I wish there were people on my side of the aisle doing what you're doing."[11]

Young conservatives in their twenties don't just serve in lower-level positions – they are channeled onto think tank boards and hired as directors of major programs. David Kirkpatrick, a journalist for the *New York Times*, writes: "Rearing new conservatives has long been a subject of keen interest to their elders. To counter what they considered the liberal dominance of the major universities and news organizations, a handful of conservative foundations have helped build a network of organizations to train young members of the movement." Austin Bramwell, 26, is one of five trustees of the *National Review*, a landmark publication of the New Right. Daniel McCarthy, 26, is an assistant editor at the *American Conservative*, a magazine founded by Pat Buchanan. Eric Cohen, 26, is the director of the biotechnology and American democracy program at the Ethics and Public Policy Center in Washington. Perhaps Richard Viguerie was right in at least one remark found in the first sentence of the first page in his 1979 blueprint for the New Right: "The Left is old and tired. The New Right is young and vigorous ... Our leaders are mostly in their 30s and 40s."[12] That insight remains true today.

5 Strategic Funding: Conservatives Fund Infrastructure, While Progressives Fund Causes and Education

While Christian Right NGOs at the U.N. are smaller and fewer in number than those on the Left, they focus their work purely on advancing their policy objectives around a few specific issues. In contrast, many progressive NGOs at the U.N. were established decades ago to educate their constituencies about the U.N. rather than to change the U.N. itself. To be fair, many U.N. NGOs established themselves during the Cold War when the U.N. was often shut down by Cold War politics. When the Berlin Wall came down in the 1990s, the U.N.'s work on social issues blossomed and access for NGOs increased, attracting a new generation of humanitarian

NGOs. These NGOs, as well as some of the older, progressive NGOs, took advantage of the thawing of the Cold War and launched policy initiatives through friendly U.N. delegates. However, a large number of NGOs never shifted their work in light of their new U.N. context; they continued to focus largely on educating people about the U.N. Although such work should not be diminished, this means that a high percentage of progressive NGOs with ECOSOC status are not focusing on influencing international policy. In addition, progressives focus on a vast number of issues, crippling their effectiveness, whereas conservatives focus largely on opposing abortion, homosexuality and gender equality (as defined by feminism).

The efficiency of the Christian Right NGOs echoes a larger conservative strength identified by Jean Hardisty, founding president of Political Research Associates. Hardisty, one of the first to call attention the New Right's emergence, recognized early that the New Right (including the Christian Right) put much of its resources into building an infrastructure that could directly influence public policy. The Left, in contrast, largely put its resources into social service and humanitarian aid. Hardisty pointed out that "The Right's funders got greater political mileage for each dollar invested because the organizations and individuals funded focused on a strategic plan for seizing power."[13] While liberals like to complain that the Right has more money, their influence is actually a matter of how conservatives invest their money, in fact, their funding priorities are simply more effective in changing policy. Ironically, Micklethwait and Wooldridge write in *Right Nation*, "there is more brainpower on the Left, more money, and more resources. Yet the Left does not exercise the same influence as the Right, either in coming up with specific policies or in changing the general climate of opinion."[14]

Many of the New Right think tanks initially were supported by start-up money from the so-called "four sisters" of the conservative foundation world: the John M. Olin Foundation, the Lynde and Harry Bradley Foundation, Smith Richardson and the Scaife Foundations. Oil and banking heir Richard Mellon Scaife has been called "the financial archangel of the New Right's intellectual underpinnings." The *Washington Post* found that over the past four decades Scaife and his family's charitable entities gave at least $340 million to conservative causes and institutions – about $620 million in current dollars, adjusted for inflation:

> In the world of big-time philanthropy, there are many bigger givers. The Ford Foundation gave away $491 million in 1998 alone. But by concentrating his giving on a specific ideological objective for nearly 40 years, and making most of his grants with no strings attached, Scaife's philanthropy has had a disproportionate impact on the rise of the Right, perhaps the biggest story in American politics in the last quarter of the 20th century.[15]

The New Right also helped finance the development of religious organizations that would promote their agenda. Progressive philanthropists, in contrast, shy away from funding progressive Christian or interfaith causes. Those that fund religion usually give to denominations or humanitarian projects rather than religious activist organizations. For instance, during my time working in the global feminist movement, there was only one foundation that identified feminist religious organizing as a major priority: the Sister Fund, a small family foundation established by Helen Hunt. The New Right through its alliance with the Christian Right has therefore garnered the support of that large portion of the U.S. that views religious belief and strong values as important in national leaders.[16]

6 Rhetoric: Conservatives Speak to People's Passions, While Progressives Speak in Academic Abstractions

Most importantly, the New Right and the Christian Right identified issues that would mobilize masses of Americans who felt disenfranchised as well as resentment towards others.[17] It fanned the flames of their anger and gave them skills and messages to address their grievances. For instance, they recognized the mass of working-class males angry about job competition from minorities and immigrants, and mobilized them to attack affirmative action as taking away jobs from more qualified people. They recognized the frustrations of working mothers and divorced women and blamed the feminist social revolution. There was little response to these changes. In the words of Wilma Mankiller, a civil rights activist, the Left's "underestimation of the right's ability to organize families around issues they care[d] about" was nothing less than "staggering."[18] While conservatives dominate the language of "family values," progressives and the Democratic Party, who gave us concepts like the living wage and the social safety net to support families, have abdicated their role as guardians of the American family. Instead, progressives in the U.S. and at the U.N. rarely speak of families unless it is to deconstruct it or insist on its diversity. While analyzing social relationships through the category of gender and reminding audiences of the diversity in family types are always important goals, we cannot lose sight of the fact that the majority of U.S. families increasingly struggle to make ends meet. The crisis is even more profound when viewed in an international context.

Progressives and conservatives have developed different rhetorical strategies and progressives need to recognize the limitations of their rhetorical choices. Progressives tend to give people statistics, while conservatives try to communicate to the emotions. Progressives believe that you can convince people with facts alone without also appealing to the emotions through stories.[19] Progressives have begun to address these issues more energetically over the past few years, especially after the last presidential election. This style of rhetoric will have to change, primarily to incorporate the emotions, if we are to reach and mobilize grass-roots constituencies.

Conclusion

The progressive vision is critical to the future of the world, but these six areas suggest that progressives themselves will have to regroup and retool to meet the growing Christian Right challenge. The progressive vision has brought us the values of human rights, tolerance, inclusion, respect for diversity, an awareness of our interconnectedness, and of caring for those who are vulnerable and victimized. Progressives have put issues on the international agenda that would never have been addressed otherwise: protecting the environment, advancing women, banning landmines, bringing war criminals to justice, disarmament, preventing mass nuclear destruction, mobilizing the world to end AIDS, poverty, and much more. Progressive religious leaders have been integral to many of these movements. Their voice on moral matters, silent and silenced in recent decades, is desperately needed more than ever in national and global debates.

Political polarization does to a culture what having a split personality does to a healthy person – people are estranged from important parts of themselves. In the past few decades of political battles, progressives lost touch with important parts of their history and values. The Christian Right has much to teach – not just in terms of its organizing tactics, but also in terms of the issues it cares about. At the very least, progressives should learn from the Christian Right that they need to return to their roots and remember the valuable role religion can play in holding societies together. The Christian Right can also help us return to our progressive roots in recapturing a proactive rather than deconstructionist vision for supporting families, which in this era of rapid social change and globalization need support and protection. These two terrains – morality and the family – need not be dominated exclusively by conservatives.

In the last part of the last century, conservatives emulated progressive strategies and took them to a higher level of effectiveness. Progressives can choose to return the favor, or stay rooted in their past successes. Whether or not progressives respond to this challenge will determine the success of Christian Right global activism for the next decade.

Notes

Introduction

1. Doris Buss and Didi Herman, *Globalizing Family Values: the Christian Right in International Politics* (Saint Paul: University of Minnesota, 2003).
2. Mercy Oduyoye, *Who Will Roll the Stone Away? – The Ecumenical Decade of the Churches in Solidarity with Women* (Geneva: World Council of Churches Publications, 1990), and Press Release, World Council of Churches, "Ecumenical Decade Festival Begins In Harare," Ecumenical Decade Festival Press Release No. 1 for November 28, 1998 <http://www.wcc-coe.org/wcc/assembly/festiv-e.html> (accessed on October 5, 2003).
3. The exceptions to this oversight can be found in Philip Jenkins, *The Next Christendom: The Coming of Global Christianity* (New York: Oxford University Press, 2002); Peter Singer, *The President of Good and Evil: The Ethics of George W. Bush* (New York: Dutton, 2004), and Jim Wallis, *God's Politics: Why the Right Gets it Wrong and the Left Doesn't Get It* (San Francisco, CA: HarperSanFrancisco, 2005).
4. Bruce Benson and Peter Heltzel (eds) *Evangelicals and Empire* (New York: Oxford University, forthcoming 2006); Steve Brouwer, Paul Gifford and Susan D. Rose (eds) *Exporting the American Gospel: Global Christian Fundamentalism* (New York: Routledge, 1996), and Jane H. Bayes and Nayereh Tohidi (eds) *Globalization, Gender, and Religion: The Politics of Women's Rights in Catholic and Muslim Contexts* (New York: Palgrave, 2001).
5. How this might be done is modeled by the contributors to *Evangelicals and Empire*.
6. Peter Van der Veer, "The Moral State: Religion, Nation, and Empire in Victorian Britain and British India," 22–23, in *Nation and Religion: Perspectives on Europe and Asia*, edited by Peter Van der Veer and Hartmut Lehman (Princeton: Princeton University, 1999).
7. Ibid.
8. Clyde Wilcox, *Onward Christian Soldiers? The Religious Right in American Politics* (Boulder, CO: Westview Press, 1996), pp. 43–47.
9. Robert Parham, "Evangelicals Pledge to Hold Governments Accountable for Poverty," *Ethics Daily*, October 18, 2004.
10. James Davison Hunter, *Culture Wars: The Struggle to Define America* (New York: Basic Books, 1991).
11. Ibid.
12. Morris P. Fiorina, *Culture War? The Myth of a Polarized America* (New York: Pearson Longman, 2005), pp. ix–32.

13. Ibid.
14. Rosalind Pollack Petchesky, *Global Prescriptions: Gendering Health and Human Rights* (New York: Zed Books, 2003), p. 50.
15. Ibid., p. 60.
16. Thomas Frank, *What's the Matter with Kansas? How Conservatives Won the Heart of America* (New York: Metropolitan Books, 2004).
17. Jean Hardisty, *Mobilizing Resentment: Conservative Resurgence from the John Birch Society to the Promise Keepers* (Boston, MA: Beacon Press, 1999); Clyde Wilcox, *Onward Christian Soldiers?*, Nancy T. Ammerman, "North American Protestant Fundamentalism," pp. 1–65, in *Fundamentalism Observed,* Martin E. Marty and R. Scott Appleby (eds) (Chicago, IL: University of Chicago Press, 1991).
18. Buss and Herman, *Globalizing Family Values* (2003), pp. 53–54.
19. Ibid., p. 133.
20. Ibid.
21. Buss and Herman, p. 88.
22. Stephanie Porowski, <http://www.cwfa.org/articles/4641/CWA/misc/> Concerned Women for America, September 29, 2003.
23. Allan Carlson, *The American Way: Family and Community in the Shaping of the American Identity* (Wilmington: ISI Books. 2003), pp. 11–12.
24. Ibid., p. 169.
25. Katherine Balmforth, former director of the conservative Mormon organization, World Family Policy Center quoted in Buss and Herman, p. 111.
26. Concerned Women for America, quoted in Buss and Herman, p. 111.
27. Buss and Herman, pp. 111–112.
28. Ibid., pp. 112–113.
29. Ibid., p. 125.

1 Born Again: Three Reasons the Christian Right is Globalizing

1. Jeffery K. Hadden, "Desacralizing secularization theory," p. 116, in *Secularization and Fundamentalism Reconsidered* (New York: Paragon House, 1989).
2. Gerhard Lenski, *The Religious Factor*, rev. edn (New York: Anchor Books, 1963), p. 130, quoted in Hadden, "Desacralizing secularization theory," (1989).
3. The cover of *Time* magazine for April 8, 1966 featured the question "Is God Dead?" For the difference between secularism and secularity, see Jacques Berlinerblau, *The Secular Bible: Why Nonbelievers Must Take Religion Seriously* (New York: Cambridge University, 2005), pp. 132–133.
4. See *Secularization and Fundamentalism Reconsidered*, eds Hadden and Shupe (1989); Rodney Stark and William S. Bainbridge, *The Future of Religion* (Berkeley and Los Angeles: University of California Press, 1985); and *The Desecularization of the World: Resurgent Religion and World Politics*, Peter Berger (ed.) (Grand Rapids, MI: Ethics and Public Policy Center and Eerdmans Publishing Co., 1999).

5. Hadden, "Desacralizing secularization theory," p. 4.
6. Martin E. Marty and R. Scott Appleby, "Introduction," p. vii, in *Fundamentalisms Observed*, Marty and Appleby (eds) (Chicago, IL: University of Chicago Press, 1991).
7. Anson Shupe and Jeffrey K. Hadden, "Is there such a thing as global fundamentalism?," p. 110, in *Secularization and Fundamentalism Reconsidered*, Hadden and Shupe (eds) (1989).
8. Some sociologists note that stereotypical characteristics of what constitutes "fundamentalism" could be applied to both right-wing and left-wing religious movements. For example, Hadden and Shupe observe that the liberation theology which spawned widespread "base communities" and political organization throughout Third World Catholic countries fits some definitions of "fundamentalism." Some of its followers supported a violent political revolution in Nicaragua and helped overthrow dictators Duvalier in Haiti and Marcos in the Philippines. The point is that if one takes a broad approach to the uses of religion in instances of political mobilization, those who are described as "fundamentalist" are acting in a way that is similar to other groups. Consequently, "fundamentalist" groups are not so "odd" and "out of the mainstream" as the comments of many journalists and academics would leave one to believe.
9. Peter Berger, "The Desecularization of the World: A Global Overview," p. 2, in *The Desecularization of the World: Resurgent Religion and World Politics*, Peter Berger (ed.) (Grand Rapids, MI: Ethics and Public Policy Center and Eerdmans Publishing Co., 1999).
10. Marty and Appleby, "Introduction," p. vii, (1991).
11. Shupe and Hadden, "Is there such a thing as global fundamentalism?," pp. 109–122, (1989).
12. Marty and Appleby, "Introduction," pp. vii–x, (1991).
13. See *Fundamentalism and Gender*, John Stratton Hawley (ed.) (New York: Oxford University Press, 1994), Margaret Lamberts Bendroth, *Fundamentalism and Gender, 1875 to the Present* (New Haven, CT: Yale University, 1993), Betty A. DeBerg, *Ungodly Women: Gender and the First Wave of American Fundamentalism* (Minneapolis, MN: Fortress Press, 1990).
14. Jean Hardisty, *Mobilizing Resentment: Conservative Resurgence from the John Birch Society to the Promise Keepers* (Boston: Beacon Press, 1999), pp. 80, 85.
15. Rosalind Petchesky, *Global Prescriptions: Gendering Health and Human Rights* (London: Zed Books, 2003), pp. 43–70. Also, for a domestic parallel see Elizabeth Warren, *The Two Income Trap* (New York: Basic Books, 2003), p. 161. The websites for the following organizations in Washington, DC reveal an interest in addressing the problem of economic self-sufficiency for low-income families, and especially single-mother families, but not the more general issue of how economics affects family stability: Wider Opportunities for Women, National Women's Law Center, Center for Law and Social Policy, and Center for Family and Practice.
16. Philip Jenkins, *The Next Christendom: The Coming of Global Christianity* (New York: Oxford University Press, 2002), pp. 1–14;

Berger, "The Descularization of the World," pp. 1–18 (1999), and Pablo A. Deiros, "Protestant Fundamentalism in Latin America," pp. 142–182, in *Fundamentalisms Observed*, Marty and Appleby (eds) (Chicago, IL: University of Chicago Press, 1991).

17. The John Mbiti quote was originally found in Kwame Bediako, *Christianity in Africa* (Edinburgh and New York: Edinburgh University Press/Orbis, 1995), p. 154. Jenkins uses the quote in his *The Next Christendom* (2002), p. 2.

18. Jenkins, *The Next Christendom* (2002), p. 3.

19. Ibid., p. 56.

20. Ibid., p. 61.

21. Ibid.

22. Philip Jenkins, "A New Christendom," *Chronicle of Higher Education*, March 29, 2002 <http://chronicle.com/free/v48/i29/29b00701.htm> (accessed on January 1, 2006).

23. Jenkins, *The Next Christendom* (2002), p. 195.

24. Diana Jean Shemo, "Nearing retirement, priests of the 60's fear legacy is lost," *New York Times*, September 10, 2000.

25. Jenkins, *The Next Christendom* (2002), p. 160.

26. Ibid., p. 162.

27. George Lakoff, *Don't think of an Elephant! Know your Values and Frame the Debate* (White River Junction, VT: Chelsea Green Publishing, 2004).

28. Nicholas D. Kristof, "Living Poor, Voting Rich," *New York Times*, November 3, 2004.

29. Luis Lugo, "Religion as political issue extends beyond bible belt," *Atlanta Journal-Constitution*, January 30, 2004.

30. Katharine Q. Seelye, "Moral values cited as a defining issue of the election," *New York Times*, November 4, 2004.

31. Clyde Wilcox, *Onward Christian Soldiers? The Religious Right in American Politics* (Boulder, CO: Westview, 1996), pp. 137–138.

32. One-third of Americans are evangelical (which includes black evangelicals). White evangelicals make up nearly a quarter of American citizenry. Not all white evangelicals endorse the Christian Right's agenda. See Wilcox, *Onward Christian Soldiers?* (1996), pp. 45–57.

33. The National Opinion Research Center at the University of Chicago, cited in Michael Hout and Andrew M. Greeley "A hidden swing vote: evangelicals," (op-ed), *New York Times*, September 4, 2004.

34. Hout and Greeley, "A hidden swing vote" (2004).

35. Robert Wuthnow, *Restructuring of American Religion* (Princeton, NJ: Princeton University Press, 1988), p. 188.

36. Mary E. Bendyna and Mark J. Rozell, "Uneasy alliance: conservative Catholics and the Christian right," *Sociology of Religion*, Spring 2001.

37. Ralph Reed, *Active Faith: How Christians are changing to Soul of American Politics* (New York: The Free Press, 1996).

38. Roberto R. Ramirez and G. Patricia de la Cruz, *Current Population Reports* (Washington, DC: US Census Bureau, June 2003).

39. John Micklethwait and Adrian Wooldridge, *The Right Nation: Conservative Power in America* (New York: Penguin Press, 2004), p. 240.

40. Carolyn Curiel, "How Hispanics Voted Republican," *New York Times*, November 8, 2004, p. A22; William Yardley, "The 2004 Elections: The Voting Process – The Minority Vote; Energized Black Voters Flock to Polls to Back Kerry," *New York Times*, November 3, 2004, p. A7.

41. Richard N. Ostling and Joan K. Ostling, *Mormon America: The Power and the Promise* (New York: Harper Collins, 1999), pp. 114–115.

42. Ibid.

43. Ibid.

44. Ibid.

45. Wuthnow, *Restructuring of American Religion* (1988), pp. 71–99.

46. Wilcox, *Onward Christian Soldiers?* (1996), p. 75.

47. Jean Hardisty, *Mobilizing Resentment* (1999), p. 56.

48. Robert Wuthnow and John H. Evans, "Introduction," p. 2, and Peter Thuesen, "The Logic of Mainline Churchliness," p. 44, in *The Quiet Hand of God: Faith-Based activism and the Public Role of Mainline Protestantism*, Wuthnow and Evans (eds) (Berkeley: University of California, 2002).

49. Wuthnow and Evans, "Introduction," 5, in *The Quiet Hand of God* (2002).

50. Nancy T. Ammerman, "North American Protestant Fundamentalism," pp. 1–28, in *Fundamentalism Observed*, Marty and Appleby (eds) (1991).

51. Steven Waldman and John Green, "Tribal Relations," *Atlantic Monthly*, February 18, 2006 <http://www.theatlantic.com/doc/prem/200601/tribal-relations>.

52. Parachurch organizations stand outside the organizational structure of well-established religious bodies.

53. Personal conversations with progressive national religious leaders.

54. DART stands for Direct Action and Research Training; PICO was originally the Pacific Institute for Community Organizations, but in 2004 changed its name to PICO National Network to reflect its growth into a national organizing effort.

55. Dennis Jacobsen, *Doing Justice: Congregations and Community Organizing* (Minneapolis, MI: Augsburg Fortress, 2001), pp. 23–26.

56. Ammerman, "North American Protestant Fundamentalism" (1991) pp. 1–28, and Wuthnow, *Restructuring of American Religion* (1988), pp. 137–138, 173–207.

57. Wuthnow, ibid.

58. A few progressive religious advocacy groups do exist, such as Call to Renewal, Catholics for a Free Choice, Faithful America, the Interfaith Alliance, the Foundation for Ethics and Meaning. They are small in comparison to conservative religious NGOs, which are growing in size and number and global outreach.

59. Thuesen, "The Logic of Mainline Churchliness" (2002), pp. 46–47.

60. Ibid., p. 47.

61. Wuthnow and Evans, "Introduction," p. 18, in *The Quiet Hand of God* (2002).

62. Wuthnow, *Restructuring of American Religion* (1988), p. 124.

63. Derek Davis, "From Engagement to Retrenchment: An Examination of First Amendment Activism by America's Mainline Churches, 1980–2000," p. 323, in *The Quiet Hand of God* (2002).

64. Wuthnow, *Restructuring of American Religion* (1988), pp. 147–148.

65. Davis, "From Engagement to Retrenchment," (2002), p. 323. Davis reports that the Evangelical Lutheran Church has more than 5 million members, yet its Legislative Update goes to around only 5,000.

66. Wuthnow, *Restructuring of American Religion* (1988), p. 189.

67. Wuthnow and Evans, (2002), pp. 17–22.

68. Wuthnow, *Restructuring of American Religion* (1988), p. 238.

69. Ibid., p. 196.

70. See discussions in Richard A. Viguerie and David Franke, *America's Right Turn: How Conservatives Used New and Alternative Media to Take Power* (Chicago, IL: Bonus, 2004), pp. 1–8; Robert Wuthnow, *The Struggle for America's Soul: Evangelicals, Liberals and Secularism* (Grand Rapids, MI: Eerdmans, 1989), pp. 115–141, and *The Quiet Hand* (2002).

71. Viguerie and Franke, *America's Right Turn* (2004), pp. 9–39.

72. Ann M. Florini and P.J. Simmons, "What the World Needs Now?," pp. 8–9, in *The Third Force: The Rise of Transnational Civil Society*, Ann M. Florini (ed.) (Washington, DC: Carnegie Endowment for International Peace, 2000). See Religion Counts, *Religion and Public Policy at the U.N.* (New York: Religion Counts, 2002), pp. 41–42.

73. See Jennifer Block, "Sex trafficking: why the faith trade is interested in the sex trade," *Conscience* (Catholics for Free Choice), Summer/Autumn 2004 <http://www.catholicsforchoice.org/conscience/archived/SexTrafficking.htm>; Susan Jones, "Conservative Group Gets Federal Money to Combat Sex Trafficking," *CNSNews.com Morning Editor*, December 1, 2004, CNSNews.com (Cybercast News Service is a conservative news source founded in 1998); and Esther Kaplan, "Follow the Money," *The Nation*, posted October 14, 2004 <http://www.thenation.com/doc/20041101/Kaplan>.

74. Wuthnow and Evans, *The Quiet Hand* (2002), p. 188.

75. Research Services Program Area, General Assembly Council, Presbyterian Church (USA), "A Presbyterian Panel Snapshot," Presbyterian Panel Surveys of Members, 1993–1999 <http://www.pcusa.org/research/reports/trend12.htm> (accessed on January 1, 2006).

76. National Council of Churches in Christ, *Yearbook of American and Canadian Churches* (New York: National Council of Churches in Christ, 2003), p. 2.

77. Benton Johnson, Dean R. Hoge and Donald A. Luidents, "Mainline Churches: The Real Reason for decline," No. 31 *First Things* (1993), pp. 13–18.

78. Donald Luidens, "Fighting 'decline': mainline Churches and the tyranny of aggregate data'", *Christian Century*, No. 113 (April 17, 1996), p. 1075.

79. Ibid., p. 1077.

80. Ibid.

81. For more information see Kirk C. Hadaway, "Denominational Defection: Recent Research on Religious Disaffiliation in America," p. 188, and

Mark Wilhelm, "Membership Decline and Congregational Identity in Yonkers, New York: A Case Study in the Presbyterian Church (USA)," pp. 150–176, in *The Mainstream Protestant "Decline:" The Presbyterian Experience*, Milton J. Coalter, John M. Mulder and Louis B. Weeks (eds) (Louisville, KY: Westminster, John Knox Press, 1990); Dean R. Hoge, "National Contextual Factors Influencing Church Trends," pp. 13–18, in *Understanding Church Growth and Decline: 1950–1979*, Dean R. Hoge and David R. Roozen (eds) (New York: Pilgrim, 1979); Johnson et al., "Mainline Churches" (1993), pp. 13–18; Dean M. Kelly, *Why Conservative Churches are Growing* (Macon, GA: Mercer University Press, 1977); Luidens, "Fighting 'decline'" (1996), pp. 1075–1079; James H. Smylie, "Church growth and decline in historical perspective: Protestant Quest for Identity, Leadership and Meaning", *American Presbyterians*, No. 73, 1995, pp. 203–218, in Carter et al., *The Mainstream Protestant Decline* (1990).

82. Wuthnow, *Restructuring of American Religion* (1988), pp. 71–72.

83. Jim Wallis, *God's Politics: Why the Right Gets it Wrong and the Left Doesn't Get It* (San Francisco, CA: HarperSanFrancisco, 2005).

84. See for example Florini (ed.), *The Third Force* (2000); Margaret E. Keck and Kathryn Sikkink, *Activists Beyond Borders* (Ithaca, NY: Cornell University Press, 1998); William Korey, *NGOs and the Universal Declaration of Human Rights* (New York: Palgrave, 2001); Peter Willets (ed.), *The Conscience of the World: The Influence of Non-Governmental Organizations in the UN System* (London: Hurst, 1996); and Jessica Matthews, "Power shift," *Foreign Affairs*, Vol. 6, No. 1 (January/February 1997), pp. 50–66.

85. Motoko Mekata, "Building partnerships toward a common Goal: Experiences of the International Campaign to Ban Landmines," in Florini (ed.), *The Third Force* (2000), pp. 143–176.

86. Keck and Sikkink, *Activists Beyond Borders* (1998), pp 39–78.

87. Religion Counts, *Religion and Public Policy at the UN*, April 2002: ISBN 0–915365–48–0, p. 5; *Student Bodies: Reproductive Health Care at Catholic Universities* (Washington, DC: The Access Series, 2002); Benjamin Rivlin, "Thoughts on religious NGOs at the UN: a component of global civil society," reprinted in *Civil Society in the Information Age*, Peter I. Hajnal (ed.) (Burlington, VT: Ashgate Publishing, 2002), pp. 155–173.

88. Keck and Sikkink, *Activists Beyond Borders* (1998), pp 39–79.

89. Allen D. Hertke, *Freeing God's Children: The Unlikely Alliance for Global Human Rights* (New York: Rowman & Littlefield, 2004).

90. Laurie Goodstein, "The persecution facing Christians: concern is worldwide, lobbying effort swells, though some warn against label on a complex problem," *New York Times*, November 9, 1998, p. A16.

91. Progressive organizations like Coalition Against Trafficking in Women (CATW), a feminist organization, and ECPAT (End Child Prostitution and Trafficking in Children for Sexual Purposes), founded by a Catholic priest and supported by child rights proponents, helped catalyze movements to draw attention to women and children. More recently activists and academics have drawn attention to the problem of human trafficking

more broadly, not just for sexual purposes. Progressive campaigns found it difficult to mobilize resources and political will around the sexual exploitation of women and children. Complicating matters, feminists were sharply divided on a debate over whether or not legalizing prostitution would help or hurt women. During the 1990s, in part thanks to the U.N. conferences of that decade, especially the Beijing Women's Conference, the issue received greater attention. The government of Sweden worked with NGOs to hold the First World Congress on the Sexual Exploitation of Children in Stockholm, Sweden (1996) and a Second World Congress in Yokohama, Japan (2002).

92. Jennifer Block, "Sex trafficking," *Conscience* (Catholics for Free Choice), Summer/Autumn 2004 <http://www.catholicsforchoice.org/conscience/archived/SexTrafficking.htm>.
93. CBS Nightly News, "Jesse Helms to tackle AIDS," February 21, 2002 <http://www.cbsnews.com/stories/2002/02/26/politics/main502106.shtml> (accessed January 8, 2006).
94. Holly Burkhalter, "The Politics of AIDS: Engaging Conservative Activists," *Foreign Affairs*, January/February 2004, Vol. 83, no. 1 <http://www.foreignaffairs.org/20040101facomment83102/holly-burkhalter/the-politics-of-aids-engaging-conservative-activists.html>.
95. Heather Boonstra, "US AIDS policy: priority on treatment, conservative's approach to prevention," *The Guttmacher Report on Public Policy*, Vol. 6, No. 3 (August 2003), p. 2.
96. Quoted in ibid.

2 The Christian Right's Challenge to Global Democracy

1. Richard Bernstein, "Europe's groundswell: public opinion," *New York Times*, February 17, 2003.
2. Panel of Eminent Persons on U.N.-Civil Society Relationships, *We the Peoples: Civil Society, the U.N. and Global Governance* (New York: United Nations Department of Public Information, June 2004).
3. Heritage Foundation, "Heritage Foundation Quest for U.N. Consultative Status," online posting July 26, 2001 <www.heritage.org>. On file with author.
4. Austin Ruse, "Urgent lobbying alert/ Beijing+5" online posting December 17, 1999; *Friday Fax*, 2: 48 <http://www.c-fam.org/FAX/index.html>.
5. Austin Ruse, President of C-FAM, interview with author, July 20, 2000. Ruse claims that they had around 300 registered but no more than 100 present at a time.
6. Personal observation.
7. Austin Ruse, "Toward a permanent United Nations Pro-Family Bloc," World Congress of Families II Conference, Geneva: 14–17 November 1999. November 19, 2005. <http://www.worldcongress.org/wcf2_spkrs/wcf2_ruse.htm> (accessed on November 19, 2005).
8. Austin Ruse, July 20, 2000, interview.
9. Allen D. Hertke, *Freeing God's Children: The Unlikely Alliance for Global Human Rights* (New York: Rowman & Littlefield, 2004).

10. Charlotte Bunch, founder and director, Center for Women's Global Leadership, interview President of Women's Tribunal, with author, August 27, 2004.

11. Pat Humphries wrote the song "Keep on Moving Forward (Never turning Back)," which opened the fourth World Conference on Women in 1995 and made headlines. See <http://www.fssgb.org/humph.html> (accessed on December 29, 2005).

12. Direct observation.

13. TV broadcast, Federalist Society, "Non-Governmental Organizations Forum," Federalist Society, Washington, DC (Aired on C-SPAN, November 15, 2003).

14. Charlotte Bunch, interview.

15. Julie Stone Peters and Andrea Wolper (eds), *Women's Rights, Human Rights: International Feminist Perspectives* (New York: Routledge, 1994), pp. 11–36.

16. Jennifer Butler, "For Faith and Family: Christian Right Advocacy at the United Nations," *Public Eye*, Summer/Fall 2000, pp. 10–11.

17. "Maryland For Bush Campaign Chairperson, Ellen R. Sauerbrey," Maryland for George W. Bush Homepage <http://www.aptusit.com/MarylandforBush/EllenSauerbrey.htm> (accessed on November 19, 2005).

18. Quoted in Douglas A. Sylva, "Bush Administration calls strong families key for development," *Friday Fax* 7, 13 (March 19, 2005).

19. Richard Wilkins, Austin Ruse, interviews; Richard Wilkins, Managing Director of World Family Policy Center, June 28, 2005, interview.

20. United Nations Commission on the Status of Women, Forty-Seventh Session, 3–14 March 2003, 5:30 p.m. "Women's human rights and elimination of all forms of violence against women and girls as defined in the Beijing Platform for Action and the outcome document of the twenty-third special session of the General Assembly, Agreed Conclusions." See also Karey Vaughn (ed.), "Report on the 47th Session of the UN Commission on the Status of Women 3–14 March 2003 UN Headquarters in New York," in *Women's Voice*, September 2003, a newsletter published by Worldwide Organization of Women.

21. Vaughn (ed.), "Report on the 47th Session of the UN Commission on the Status of Women," (2003), p. 7.

22. Press Release WOM/1400, Commission on the Status of Women, Forty-seventh Session (Resumed), "Commission on Status of Women fails to Adopt Draft agreed Conclusions on Violence against Women, As it Closes Forty-Seventh Session," March 25, 2003, available December 31, 2005 <http://www.un.org/News/Press/docs/2003/wom1400.doc.htm>(accessed December 31, 2005).

23. Lydia la Riviere-Zijdel (president of the EWL), "EWL letter to U.N. Secretary General Kofi Annan: stop the global backlash against women's rights," from the European Women's Lobby (Brussels), letter dated February 4, 2003. (Open letter circulated by email, on file with author).

24. Ibid.

25. Parvina Nadjibulla, representative for the United Methodist General Board of Global Minorities, August 8, 2004, interview with author.

26. Jean Hardisty, *Mobilizing Resentment: Conservative Resurgence from the John Birch Society to the Promise Keepers* (Boston, MA: Beacon Press, 1999), pp. 93–96.

27. Ibid.

28. Ibid.

29. Flyer on file with author from NGO workshop. "Biological Differences Summary", information reprinted from Joe Tanenbaum, *Male and Female Realities* (Sugarland, TX: Candle Publishing Company), p. 48.

30. Flyer on file with author. Speakers included Dr. Ken Canfield, president of the National Center for Fathers, Dr. David Blankenhorn, president of the Institute for American Values, and Dr. Janice Shaw Crouse, Senior Fellow, The Beverly LaHaye Institute.

31. Wendy Wright, "U.S. Proposes adding Fathers to UN Document," CWA website, March 5, 2004 <http://www.cwfa.org/articles/5342/CWA/nation/> (accessed December 30, 2005).

32. Parvina Nadjibulla, interview.

33. Ibid.

34. DAWN (Development Alternatives with Women for a New Era), "No to negotiations for B+10?," in *DAWN Informs*, September 2003, p. 13.

35. Ibid.

36. Ibid.

37. Ibid.

38. Parvina Nadjibulla, interview.

39. Center for Women's Global Leadership, the NGO Committee on the Status of Women, and the Women's Environment and Development Organization. "2005 CSW Review of the Beijing Platform for Action (Beijing+10) NGO Discussions at the 48th Session of the Commission on the Status of Women, March 1–12, 2004" <http://www.cwgl.rutgers.edu/globalcenter/policy/b10/ReportB10March2004.pdf>.

40. United Nations, Commission on the Status of Women, 48th Session, Press Release WOM/1440, "*Review of the 1995 Beijing Action Plan Should Focus on National Implementation. Avoid Lengthy Negotiations, Women's Commission Told*," (New York: Department of Public Information, March 5, 2003). See also (unpublished working paper) Center for Women's Global Leadership, "Beijing+10 Review: A Feminist Strategy for 2004–05, A working paper for NGOs on how to move forward," <http://www.cwgl.rutgers.edu/globalcenter/policy/csw04/B10strategy-CSW04.pdf>.

41. Suzanne Goldenberg, "America urges U.N. to renounce abortion rights," *Guardian*, March 1, 2005.

42. Warren Hoge, "Panel Backs Women's Rights After U.S. Drops Abortion Issue," *New York Times*, March 5, 2005.

43. Ambassador Ellen Sauerbrey, at the Security Council Stakeout, March 4, 2005, "U.S. U.N. Press Release # 39 (05)" (New York: U.S. Mission to the United Nations, March 4, 2005).

44. Women's Media Pool, "Governments pledge to accelerate efforts to achieve equality for women and fulfill Beijing commitments, as UN Commission

concludes," New York, 11 March 2004, <www.womensmediapool.org/notas/unend.htm> (accessed June 23, 2005).

45. Dr. Farooq Hassan, Special Ambassador for the World Family Alliance, July 15, 2005, interview with the author.

46. Center for Women's Global Leadership ... Development Organization, "2005 CSW Review".

47. Ibid.

48. Susan Hartman, *The Other Feminists* (New Haven, CT: Yale University Press, 1998), and Helen Hunt, *Faith and Feminism: A Holy Alliance* (New York: Atria Books, 2004).

49. Charlotte Bunch, interview.

50. Eman Ahmed, "Not the only way: Dr. Hashmi's hold on Pakistani women," *Women's Human Rights Net,* November 2004, Reader No. 1, p. 13. This is published in Toronto by the Association of Women in Development (AWID).

51. "U.S. Contempt for Convention Brings 'Spoiler' Charge from NGOs," *On the Record for Children (Your link to the UN General Assembly Special Session on Children)*, 14: 5, February 2, 2001.

52. Ibid.

53. See Family Research Council, "UN Committee Takes Aim at Family Structure and Morality," *Culture Facts*, February 21, 2001, <http://www.frc.org/get/cu01b4.cfm#title7>. See also the National Center for Home Education, "UN News Update," *HSLDA News*, June 14, 2001, <http://nche.hslda.org/docs/news/hslda/200106140.asp>. The update states, "Among the United Nations international treaties and activities monitored by Home School Legal Defense Association is one of the most dangerous attacks on parental rights ever – the United Nations Convention on the Rights of the Child (CRC). Because the UN is holding a Child Summit this September, the CRC is taking center stage worldwide this year." For liberal source see Sharon Lerner, "Saviors of the Children," *Village Voice*, May 8, 2002, <www.villagevoice.com/issues/0219/lerner.php>, viewed May 8, 2002.

54. CRIN (Child Rights Information Network), "Battle-Lines Drawn," *PrepCom Update*, Number 1, June 11, 2004. This was a daily morning update managed by a coalition of progressive NGOs at the UN Special Session on Children Prepcom. The update reported, "Because of its power in the world and in the UN, the U.S. position will be crucial on several issues. It dislikes references to poverty and rights for example and supports the death penalty. The new Administration's domestic links with Christian fundamentalists is likely to colour its attitude to reference to the family, sex education and a range of other issues."

55. Karen De Young and Colum Lynch, "War of Words at Youth Summit: U.S. Says Document Endorses Abortion," *Washington Post*, May 9, 2002, p. A18.

56. On the Record Staff, "European Patience Wears Thin," *On the Record for Children (Your Link to the UN General Assembly Special Session on Children)*, 2: 6, June 15, 2001, p. 1 and "U.S. says Bejing and Cairo Reference Must Come Out," p. 3.

57. "U.S. Contempt for Convention Brings 'Spoiler' Charge from NGOs," *On the Record for Children* (2001).

58. William Orme, "UN Forum on Children Takes up Abortion: Controversy: Delegates argue about whether phrase 'reproductive health services' should be included in conference documents," *Los Angeles Times*, May 9, 2002, p. A3. <http://www.latimes.com/templates/misc/> (accessed on May 9, 2002). See also Sharon Lerner, "Far Right Bush Delegates Ally with Religious Conservatives at UN Conference: Saviors of the Chilren," *Village Voice*, May 14, 2002.

59. Orme, "UN Forum on Children Takes up Abortion," (2002).

60. On the Record Staff, "Language on Reproductive Health Care Alarms Pro Life and Pro choice Advocates," *On the Record for Children*, p. 3 June 14, 2001, Vol. 2, No. 5. (*On the Record* was the official NGO publication for the conference.

61. Center for Reproductive Rights. "U.N. Special Session on Children: Missed Opportunities and Neglected Realities," briefing paper, <www.reproductive rights.org>, December 2002.

62. On the Record Staff, "European Patience Wears Thin" and "U.S. says Bejing and Cairo Reference Must Come Out," (2001).

63. See, "A World Fit for Children," U.N. GAOR, 27th Special Session, New York, United States, May 8–10, 2002, Supp. No. 3, Para. 15, U.N. Doc. A/s-27/19/Rev 1 (2002).

64. Mary Jo Anderson, "The UN's War Against Children," *Crisis: Politics, Culture and the Church*, September 2001, <http://www.nrlc.org/news/2002/NRL06/un.html> (accessed November 19, 2005) and Dave Andrusko, "Huge Pro-Life Win at Children's Summit," *National Right to Life News*, June 2002, <http://www.nrlc.org/news/2002/NRL06/un.html> (accessed November 19, 2005).

65. Child Rights Caucus press advisory, "NGOs Disappointed by Outcome of the Children's Summit," <www.crin.org/resources/infodetail.asp?ID+2613&flag=news> (accessed on December 29, 2005). The Child Rights caucus was the main NGO caucus at the Special Session.

66. Ibid.

67. Orme, "UN Forum on Children Takes up Abortion," *Los Angeles Times*, May 9, 2002.

68. David Roth, co-chair, NGO Committee on the family, May 27, 2004.

69. Ellen Sauerbrey, "The Status of Family Issues at the UN," <http://www.unitedfamilies.org/ellen.asp>.

70. Emily Freeburg, Lutheran World Federation UN Office, July 28, 2004, interview with author.

71. U.N. General Assembly Resolution 58/15, December 3, 2003, paragraph 2 welcomed Qatar's decision to host "an international conference in November 2004 to celebrate the tenth anniversary and encourages governments to make every possible effort to realize the anniversary's objectives." Such language is a polite nod to the desire of a government to draw attention to a special year.

72. Douglas A. Sylva, "Qatar seeks worldwide scholarship on family life," *Friday Fax*, 7, 21 (14 May 2004).

73. Sauerbrey, "The status of family issues at the United Nations."
74. Website of the WFPC, "Processes and Outcomes for the Doha International Conference for the Family," <http://www.worldfamilypolicy.org/intl_conf. htm> (accessed on December 28, 2005). Also Farooq Hassan, interview.
75. Dr. David Popenoe from Rutgers University, interview, January 28, 2004.
76. Doha International Conference for the Family Participants list on the official Doha International Conference for the Family website (sponsored by the government of Qatar), <www.dicf.org.qa/english/Participants/index.html>.
77. David Roth, co-chair of the NGO Committee on the Family, May 27, 2004.
78. "The Doha Declaration." WFPC website <http://www.worldfamilypolicy. org/intl_conf_doha.html>.
79. Ibid.
80. WFPC website, "Summary: Processes and Outcomes of Doha International Conference for the Family."
81. Sharon Slater, "Meridian readers made a big difference at the United Nations," *Meridian Magazine*, 2004, <http://meridianmagazine.com/familywatch/041208difference.html> (accessed on January 8, 2006).
82. Dr. Farooq Hassan, "After Doha: the future of family internationally," *Islam Online Live Dialogue*, December 8, 2004 <http://www.islamonline. net/livedialogue/english/Browse.asp?hGuestID=ZEeWV6>.
83. Dr. Farooq Hassan, Special Ambassador for the World Family Alliance, interview, July 15, 2005.
84. Ibid.
85. Ælfwine Mischler, "Limitations of the Doha Conference: An Interview with Dr Farooq Hassan," IslamOnline.net, November 25, 2004 <http:// www.islamonline.net/English/In_Depth/Doha_Conference/Views/03. shtml>.
86. Ælfwine Mischler, "Was Doha a victory?," IslamOnline.net, November 25, 2004, archived <www.islamonline.net/English/In_Depth/Doha_conference/views/04.shtml>.
87. United Nations, General Assembly, 59th Session, "General Assembly commemorates 10th Anniversary of International Year of the Family," *Press Release GA/10311* (December 6, 2004).
88. Charlotte Bunch, interview.
89. Christopher Marquis, "U.S. Is Accused of Trying to Isolate U.N. Agency," *New York Times*, June 21, 2004. p. A3.
90. John Washburn, Convener, American Non-governmental Organizations Coalition on the International Criminal Court, interview, August 4, 2004.
91. Not only has the United States not ratified the Rome statute that brought the court into being, it has become the first country to ever "unsign" a treaty – establishing a dangerous precedent in international law. The Bush Administration vigorously sought to have other nations sign bilateral agreements with the U.S. exempting U.S. citizens from the treaty and has gone so far as to sanction allies for belonging to the court. It has withheld military aid from at least 25 countries and economic and development

aid to countries including Bosnia, Honduras and Niger. It threatened to deny Croatia admission to NATO. This heavy-handed strategy has often backfired as countries deeply offended by such intervention only dug in their heels in resistance. See William Driscoll, Joseph P. Zompetti, and Suzette Zompetti, *The International Criminal Court and the Quest for Justice* (New York: International Debate Education Association, 2004), p. 21.

92. Washburn, interview.

93. The National Security Strategy of the United States of America, *Rebuilding America's Defenses: Strategy, Forces and Resources for a New Century: A Report*, September 2002 <www.whitehouse.gov/nsc/nss.html/> (accessed November 3, 2004).

94. Douglas Sylva, "Muslim allies at the U.N. fight for the 'Right Stuff'," *Insight on the News – Fair Comment*, September 17, 2001, p. 44.

95. Richard Wilkins, "Ramifications of the International Criminal Court for war, peace and social change," *Federalist Society White Paper* (Washington, DC: Federalist Society for Law and Public Policy Studies) <http://www.fed-soc.org/Intllaw&%20AmerSov/WilkinsICC.pdf> (accessed April 5, 2006).

96. Washburn, interview.

97. Ibid.

98. Ibid.

99. Ibid.

100. Ibid.

101. Quoted in Jean Hardisty and Elizabeth Furdon, "Policing civil society: NGO watch," *The Public Eye*, 18:1, Number 1 (Spring 2004), p. 7.

102. NGO Watch homepage, American Enterprise Institute and Federalist Society for Law and Public Policy Studies, November 19, 2005 < http://www.ngowatch.org/info.htm>.

103. David Brock, *The Republican Noise Machine* (New York: Crown Publishing Group, 2005).

104. TV broadcast: Federalist Society, "Non-Governmental Organizations Forum," Federalist Society, Washington, DC (aired on C-SPAN, November 15, 2003). C-SPAN provides coverage of a variety of public affairs events. C-SPAN is a private, non-profit company, created in 1979 by the cable television industry as a public service. Its mission is to provide public access to the political process. C-SPAN receives no government funding; operations are funded by fees paid by cable and satellite affiliates who carry C-SPAN programming.

105. Ibid.

106. NGO Watch, "Corrupting U.S.AID's mission?" <www.ngowatch.org>, August 15, 2004, on file with author.

107. Hardisty and Furdon, "Policing civil society." See also Naomi Klein, "Bush to NGOs: Watch Your Mouths," *Globe and Mail* (Canada), June 20, 2003, viewed at <http://www.commondreams.org/views03/0620–06.htm> (accessed on December 31, 2005), and Alan Beattie, "NGOs Under Pressure on Relief Funds," *Financial Times,* June 13, 2003, <http://

www.globalpolicy.org/ngos/fund/2003/0610control.htm> (accessed on December 31, 2005).

108. Quoted by Jerome Shestack, during TV broadcast, Federalist Society, "Non-Governmental Organizations Forum" (2003).

109. TV broadcast: Federalist Society, "Non-Governmental Organizations Forum" (2003).

110. Doris Buss and Did Herman, *Globalizing Family Values: the Christian Right in International Politics* (Saint Paul: University of Minnesota Press, 2003), p. 137.

111. Keck and Sikkink, *Activists Beyond Borders* (1998), pp 1–38. Also Julie Fisher, *NGOs and the Political Development of the Third World* (Bloomfield, CT: Kumarian Press, 1998), pp. 1–38.

112. Robert Parham, "Evangelicals pledge to hold governments accountable for poverty," *Ethics Daily*, October 18, 2004.

113. <www.micahchallenge.org>.

3 Assembling a Pro-Family Alliance

1. Daniel Williams and Alan Cooperman, "Long-Serving and Well-Traveled Pope Persevered Despite Illness," *Washington Post*, April 3, 2005, p. A1.

2. Timothy George (interview by Collin Hansen), "Pope gave Evangelicals the moral impetus we didn't have," *Christianity Today*, April 2005, <http://www.christianitytoday.com/ct/2005/114/32.0.html>.

3. Ibid.

4. David Scott, "The Pope we never knew: The unknown story of how John Paul II ushered campus Crusade into Catholic Poland." *Christianity Today*, April 2005, <http://www.christianitytoday.com/ct/2005/005/13.34.html>.

5. George Weigel, "What Really Happened at Cairo," *First Things*, February 1995, pp. 24–31.

6. Austin Ruse, President of C-FAM, July 7, 2004, interview with author.

7. Weigel, "What Really Happened at Cairo," p. 24.

8. I attended this gathering at the invitation of a colleague. Invitation on file with author.

9. Austin Ruse, "Urgent Lobbying Alert/Bejing+5," *Friday Fax List* 3:5 (December 17, 1999).

10. Ibid.

11. Personal observation from public presentations on the subject and discussions with NGO leaders, U.N. staff.

12. Austin Ruse, July 7, 2004, interview.

13. Ibid.

14. Ibid.

15. Ibid.

16. Ibid.

17. In 1993 HLI was denied accreditation as an NGO with consultative status with the U.N. Economic and Social Council (ECOSOC). See United Nations Economic and Social Council, "Non-Governmental Organizations: Report of the Committee on on-Governmental Organization," E/1993/63 (New York: United Nations, 7 June 1993), p. 15. Earlier in 1991, the ECOSOC

had not granted HLI's request but referred its application back to the Committee on Non-governmental Organizations for further consideration. See United Nations General Assembly, "Official Records 46th Session 1991/92, 46:14 Supp.1–4," (New York: United Nations Department of Public Information, 1992).

18. Austin Ruse, May 27, 2004, interview.
19. Austin Ruse, July 7, 2004, interview.
20. Richard N. Ostling and Joan K. Ostling, *Mormon America: The Power and the Promise* (New York: Harper Collins, 1999), pp. 113–129.
21. Ibid., pp. 114–115.
22. Philip Jenkins, *The Next Christendom: The Coming of Global Christianity* (New York: Oxford University Press, 2002), p. 66.
23. Ostling and Ostling, *Mormon America* (1999), pp. 159–172.
24. Ibid., p. 172.
25. Ibid., p. 364.
26. Ibid., p. 172.
27. Ibid. (1999), pp. 118–119.
28. Ibid., p. xxvii.
29. Bryan Waterman and Brian Kagel, *The Lord's University: Freedom and Authority at BYU* (Salt Lake City, UT: Signature Books, 1998).
30. Richard Viguerie and David Franke, *America's Right Turn* (Chicago, IL: Bonus Books, 2004), p. 141.
31. Ostling and Ostling, *Mormon America* (1999), p. 171.
32. The proclamation was read by President Gordon B. Hinckley as part of his message at the General Relief Society Meeting held September 23, 1995, in Salt Lake City, Utah. The complete document can be found at "The Family: A Proclamation to the World." <http://www.lds.org/library/display/0,4945,161–1–11–1,00.html> (written by The First Presidency and the Council of the Twelve Apostles of The Church of Jesus Christ of Latter-Day Saints.) When the LDS president (who serves for life) takes office, he chooses seasoned churchmen to be his first counselor and second counselor, and these three men then lead as a collective trio called the First Presidency. They are advised by the Quorum of the Twelve Apostles. The Quorum of the Twelve chooses the next president who is from among the Twelve.
33. Ibid.
34. Waterman and Kagel, *The Lord's University* (1998).
35. Susan Roylance, founder of United Families International, August 20, 2004, interview with author.
36. Ibid.
37. Ibid.
38. Ibid.
39. Ibid.
40. Dr. Richard Wilkins, Managing Director of the World Family Policy Center, June 28, 2005, interview with author.
41. Ibid.
42. Ibid.
43. Ibid.
44. Ibid.

45. Ibid.
46. Ibid.
47. Ibid.
48. Ibid.
49. Tad Walch, "Richard G. Wilkins: defending the Family," *Brigham Young Magazine* 51:3 (Fall 1997), <http://magazine.byu.edu/bym/1997/97fall/closerlook.html>.
50. Richard Wilkins, interview.
51. Ibid.
52. Ibid.
53. Allan Carlson, President of the Howard Center, July 11, 2004, interview with author.
54. Ibid.
55. Ibid.
56. Ibid.
57. Carlson, interview.
58. Ibid.
59. Jesus Hernandez, Co-Founder of Red Familia, August 26, 2004, interview with author.
60. Ibid.
61. Carlson, interview.
62. Allan Carlson, *The New Agrarian Mind: The Movement toward Decentralist Thought in Twentieth-Century America* (New Brunswick, NJ: Transaction, 2000).
63. Carlson, interview.
64. Interhemispheric Resource Center, "Richard Neuhaus," *Right Web Profiles* (Silver City, NM: March 2004), <http://rightweb.irc-online.org/ind/neuhaus/neuhaus.php>.
65. Allan Carlson, interview.
66. This section is based on informal conversations with U.N. staff.
67. Jean Hardisty and Elizabeth Furdon, "Policing civil society: NGO watch," *The Public Eye*, 18:1 Number 1 (Spring 2004), p. 7; Naomi Klein, "Bush to NGOs: Watch Your Mouths," *Globe and Mail* (Canada), June 20, 2003, <http://www.commondreams.org/views03/0620–06.htm> (accessed on December 31, 2005) and Alan Beattie, "NGOs Under Pressure on Relief Funds," *Financial Times,* June 13, 2003, <http://www.globalpolicy.org/ngos/fund/2003/0610control.htm> (accessed on December 31, 2005).
68. William Martin, *With God on Our Side: the Rise of the Religious Right in America* (New York: Broadway, 1997), p. 184.
69. Micklethwait and Wooldridge, *Right Nation: Conservative Power in America* (New York: Penguin Press, 2004). According to Micklethwait and Wooldridge (p. 147), 85 per cent of the American people profess religious belief. Moreover, polls show that 60 to 70 per cent of the American population responds positively to political leaders referring to religion. Thirty-nine per cent describe themselves as "born-again" and a third of registered voters are white Evangelical Protestants (p. 150). Finally, Bush also won the votes of a majority of religiously active Catholics in 2000 (p. 147).

70. Peter Singer, *The President of Good and Evil: The Ethics of George W. Bush* (New York: Dutton, 2004) pp. 1–2.

71. Ibid.

72. Jack Beaty, "The faith-based presidency," *Atlantic Monthly Online*, March 25, 2004, <http://www.theatlantic.com/doc/200403u/pp2004-03-25> (accessed on October 11, 2005).

73. Kenneth Chang, "Scientists say White House questioned their politics," *New York Times*, July 9, 2004.

74. Beaty, "The faith-based presidency."

75. Micklethwait and Wooldridge, *Right Nation* (2004), p. 188.

76. Ibid.

77. David Kirkpatrick, "Bush campaign seeks help from thousands of congregations," *New York Times*, June 3, 2004.

78. Micklethwait and Wooldridge, *Right Nation* (2004), p. 147.

79. George Bush, *A Charge to Keep* (New York: Harper Publishing, 2001), pp. 138–139.

80. Other less prominent but significant appointments include Kay Coles James, former dean of the government school at Pat Robertson's Regent University who oversees the federal workforce. Claude Allen is the Deputy Secretary of Health and Human Services.

81. Micklethwait and Wooldridge, *Right Nation* (2004), p. 146.

82. Wade Horn spoke at the World Congress of Families Special Session on the family held May 3, 2002 in New York City, announcement on World Congress of Families website <http://www.worldcongress.org/WCFreg/wcf_reg_nyc_ufi_0205.htm>, and see also Wendy Wright, Concerned Women for America, "World Congress of Families Equips Delegates for Battle at World Summit on Children," January 1, 2002, <http://www.cwfa.org/articledisplay.asp?id=1958&department=CWA&categoryid=nation>. He also spoke at the World Congress of families in Mexico.

83. David D. Kirkpatrick, "Warily, a religious leader lifts his voice in politics," *New York Times*, May 13, 2004.

84. Ibid.

85. Ibid.

86. Martin, *With God on Our Side* (1997), pp. 341–343.

87. Kirkpatrick, "Warily, a religious leader lifts his voice in politics."

88. Austin Ruse, July 7, 2004, interview.

89. Thomas Jacobson, July 31, 2004, interview.

90. Ibid.

91. Ibid.

92. Ibid.

93. Austin Ruse, interview.

94. Thomas Jacobson, interview.

95. Ibid.

96. Ibid.

97. Micklethwait and Wooldridge, *Right Nation* (2004), p. 187.

98. Hardisty, *Mobilizing Resentment* (1999), p. 80.

99. Concerned Women for America deserves more attention and study. See Kirstin Isgro's dissertation on Concerned Women for America

Department of Communication/Women's Studies Program, University of Massachusetts–Amherst (forthcoming).

100. Matt Bai, "Wiring the Vast Left-Wing Conspiracy," *New York Times Magazine*, July 25, 2004, <http://www.nytimes.com/2004/07/25/magazine/25DEMOCRATS.html?pagewanted=11&ei=5088&en=13ada 638bbe542f0&ex=1248494400&partner=rssnyt>, and Micklethwait and Wooldridge, *Right Nation* (2004), p. 188.

4 A Global Religious Right?

1. Anonymous flyer handed out by Christian Right NGO delegates at the Lesbian Caucus, "What is Going On," June 2000, in author's possession.

2. Catherine Hurlburt and Wendy Wright, "The Hand That Robbed the Cradle," *Family Voice*, July/August 2000, pp. 18–23.

3. Austin Ruse, July 7, 2004, interview.

4. LeRoy Walters, "The United Nations and Human Cloning: A Debate on Hold," *The Hastings Report*, January/February 2004, p. 5–6, pamphlet on file with author.

5. United Nations, "General Assembly votes to ban all forms of human cloning," press release, March 8, 2005, <http://www.care.org.uk/press/08-0302005.htm> (accessed on April 1, 2005).

6. Ibid.

7. Wendy Wright, "United Nations Debates Cloning Ban," Concerned Women for America, <www.cwfa.org/articledisplay.asp?id=2582&department=CWA&categoryid=life> (accessed on October 3, 2002).

8. Our Bodies Ourselves, Letters to the Editor, *New York Times*, January 31, 2002. See website at <www.ourbodiesourselves.org/clonyt.htm> (accessed on January 1, 2006). See also "Statement on Human Cloning," June 2001 on same website.

9. Celeste Biever, "U.N. postpones global human cloning ban," *New Scientist*, November 16, 2003, <http://www.newscientist.com/article.ns?id=dn4359 &print=true>.

10. Maggie McKee, "U.N. human cloning vote stalls yet again," *New Scientist*, October 24, 2004.

11. Ibid.

12. Paul Webster and John Hooper, "France and Germany Seek U.N. Ban on Cloning of Humans," *Guardian*, August 10, 2001, < http://www.guardian.co.uk/international/story/0,3604,534794,00.html>.

13. LeRoy Walters, "The United Nations and Human Cloning: A Debate on Hold," *Hastings Center Report*, January–February 2004, p. 5. See also Webster and Hooper, "France and Germany Seek U.N. Ban."

14. Wendy Wright, "Countries Take Sides on U.N. Cloning Ban," Concerned Women for America, October 3, 2003, <http://www.cwfa.org/articles/4674/CWA/life/> (accessed on December 4, 2005).

15. Biever, "U.N. postpones ... ban," November 16, 2003.

16. Thomas Jacobson, Focus on the Family Representative to the U.N., interview with author, July 31, 2004. For a list of Focus on the Family

international affiliates, see their website < http://www.family.org/welcome/intl/>.

17. Colum Lynch, "U.N. Split on Human Cloning Ban," *Washington Post*, October 22, 2004, p. A22.

18. United Nations General Assembly, "International convention against the reproductive cloning of human beings," Costa Rica: draft resolution. A/58/L.37. December 5, 2003.

19. Ibid.

20. Douglas Sylva, vice-president, C-FAM, July 30, 2004, interview with author.

21. Webster and Hooper, "France and Germany Seek U.N. Ban."

22. Gregory M. Lamb, "U.N. delay: a boost for cloning advocates," *Christian Science Monitor*, October 25, 2004, <http://www.csmonitor.com/2004/1025/p12s01-stgn.html>.

23. For a history and collection of documents on the controversy see the Ad Hoc Committee on an International Convention against the Reproductive Cloning of Human Beings, <www. U.N.org/law/cloning>.

24. BBC News, "U.N. Derails ban on human Cloning," November 6, 2003, <http://newsvote.bbc.co.uk/mpapps/pagetools/print/news.bbc.co.uk/2/hi/science/nature/32479> (accessed on January 18, 2006).

25. Katie Mantell, "Global human cloning ban put on ice," SciDevNet.org, November 7, 2002, <http://www.scidev.net/Editorials/index.cfm?fuseaction=readEditorials&itemid=85&language=1> (accessed on December 5, 2005).

26. Gregory M. Lamb, "The Cloning Clash. Does the world need cloning research? U.N. members tackle a topic that leaves many Uneasy," *Christian Science Monitor*, November 6, 2003, <www.csmonitor.com/2003/1106/p12s01-stct.html>.

27. Jeanne Head, "Update on the United Nations and Cloning," International Right to Life Federation, November 6, 2003, <http://www.nrlc.org/news/2003/NRL11/update_on_the_united_nations_and.htm>.

28. Lynch, "U.N. Split."

29. LeRoy Walters, "The United Nations and Human Cloning."

30. U.N. News Centre, "General Assembly approves declaration banning all forms of cloning," March 8, 2005, <http://www.un.org/apps/news/story.asp?News ID=13576&CR=cloning&Cr1> (accessed on March 9, 2005).

31. U.N. General Assembly A/RES/59/280, March 23, 2005, "United Nations Declaration on Human Cloning," Resolution Adopted by the General Assembly.

32. Ibid.

33. U.N. Press Release General Assembly/10333, 59th General Assembly, Plenary, 82nd Meeting (AM), General Assembly adopts United Nations Declaration on Human Cloning by Vote of 84-34-37, <http://www.un.org/News/Press/docs/2005/ga10333.doc.htm> (accessed March 3, 2005).

34. "Trade in embryos and egg cell donation," Motions for resolutions – Planned egg cell trade, Doc.: B6-0199/2005 to B6-0205/2005, vote October 3, 2005. *European Parliament Daily Notebook*, October 3, 2005, < http://www.europarl.eu.int/omk/sipade3?PUBREF=-//EP//TEXT+PRESS+DN-

20050310-1+0+DOC+XML+V0//EN&LEVEL=2&NAV=S>   (accessed
January 1, 2006), See also Chris Morris, "MEPs seek inquiry into
donor pay," BBC News, March 8, 2005, <http://news.bbc.co.uk/2/hi/
health/4328079.stm> (accessed on April 12, 2005).

35. Press Release, "International Ban on Human Cloning," Family Research
Council, February 18, 2005, <www.frc.org/get.cfm?i=PR05B04> (accessed
on January 1, 2006.)

36. Jesus Hernandez, co-founder of Red Familia, interview with author,
August 26, 2004.

37. "Mexico's political earthquake – election of Vincente Fox," *Christian
Century*, July 19, 2000.

38. Allan Carlson, President of the Howard Center, interview with author,
July 11, 2004.

39. Howard Center for Family, Religion and Society, "Special Issue: WCF III
Update," March 29–31, 2004, p. 4, Pamphlet on file with author.

40. Ibid.

41. Jesus Hernandez, interview.

42. Luis Manuel Arellano, "Lorenzo Servitje, doble moral," Cimacnoticias.
com, April 17, 2002, <www.cimacnoticias.com/noticias/02abr/02041709.
html > (accessed on December 3, 2005).

43. Mario Reyes, "La institucion matrimonial, amenazada por el avance do la
mujer: Lorenzo Servitje," *NotieSe*, March 30, 2004, on file with author.

44. Jesus Hernandez, interview. This is confirmed by conference materials in
possession of the author. See also Reyes, "La institution matrimonial,"
NotieSe, March 30, 2004.

45. Reyes, "La institution."

46. Diego Cevallos, "Population: Natural Family Definition Rankles Rights
Activists," *Inter Press Service*, April 1, 2004.

47. Ibid.

48. Some organizers of the WCF Mexico say it drew over 3,500 participants
from 75 countries (Jesus Hernandez, interview); Mexican press reported
over 2,000 participants from 40 to 60 countries. See also Reyes, "La
institution matrimonial," *NotieSe*, March 30, 2004.

49. The Information Site on Philippine Politics and Government, <http://
www.i-site.ph/Databases/ElectionFiles/Senatoriables/KNP/tatad-personal.
html>.

50. Gordon Urquhart, "Rome's Hard Road for Women," *Guardian*, October
23,1999,<http://www.guardian.co.uk/comment/story/0,,256836,00.html>
(accessed April 9, 2006).

51. Milanes, interview.

52. Doha International Year of the Family website sponsored by "pro-family"
NGOs, <http://www.yearofthefamily.org/> (accessed November 19, 2005).
Interview with Dr. Farooq Hassan, July 15, 2005.

53. World Family Policy Center, "Summary: Process and Outcomes of Doha
International Conference for the family," <http://www.worldfamilypolicy.
org/wfpc/intl conf.htm>.

54. Hassan, interview.

55. Dr. Farooq Hassan, "Muslim Ulama and Implementing Restrictive Family and Population Policies," Islam Online, May 18, 2005, <http://www.islamonline.et/English/contemporary/2005/05/article03.shtml> (accessed November 6, 2005).

56. Hassan, interview.

57. Ibid.

58. Ibid.

59. Ibid.

60. Ibid.

61. "Can Clerics Help Control the Baby Boom?" *Daily Times Site Edition*, May 23, 2005 < http://www.dailytimes.com.pk/print.asp?page=2005\05\23\story_23-5-2005_pg7_35> (accessed November 6, 2005).

62. Hassan, interview.

63. Ibid.

64. Ibid.

65. Brian Whitaker, "Fundamental Union," *Guardian*, January 25, 2005, <www.guardian.co.uk/elsewhere/journalist/story/0,7792,1398055,00.html>.

66. Ælfwine Mischler, *Islam Online,* "Questions on pro-family movement," communication by email, in author's possession, June 2, 2005.

67. See, for example, Nathan Glazer and Daniel Bell, Op-eds, *New York Times,* October 26, 2003, p. 10; responding to Michael Lind, "A Tragedy of Errors," *The Nation*, February 5, 2004, <http://www.thenation.com/doc.mhtml?i=20040223&s=lind>.

68. William Kristol and Robert Kagan, *Rebuilding America: Strategy, Forces and Resources for a New Century.* (Project for the New American Century (PNAC), 2000), and their article "Towards a NeoReaganite Foreign Policy," 75:4 *Foreign Affairs,* (July/August 1996), pp. 18–32.

69. See Kristol and Kagan, *Rebuilding America* (2000).

70. John Micklethwait and Adrian Wooldridge, *The Right Nation: Conservative Power in America* (New York: Penguin Press, 2004), p. 218.

71. Tom Barry and Jim Lobe, "The Men Who Stole the Show," *Foreign Policy in Focus.* Albuquerque, NM, October 1, 2002, Special Report 18. Other members of the PNAC include famous social conservatives Gary Bauer, former presidential candidate and the first director of the Family Research Council, William J. Bennett, former Secretary of Education, and George Weigel, political commentator and papal biographer. Following the election of President George W. Bush in 2000, many of the PNAC's members were appointed to key positions within the new Bush Administration, for example, Elliott Abrams (National Security Council Representative for Middle Eastern Affairs), John R. Bolton (U.S. Ambassador to the United Nations), Paul Wolfowitz (Deputy Secretary of Defense, 2001–05, and now World Bank President), Donald Rumsfeld (Secretary of Defense) and Richard Cheney (U.S. Vice-President).

72. Ibid., p. 2.

73. The National Security Strategy of the United States of America, September 2002, "Rebuilding America's Defenses: Strategy, Forces and Resources

for a New Century", A Report, <www.whitehouse.gov/nsc/nss.html> (accessed November 3, 2004).

74. Barry and Lobe, "The Men who Stole the Show," p. 6.

75. Norman Podhoretz and Thomas L. Jeffers, *The Norman Podhoretz Reader* (New York: Simon and Schuster, 2004), pp. 272–273, and Murray Friedman, *The Neoconservative Revolution: Jewish Intellectuals and the Shaping of Public Policy* (New York: Columbia University Press, 2005), pp. 116–136, 185–204.

76. Shadia B. Drury, *Leo Strauss and the American Right* (New York: St. Martin's Press, 1999). On neoconservative attitudes toward religion and the Christian Right, see Friedman, *Neoconservative Revolution* (2005), pp. 205–222.

77. Walter Russell Mead, "Q and A: Neocons Niche in American History," interview with *Christian Science Monitor*, <http://www.csmonitor.com/specials/neocon/mead> (accessed on January 2, 2006).

78. "Empire Builders: Neoconservatives and their Blueprint for U.S. Power," *Christian Science Monitor*, August 2003, <http://www.csmonitor.com/specials/neocon/mead.html/>.

79. Joseph Bottum, "The New Fusionism," *First Things*, June/July 2005, Number 154.

80. Kristol and Kagan, "Towards a Neo-Reaganite Foreign Policy," (1996).

81. Michael Lind, "A Tragedy of Errors," *The Nation*, February 5, 2004, <http://www.thenation.com/doc.mhtml?i=20040223&s=lind>.

82. Ibid.

83. Drury, *Leo Strauss and the American Right*, (1999), p. 152.

84. For an overview of the *Left Behind* series, see Glenn W. Shuck, *Marks of the Beast: The Left Behind Novels and the Struggle for Evangelical Identity* (New York: New York University Press, 2005), and Tim LaHaye, Jerry B. Jenkins and Sandi L. Swanson, *The Authorized Left Behind Handbook* (Wheaton, IL: Tyndale House, 2005).

85. Wes Howard-Brook, *Unveiling Empire: Reading Revelation Then and Now* (Maryknoll, NY: Orbis, 2001), p. 6.

86. Ibid.; Hal Lindsey, *The Late Great Planet Earth* (Grand Rapids, MI: Zondervan, 1970), and *The 1980s: Countdown to Armageddon* (New York: Bantam, 1983).

87. Weber quoted in Howard-Brook, *Unveiling Empire*, (2001), p. 6.

88. Howard-Brook, *Unveiling Empire*, (2001), p. 16.

89. Peter Singer, *The President of Good and Evil: The Ethics of George W. Bush* (New York: Dutton, 2004), pp. 183–187.

90. Barry and Lobe, "The Men Who Stole the Show," (2002).

91. Ruse, interview.

92. Nina Easton, *Gang of Five* (New York: Simon and Schuster, 2000), pp. 67–69.

93. Ibid.

94. See the "Our Purpose" page on the Federalist Society website <http://www.fed-soc.org/ourpurpose.htm> (accessed on January 18, 2006).

95. Easton, *Gang of Five*, (2000), pp. 67–69.

96. Information from the "Our Background" page on the Federalist Society website <http://www.fed-soc.org/ourpurpose.htm> (accessed on January 18, 2006).

97. Robert Kagan, *Of Paradise and Power: America and Europe in the New World Order* (New York: Knopf, 2004).

98. George Weigel, "Europe's Problem – and Ours," *First Things*, 140, February 2004, pp. 18–25.

99. Olle Wangborg, Swedish Association for Sexuality Education, email communication, "U.S. based Christian Right," Wednesday, May 19, 2004.

100. Ibid.

101. Olle Wangborg, Swedish Association for Sexuality Education, Listserv "update on opposition in Sweden" sent via Elfriede Harth, March 31, 2004 to the author.

102. Mary Jo Anderson, "Heroic Youth A Tonic in Tough Times: World Youth Alliance at World Youth Day," *Voices*, Online Edition (Women for Faith and Family), 17:3 (Michaelmas 2002), <http://www.wf-f.org/02-3-TOC.html> (accessed on January 18, 2006).

103. Thierry Cagianut, "Youth Leader Anna Halpine (in Top Ten People of 2004 Article)," *Inside the Vatican*, January–February 2005, pp. 18–30.

104. Interhemispheric Resource Center, "Richard Neuhaus," *Right Web Profiles* (Silver City, NM: March 2004), <http://rightweb.irc-online.org/ind/neuhaus/neuhaus.php>.

105. Cagianut, "Youth Leader," p. 30.

106. *Catholic Online*, "Aiming to Get Young People Active in International Policy, Anna Halpine's World Youth Alliance Works with U.N. and European Union," New York, December 22, 2003, *Catholic Online*, <http://www.catholic.org/featured/headline.php?ID=596> (accessed on February 12, 2006).

107. Anderson, "Heroic Youth A Tonic in Tough Times."

108. "Aiming to Get Young People Active in International Policy."

109. Anderson, "Heroic Youth A Tonic in Tough Times."

110. Carlson, interview. The next congress will be in Poland: "Europe is almost lost: to a demographic winter and to the secularists. If Europe goes, much of the world will go with it. Almost alone, Poland has maintained strong faith and strong families, though even Poland comes under severe pressure to change. Poland has saved Europe before. It is likely she will save Europe again. On family and population questions, Europe is the battleground in the early years of the 21st century and Poland is the pivot point. It makes abundant sense that The World Congress of Families IV meet among the brave people of Poland. Poland's central location will give pro-family groups across the Continent easy access to this Congress" – from the WCF IV Planning Meeting, October 23–25, 2005, Rockford, IL <http://www.worldcongress.org/WCF4/wcf4.ini.htm>.

111. Dr. Gudron Lang, regional director for Europe, World Youth Alliance, July 30, 2004, interview with the author.

112. Ibid.

113. Ed Lasky, "Arab Reform," *American Thinker*, June 25, 2004, <http://www.americanthinker.com/articles.php?article_id=3627>. The magazine is "dedicated to exploring national security in all its dimensions, strategic, economic, diplomatic, and military is emphasized. The right to exist, and the survival of the State of Israel are of great importance to us. Business, science, technology, medicine, management, and economics in their practical and ethical dimensions are also emphasized, as is the state of American culture."

114. Dr. Richard Wilkins, managing director of the World Family Policy Center, June 28, 2005, interview with the author.

115. Susan Roylance, Founder of United Families International, August 20, 2004, interview with the author.

Conclusion

1. Jim Wallis, *God's Politics: Why the Right Gets it Wrong and the Left Doesn't Get It* (San Francisco, CA: HarperSanFrancisco, 2005).

2. Richard A. Viguerie and David Franke, *America's Right Turn: How Conservatives Used New and Alternative Media to Take Power* (Chicago, IL: Bonus, 2004), p. 190.

3. During the weeks leading up to Christmas 2005, conservative news station Fox News ran scores of stories reporting on the so-called "War on Christmas," which explored allegations from Christian groups that secularists were attacking Christianity by, for example, calling for the removal of Christmas trees and Nativity scenes from public places like shopping malls, and other such stories. The topic was so popular that mainstream networks also picked up the story of the "War."

4. Viguerie and Franke, *America's Right Turn*, (2004), pp. 87–103. Viguerie spent days in the clerks office of the House of Representatives copying by hand the register of contributors to the Barry Goldwater campaign. This initial list of 15,000 donors became the foundation for building a New Right network (he copied 12,500 before the clerk got nervous about it and kicked him out). Viguerie then computerized the list. This seemingly simple invention enabled Viguerie and other conservatives to mobilize a support base that grew undetected by progressive organizers and media.

5. Viguerie and Franke, *America's Right Turn*, (2004), p. 133.

6. John Micklethwait and Adrian Wooldridge, *The Right Nation: Conservative Power in America* (New York: Penguin Press, 2004), p. 12.

7. Micklethwait and Wooldridge, *The Right Nation*, (2004), p. 163.

8. David Kirkpatrick, "College for the Home Schooled is Shaping Leaders for the Right," *New York Times*, March 8, 2004.

9. <www.witherspoonfellowship.org>.

10. The home-schooling movement took off in the U.S. during the 1980s as Christian conservatives began teaching their children at home, appalled by secular, irreligious culture in schools, as exemplified by sex education, a ban on prayer and the teaching of evolution. Michael Farris' organization, the Home School Legal Defense Association, has a membership of 81,000 families. About two-thirds of the half a million families who home-

school their children are evangelical Christians, according to home-school advocates.

11. Viguerie and Franke, *America's Right Turn*, (2004), p. 167.
12. Richard Viguerie, *The New Right: We're Ready to Lead* (Falls Church, VA: Vigurie Company, 1981), p. 1.
13. Jean Hardisty, *Mobilizing Resentment: Conservative Resurgence from the John Birch Society to the Promise Keepers* (Boston: Beacon Press, 1999), p. 16.
14. Micklethwait and Wooldridge, *The Right Nation: Conservative Power in America*, (2004), p. 166.
15. Robert G. Kaiser and Ira Chinoy, "Scaife: Funding Father of the Right," *Washington Post*, May 2, 1999, Page A1.
16. Republicans recognize what a recent Pew study revealed: a good number of Americans want more rather than less reference to religion by national leaders. The Pew Forum on Religion and Public Life reported that nearly twice as many respondents to a recent poll on religion and politics say there has been too little reference to religion by politicians (41 per cent) as say there has been too much (21 per cent). In fact, more than 70 per cent of Democrats and 50 per cent of liberal Democrats hold strong personal religious attitudes. Surprisingly, even Democrats are more religious than the overdrawn popular perception suggests.
17. Hardisty, *Mobilizing Resentment*.
18. Wilma Mankiller, "Foreword," p. x, in Hardisty, *Mobilizing Resentment*, 1999.
19. George Lakoff, *Moral Politics: How Liberals and Conservatives Think*, Second Edition (Chicago, IL: The University of Chicago Press, 2002).

Bibliography

Interviews

Charlotte Bunch, Founder and Director, Center for Women's Global Leadership, and President, Women's Tribunal, August 27, 2004.
Allan Carlson, President of the Howard Center, July 11, 2004.
Emily Freeburg, Lutheran World Federation, U.N. Office, July 28, 2004.
Dr. Farooq Hassan, Special Ambassador for the World Family Alliance, July 15, 2005.
Jesus Hernandez, co-founder of Red Familia, Mexico City, August 26, 2004.
Thomas Jacobson, Focus on the Family Representative to the U.N., July 31, 2004.
Dr. Gudron Lang, Regional Director for Europe, World Youth Alliance, July 30, 2004.
Parvina Nadjibulla, United Methodist Church Representative to the U.N., August 12, 2004.
Dr. David Popenoe, Professor of Sociology at Rutgers University, and Co-Director of the National Marriage Project, January 28, 2004.
David Roth, Co-Chair, U.N. NGO Committee on the Family (NYC), May 27, 2004.
Susan Roylance, founder of United Families International, August 20, 2004.
Austin Ruse, President of C-FAM [Catholic Families], May 27 and July 7, 2004.
John Washburn, Convener, American Non-governmental Organizations Coalition on the International Criminal Court, August 4, 2004.
Dr. Richard Wilkins, Managing Director of the World Family Policy Center, June 28, 2005.

Works Cited

Ahmed, Eman. "Not the only way: Dr. Hashmi's hold on Pakistani women," *Women's Human Rights Net*. Toronto: Association of Women in Development (AWID), November 2004.
Ammerman, Nancy. "North American Protestant Fundamentalism," in Martin E. Marty and R. Scott Appleby, eds. *Fundamentalism Observed*. Chicago, IL: University of Chicago Press, 1991.
Anderson, Mary Jo. "The UN's War Against Children," *Crisis: Politics, Culture and the Church*, September 2001.
——. "Heroic Youth A Tonic in Tough Times: World Youth Alliance at World Youth Day," *Voices* Online Edition (Women for Faith and Family), Vol. 17, No. 3, Michaelmas 2002 <http://www.wf-f.org/02-3-TOC.html> (accessed January 18, 2006).

Andrusko, Dave. "Huge Pro-Life Win at Children's Summit," *National Right to Life News*, June 2002.

Arellano, Luis Manuel. "Lorenzo Servitje, doble moral," Cimacnoticias.com, April 17, 2002 <www.cimacnoticias.com/noticias/02abr/02041709.html> (accessed on December 3, 2005).

Barry, Tom and Jim Lobe. "The Men Who Stole the Show," *Foreign Policy in Focus*. Albuquerque, NM, October 2002, Special Report #18.

Bayes, Jane H., and Nayereh Tohidi, eds. *Globalization, Gender, and Religion: The Politics of Women's Rights in Catholic and Muslim Contexts*. New York: Palgrave, 2001.

Beattie, Alan. "NGOs Under Pressure on Relief Funds," *Financial Times*, June 13, 2003.

Beatty, Jack. "The faith-based presidency," *Atlantic Monthly Online*, 25 March 2004. <http://www.theatlantic.com/doc/prem/200403u/pp2004-03-25>, (accessed April 9, 2006).

Bediako, Kwame. *Christianity in Africa*. Edinburgh: Edinburgh University Press/ Orbis, 1995.

Bendroth, Margaret Lamberts. *Fundamentalism and Gender, 1875 to the Present*. New Haven, CT: Yale University, 1993.

Bendyna, Mary E. and Mark J. Rozell. "Uneasy alliance: conservative Catholics and the Christian right," *Sociology of Religion*, Spring 2001.

Benson, Bruce, and Peter Heltzel, eds. *Evangelicals and Empire*. New York: Oxford University, forthcoming 2006.

Berger, Peter, ed. *The Desecularization of the World: Resurgent Religion and World Politics*. Grand Rapids, MI: Ethics and Public Policy Center and Eerdmans Publishing Co., 1999.

Berlinerblau, Jacques. *The Secular Bible: Why Nonbelievers Must take Religion Seriously*. New York: Cambridge University Press, 2005.

Bernstein, Richard. "Europe's groundswell: public opinion," *New York Times*, 17 February 2003.

Block, Jennifer. "Sex trafficking: why the faith trade is interested in the sex trade," *Conscience* (Catholics for Free Choice), Summer/Autumn, 2004.

Boonstra, Heather. "US AIDS policy: priority on treatment, conservative's approach to prevention", *The Guttmacher Report on Public Policy* Vol. 6, No. 3 (August 2003).

Bottum, Joseph. "The New Fusionism,' *First Things*, June/July 2005, No. 154.

British Broadcasting Corporation News staff and agencies. "U.N. Delays ban on human Cloning," November 6, 2003 <http://newsvote.bbc.co.uk/mpapps/ pagetools/print/news.bbc.co.uk/2/hi/science/nature/32479> (accessed on January 18, 2006).

Brock, David. *The Republican Noise Machine*. New York: Crown Publishing Group, 2005.

Brouwer, Steve, Paul Gifford and Susan D. Rose. *Exporting the American Gospel: Global Christian Fundamentalism*. New York: Routledge, 1996.

Bryan, Waterman and Brian Kagel. *The Lord's University: Freedom and Authority at BYU*. Salt Lake City: Signature Books, 1998.

Burkhalter, Holly. "The Politics of AIDS: Engaging Conservative Activists," *Foreign Affairs*, January/February 2004, Vol. 83, No. 1 <http://www.

foreignaffairs.org/20040101facomments83102/holly-burkhalter/the-politics-of-aids-engaging-conservative-activists.html>.

Bush, George. *A Charge to Keep*. New York: Harper Publishing, 2001.

Buss, Doris and Didi Herman. *Globalizing Family Values: the Christian Right in International Politics*. Saint Paul: University of Minnesota Press, 2003.

Butler, Jennifer. "For Faith and Family: Christian Right Advocacy at the United Nations," *Public Eye*, Summer/Fall 2000, pp. 10–11.

Butler, Jennifer. "New sheriff in town: the Christian right shapes U.S. agenda at the United Nations," *Public Eye*, Summer 2002, pp. 14–21.

Cagianut, Thierry. "Youth Leader Anna Halpine (in Top Ten People of 2004 Article)," *Inside the Vatican*, January–February 2005, pp. 18–30.

Carlson, Allan. *The New Agrarian Mind: The Movement Toward Decentralist Thought in Twentieth-Century America*. New Brunswick, NJ: Transaction, 2000.

Catholic Online. "Aiming to Get Young People Active in International Policy, Anna Halpine's World Youth Alliance Works with U.N. and European Union," New York, December 22, 2003. *Catholic Online* <http://www.catholic.org/featured/headline.php?ID=596> (accessed on February 12, 2006).

Catholics for a Free Choice. *Student Bodies: Reproductive Health Care at Catholic Universities*. Washington, DC: The Access Series, 2002.

CBS Nightly News staff. "Jesse Helms to tackle AIDS," February 21, 2002.

Center for Reproductive Rights. "U.N. Special Session on Children: Missed Opportunities and Neglected Realities," Briefing Paper, December 2002.

Center for Women's Global Leadership. "Beijing+10 Review: A Feminist Strategy for 2004-05, A working paper for NGOs on how to move forward," <http://www.cwgl.rutgers.edu/globalcenter/policy/csw04/B10strategy-CSW04.pdf>.

——, the NGO Committee on the Status of Women, and the Women's Environment and Development Organization. "2005 CSW Review of the Beijing Platform for Action (Beijing+10) NGO Discussions at the 48th Session of the Commission on the Status of Women, March 1–12, 2004."

Cevallos, Diego. "Population: Natural Family Definition Rankles Rights Activists," *Inter Press Service*, April 1, 2004.

Chang, Kenneth. "Scientists say White House questioned their politics," *New York Times*, 9 July 2004.

Child Rights Caucus press advisory, "NGOs Disappointed by Outcome of the Children's Summit" <www.crin.org/resources/infodetail.asp?ID+2613&flag='news'>.

Christian Science Monitor staff. "Empire Builders: Neoconservatives and their Blueprint for U.S. Power," *Christian Science Monitor*, August 2003 <http://www.csmonitor.com/specials/neocon/mead.html/>.

Coalter, Milton J., John M. Mulder and Louis B. Weeks. *The Mainstream Protestant "Decline:" The Presbyterian Experience*. Louisville, KY: Westminster, John Knox Press, 1990.

CRIN (Child Rights Information Network). "Battle-Lines Drawn," *PrepCom Update*, No. 1, June 11, 2004.

Curiel, Carolyn. "How Hispanics Voted Republican," *New York Times*, November 8, 2004, p. A22.

Daily Times – Site Edition. "Can Clerics Help Control the Baby Boom?" May 23, 2005 <http://www.dailytimes.com.pk/print.asp?page=2005\05\23\story_23-5-2005_pg7_35> (accessed November 6, 2005).

Davis, Derek. "From Engagement to Retrenchment: An Examination of First Amendment Activism by America's Mainline Churches, 1980–2000," in Wuthnow and Evans, eds, *The Quiet Hand of God* (2002).

DAWN (Development Alternatives with Women for a New Era), "No to negotiations for B+10?," *DAWN Informs*, September 2003.

De Young, Karen and Colum Lynch. "War of Words at Youth Summit: U.S. Says Document Endorses Abortion," *Washington Post*, May 9, 2002; p. A18.

Dean M. Kelly. *Why Conservative Churches are Growing.* Macon, GA: Mercer University Press, 1977.

Dean R. Hoge. "National Contextual Factors Influencing Church Trends," in *Understanding Church Growth and Decline: 1950–1978.* New York: The Pilgrim Press, 1979.

DeBerg, Betty A. *Ungodly Women: Gender and the First Wave of American Fundamentalism.* Minneapolis, MN: Fortress Press, 1990.

Deiros, Pablo A. "Protestant fundamentalism in Latin America," in Martin E. Marty and Scott Appleby, eds, *Fundamentalisms Observed.* Chicago, IL: University of Chicago Press, 1991.

Donald Luidens. "Fighting 'decline': mainline Churches and the tyranny of aggregate data," *Christian Century*, No. 113, April 17, 1996, pp. 1075–1079.

Driscoll, William, Joseph P. Zompetti and Suzette Zompetti. *The International Criminal Court and the Quest for Justice.* New York: International Debate Education Association, 2004.

Drury, Shadia B. *Leo Strauss and the American Right.* New York: St. Martin's Press, 1999.

Easton, Nina. *Gang of Five.* New York: Simon and Schuster, 2000.

European Parliament. "Trade in embryos and egg cell donation," Motions for resolutions – Planned egg cell trade, Doc.: B6-0199/2005 to B6-0205/2005, vote October 3, 2005. *European Parliament Daily Notebook* <http://www.europarl.eu.int/omk/sipade3?PUBREF=-//EP//TEXT+PRESS+DN-20050310-1+0+DOC+XML+V0//EN&LEVEL=2&NAV=S> (accessed January 1, 2006).

Family Research Council Press Release, "International Ban on Human Cloning," Family Research Council, February 18, 2005 <www.frc.org/get.cfm?i=PR05B04> (accessed on January 1, 2006.)

Family Research Council. "UN Committee Takes Aim at Family Structure and Morality," *Culture Facts*, February 21, 2001.

Fiorina, Morris P. *Culture War? The Myth of a Polarized America.* New York: Pearson Longman, 2005.

Fisher, Julie. *NGOs and the Political Development of the Third World.* Bloomfield, CT: Kumarian Press, 1998.

Florini, Ann, ed. *The Third Force: The Rise of Transnational Civil Society.* Washington, DC: Carnegie Endowment for International Peace, 2000.

—— and P.J. Simmons, "What the World Needs Now?," in Florini, ed., *The Third Force* (2000).

Frank, Thomas. *What's the Matter with Kansas? How Conservatives Won the Heart of America.* New York: Metropolitan Books, 2004.

Friedman, Murray. *The Neoconservative Revolution: Jewish Intellectuals and the Shaping of Public Policy*. New York: Cambridge University, 2005.

George, Timothy (interview by Collin Hansen). "Pope gave Evangelicals the moral impetus we didn't have," *Christianity Today*, April 2005 <http://www. christianitytoday.com/ct/2005/114/32.0.html>.

Goldenberg, Suzanne. "America urges UN to renounce abortion rights," *Guardian*, March 1, 2005.

Goodstein, Laurie. "The persecution facing Christians: concern is worldwide, lobbying effort swells, though Aome warn against label on a complex problem," *New York Times*, November 9, 1998.

Hadaway, Kirk C. "Denominational Defection: Recent Research on Religious Disaffiliation in America," in Coalter et al., eds, *The Mainstream Protestant "Decline"* (1990).

Hadden, Jeffery K. and Shupe, Anson, eds. *Secularization and Fundamentalism Reconsidered*, Vol. III. New York: Paragon House, 1989.

Hansen, Collin. "Pope gave Evangelicals the moral impetus we didn't have," interview with Timothy George, *Christianity Today*, April 2005.

Hardisty, Jean. *Mobilizing Resentment: Conservative Resurgence from the John Birch Society to the Promise Keepers*. Boston, MA: Beacon Press, 1999.

—— and Elizabeth Furdon. "Policing civil society: NGO watch," *The Public Eye*, Vol. 18, No. 1, Spring 2004.

Hartman, Susan. *The Other Feminists*. New Haven, CT: Yale University Press, 1998.

Hassan, Dr. Farooq. "After Doha: the future of family internationally," *Islam Online Live Dialogue*, December 8, 2004 <http://www.islamonline.net/ livedialogue/english/Browse.asp?hGuestID=ZEeWV6>.

——. "Muslim Ulama and Implementing Restrictive Family and Population Policies," *Islam Online*, May 18, 2005 <http://www.islamonline.et/English/ contemporary/2005/05/article03.shtml> (accessed November 6, 2005).

Hawley, John Stratton. *Fundamentalism and Gender*. New York: Oxford University Press, 1994.

Head, Jeanne. "Update on the United Nations and Cloning," International Right to Life Federation, November 6, 2003 <http://www.nrlc.org/news/2003/ NRL11/update_on_the_united_nations_and.htm>.

Hertke, Allen D. *Freeing God's Children: The Unlikely Alliance for Global Human Rights*. New York: Rowman & Littlefield, 2004.

Heritage Foundation. "Heritage Foundation Quest for U.N. Consultative Status," Online posting July 26, 2001 <www.heritage.org>.

Hoge, Dean R. "National Contextual Factors Influencing Church Trends," pp. 13–18, in Hoge and Roozen, eds, *Understanding Church Growth and Decline* (1979).

—— and David R. Roozen, eds. *Understanding Church Growth and Decline: 1950–1979*. New York: Pilgrim, 1979.

Hoge, Warren. "Panel Backs Women's Rights After U.S. Drops Abortion Issue," *New York Times*, March 5, 2005.

Hout, Michael and Greeley Andrew M. "A hidden swing vote: evangelicals," (op-ed) *New York Times*, September 4, 2004.

Howard-Brook, Wes. *Unveiling Empire: Reading Revelation Then and Now.* Maryknoll, NY: Orbis, 2001.

Hunt, Helen. *Faith and Feminism: A Holy Alliance.* New York: Atria Books, 2004.

Hunter, James Davison. *Culture Wars: The Struggle to Define America.* New York: Basic Books, 1991.

Hurlburt, Catherine and Wendy Wright. "The Hand That Robbed the Cradle," *Family Voice*, July/August 2000.

Interhemispheric Resource Center staff. "Profile: Richard Neuhaus," *Right Web*, Silver City, NM: March 2004 <http://rightweb.irc-online.org/ind/neuhaus/neuhaus.php>.

Jacobsen, Dennis. *Doing Justice: Congregations and Community Organizing.* Minneapolis, MN: Augsburg Fortress, 2001.

Jenkins, Philip. "A New Christendom," *Chronicle of Higher Education*, March 29, 2002.

———. *The Next Christendom: The Coming of Global Christianity.* New York: Oxford University Press, 2002.

Johnson, Benton, Dean R. Hoge and Donald A. Luidents. "Mainline Churches: The Real Reason for decline," *First Things*, Vol. 31, 1993, pp. 13–18.

Jones, Susan "Conservative Group Gets Federal Money to Combat Sex Trafficking," *CNSNews.com Morning Edition*, December 1, 2004.

Kagan, Robert. *Of Paradise and Power: America and Europe in the New World Order.* New York: Knopf, 2004.

Keck, Margaret E. and Kathryn Sikkink. *Activists Beyond Borders.* Ithaca, NY: Cornell University Press, 1998.

Kelly, Dean M. *Why Conservative Churches are Growing.* Macon, GA: Mercer University Press, 1977.

Marquis, Christopher. "U.S. Is Accused of Trying to Isolate U.N. Agency," *New York Times*, June 21, 2004, p. A3.

Kaiser, Robert G. and Ira Chinoy. "Scaife: Funding Father of the Right," *Washington Post*, May 2, 1999, p. A1.

Kaplan, Esther. "Follow the Money," *The Nation*, October 14, 2004.

Kirkpatrick, David D. "Bush campaign seeks help from thousands of congregations," *New York Times*, June 3, 2004.

———. "College for the Home Schooled is Shaping Leaders for the Right," *New York Times*, March 8, 2004.

———. 'Warily, a religious leader lifts his voice in politics', *New York Times*, May 13, 2004

Klein, Naomi. "Bush to NGOs: Watch Your Mouths," *Globe and Mail* (Canada), June 20, 2003 <http://www.commondreams.org/views03/0620-06.htm>.

Korey, William. *NGOs and the Universal Declaration of Human Rights.* New York: Palgrave, 2001.

Kristof, Nicholas D. "Living Poor, Voting Rich," *New York Times*, November 3, 2004.

Kristol, William and Robert Kagan. *Rebuilding America: Strategy, Forces and Resources for a New Century.* Project for the New American Century (PNAC), 2000.

LaHaye, Tim, Jerry B. Jenkins and Sandi L. Swanson. *The Authorized Left Behind Handbook*. Wheaton, IL: Tyndale House, 2005.

——. *Moral Politics: How Liberals and Conservatives Think*, second edn, Chicago, IL: University of Chicago Press, 2002.

Lakoff, George. *Don't think of an Elephant! Know your Values and Frame the Debate*. White River Junction, VT: Chelsea Green Publishing, 2004.

Lamb, Gregory M. "The Cloning Clash. Does the world need cloning research? U.N. members tackle a topic that leaves many uneasy," *Christian Science Monitor*, November 6, 2003 <www.csmonitor.com/2003/1106/p12s01-stct. html>.

——. "U.N. delay: a boost for cloning advocates," *Christian Science Monitor*, October 25, 2004.

Lasky, Ed. "Arab Reform," *American Thinker*, June 25, 2004 <http://www. americanthinker.com/articles.php?article_id=3627>.

Lenski, Gerhard. *The Religious Factor*, rev. edn, New York: Anchor Books, 1963.

Lerner, Sharon. "Saviors of the Children," *Village Voice*, May 8, 2002.

Lind, Michael. "A Tragedy of Errors," *The Nation*, February 5, 2004 <http:// www.thenation.com/doc.mhtml?i=20040223&s=lind>.

Lugo, Luis. "Religion as political issue extends beyond bible belt," *Atlanta Journal-Constitution*, January 30, 2004.

Lynch, Colum. "U.N. Split on Human Cloning Ban," *Washington Post*, October 22, 2004, p. A22.

Mantell, Katie. "Global human cloning ban put on ice," *SciDevNet.org*. November 7, 2002 <http://www.scidev.net/Editorials/index.cfm?fuseaction=re adEditorials&itemid=85&language=1> (accessed December 5, 2005).

Martin, William. *With God on Our Side: the Rise of the Religious Right in America*. New York: Broadway, 1997.

Marty, Martin E. and R. Scott Appleby, eds. *Fundamentalisms Observed*. Chicago, IL: University of Chicago Press, 1991.

Matthews, Jessica. "Power shift," *Foreign Affairs* Vol. 6, No. 1, January/February 1997.

Mead, Walter Russell. "Q and A: Neocons Niche in American History," interview with *Christian Science Monitor* <www.csmonitor.com>.

McKee, Maggie. "U.N. human cloning vote stalls yet again," *New Scientist*, October 24, 2004.

Mekata, Motoko. "Building partnerships toward a common Goal: Experiences of the Internaitonal Campaign to Ban Landmines," in Florini (ed.), *The Third Force* (2000).

Micklethwait, John and Adrian Wooldridge. *The Right Nation: Conservative Power in America*. New York: Penguin Press, 2004.

Mischler, Ælfwine. "Limitations of the Doha Conference: An Interview with Dr. Farooq Hassan," *Islam Online*, 25 November 2004 <http://www.islamonline. net/English/In_Depth/Doha_Conference/Views/03.shtml>.

——. "Was Doha a victory?," *Islam Online*, November 25, 2004 <www. islamonline.net/English/In_Depth/Doha_conference/views/04.shtml>.

Morris, Chris. "MEPs seek inquiry into donor pay," BBC News, March 8, 2005 <http://news.bbc.co.uk/2/hi/health/4328079.stm> (accessed on April 12, 2005).

National Center for Home Education. "UN News Update," *HSLDA News*, June 14, 2001 <http://nche.hslda.org/docs/news/hslda/200106140.asp>.

National Council of Churches in Christ. *Yearbook of American and Canadian Churches*. New York: National Council of Churches in Christ, 2003.

Oduyoye, Mercy. *Who Will Roll the Stone Away? – The Ecumenical Decade of the Churches in Solidarity with Women*. Geneva: World Council of Churches Publications, 1990.

On the Record for Children. "European Patience Wears Thin," *On the Record for Children*, Vol. 2, No. 6, June 15, 2001.

——. "U.S. Contempt for Convention Brings 'Spoiler' Charge from NGOs," *On the Record for Children*, Vol. 14, No. 5, February 2, 2001.

——. "U.S. says Bejing and Cairo Reference Must Come Out," *On the Record for Children*, Vol. 2, No. 6, June 15, 2001.

——. "Language on Reproductive Health Care Alarms Pro Life and Pro choice Advocates," *On the Record for Children*, June 14, 2001.

Orme, William. "UN Forum on Children Takes up Abortion: Controversy: Delegates argue about whether phrase 'reproductive health services' should be included in conference documents," *Los Angeles Times*, May 9, 2002, p. A3.

Ostling, Richard N. and Joan K. Ostling *Mormon America: The Power and the Promise*. New York: Harper Collins, 1999.

Our Bodies Ourselves, Letter to the Editor, *New York Times*, January 31, 2002.

Panel of Eminent Persons on UN-Civil Society Relationships, *We the Peoples: Civil Society, the UN and Global Governance*. New York: United Nations Department of Public Information, June 2004.

Parham, Robert. "Evangelicals pledge to hold governments accountable for poverty," *Ethics Daily*, October 18, 2004.

Petchesky, Rosalind Pollack. *Global Prescriptions: Gendering Health and Human Rights*. New York: Zed Books, 2003.

Peters, Julie Stone and Andrea Wolper, eds. *Women's Rights, Human Rights: International Feminist Perspectives*. New York: Routledge, 1994.

Podhoretz, Norman, and Thomas L. Jeffers. *The Normon Podhoretz Reader*. New York: Simon and Schuster, 2004.

Presbyterian Church (USA). *The Background Report for the 1997–1999 Presbyterian Panel* (Louisville, KY: Research Services, 2000).

Presbyterian Church (USA) Research Services Program Area. "A Presbyterian Panel Snapshot," Presbyterian Panel Surveys of Members, 1993–99.

Ramirez, Roberto R. and G. Patricia de la Cruz. *Current Population Reports*. Washington, DC: U.S. Census Bureau, June 2003.

Reed, Ralph. *Active Faith: How Christians are changing to Soul of American Politics*. New York: The Free Press, 1996.

Religion Counts. *Religion and Public Policy at the U.N.* New York: Religion Counts, 2002.

Reyes, Mario. "La institucion matrimonial, amenazada por el avance do la mujer: Lorenzo Servitje," *NotieSe*, March 30, 2004.

Riviere-Zijdel, Lydia (President of the EWL). "EWL letter to U.N. Secretary General Kofi Annan: stop the global backlash against women's rights," from the European Women's Lobby (Brussels), letter dated February 4, 2003, open letter circulated by email, on file with author.

Rivlin, Benjamin. "Thoughts on religious NGOs at the UN: a component of global civil society," in Peter I. Hajnal, ed. *Civil Society in the Information Age*. Burlington, VT: Ashgate Publishing, 2002.

Ruse, Austin. "Toward a permanent United Nations Pro-Family Bloc," World Congress of Families II Conference, Geneva, November 14–17, 1999.

——. "Urgent Lobbying Alert/Bejing+5," *Friday Fax List*, Vol. 3, No. 5, December 17, 1999.

Sauerbrey, Ambassador Ellen. "The status of family issues at the United Nations," speech given at United Families International, on file with author <http://www.unitedfamilies.org/ellen.asp>.

——. At the Security Council Stakeout, "USUN Press Release # 39 (05)," New York: U.S. Mission to the United Nations, March 4, 2005.

Scott, David. "The Pope we never knew: The unknown story of how John Paul II ushered campus Crusade into Catholic Poland," *Christianity Today*, April 2005.

Seelye, Katharine Q. "Moral values cited as a defining issue of the election," *New York Times*, November 4, 2004.

Shemo, Diana Jean. "Nearing retirement, priests of the 60's fear legacy is lost," *New York Times*, September 10, 2000.

Shestack, Jerome. "Non-Governmental Organizations Forum," Federalist Society, Washington, DC (aired on C-Span, November 15, 2003 – C-Span Archives ID:179131-3: <c-span.org>.

Shuck, Glenn W. *Marks of the Beast: The Left Behind Novels and the Struggle for Evangelical Identity*. New York: New York University Press, 2005.

Shupe, Anson and Jeffrey K. Hadden. "Is there such a thing as global fundamentalism?," in Anson Shupe and Jeffrey K. Hadden, eds, *Secularization and Fundamentalism Reconsidered*. New York: Paragon House, 1989.

Singer, Peter. *The President of Good and Evil: The Ethics of George W. Bush*. New York. Dutton, 2004.

Slater, Sharon. "Meridian readers made a big difference at the United Nations," *Meridian Magazine*, 2004 <http://meridianmagazine.com/familywatch/041208difference.html>.

Smylie, James H. "Church growth and decline in historical perspective: Protestant Quest for Identity, Leadership and Meaning," *American Presbyterians*, No. 73, 1995, pp. 203–218.

Stark, Rodney and Bainbridge, William S. *The Future of Religion*. Berkeley and Los Angeles: University of California Press, 1985.

Sylva, Douglas A. (vice-president of C-FAM). "Bush Administration calls strong families key for development," *Friday Fax*, Vol. 7, No. 13, March 19, 2005.

——. "Muslim allies at the UN fight for the 'Right Stuff," *Insight on the News – Fair Comment*, September 17, 2001.

——. "Qatar seeks worldwide scholarship on family life," *Friday Fax*, Vol. 7, No. 21, May 14, 2004.

——. "United Nations Children's Fund: women or children first?," *White Paper Series* No. 3, New York: International Organization Research Group (C-FAM), 2003.

Tanenbaum, Joe. *Male & Female Realities: Understanding the Opposite Sex.* Sugarland, TX: Candle Publishing Co., 1989.

Thuesen, Peter. "The Logic of Mainline Churchliness," in Wuthnow and Evans, eds, *The Quiet Hand of God* (2002).

United Nations Commission on the Status of Women, 47th Session (Resumed), Press Release. "Commission on Status of Women fails to Adopt Draft agreed Conclusions on Violence against Women, As it Closes Forty-Seventh Session," March 25, 2003.

——, 48th Session. Press Release WOM/1440, "Review of the 1995 Beijing Action Plan Should Focus on National Implementation. Avoid Lengthy Negotiations, Women's Commission Told." New York: Department of Public Information, March 5, 2003.

——, 47th Session. "Women's human rights and elimination of all forms of violence against women and girls as defined in the Beijing Platform for Action and the outcome document of the twenty-third special session of the General Assembly, Agreed Conclusions," March 3–14, 2003, 5:30 p.m.

United Nations Economic and Social Council, "Non-Governmental Organizations: Report of the Committee on on-Governmental Organization," E/1993/63, New York: United Nations, June 7, 1993, p. 15.

United Nations General Assembly, 10333, 59th General Assembly. Plenary, 82nd Meeting (AM), "General Assembly adopts United Nations Declaration on Human Cloning by Vote of 84-34-37," press release <http://www.un.org/News/Press/docs/2005/ga10333.doc.htm> (accessed March 3, 2005).

——, 59th Session. 'General Assembly commemorates 10th Anniversary of International Year of the Family," Press Release GA/10311, December 6, 2004.

——, "General Assembly votes to ban all forms of human cloning," press release, March 8, 2005.

——. "International convention against the reproductive cloning of human beings," Costa Rica: draft resolution. A/58/L.37, December 5, 2003.

——, "Official Records: A World Fit for Children, 27th Special Session," New York, May 8–10, 2002, Supp. No. 3, Para. 15, UN Doc. A/s-27/19/Rev 1 (2002).

——. "Official Records 46th Session 1991/92, 46:14 Supp. 1–4." New York: United Nations Department of Public Information, 1992.

——. A/RES/59/280, March 23, 2005, "United Nations Declaration on Human Cloning," Resolution Adopted by the General Assembly.

United Nations News Centre, "General Assembly approves declaration banning all forms of cloning," March 8, 2005 <http://www.un.org/apps/news/story.asp?News ID=13576&CR=cloning&Cr1> (accessed on March 9, 2005).

United States government. The National Security Strategy of the United States of America, September 2002, "Rebuilding America's Defenses: Strategy, Forces and Resources for a New Century: A Report" <www.whitehouse.gov/nsc/nss.html> (accessed November 3, 2004).

Urquhart, Gordon. "Rome's Hard Road for Women," *Guardian*, October 23, 1999 <http://www.guardian.co.uk/comment/story/0,,256836,00.html> (accessed April 9, 2006).

Vaughn, Karey, ed. "Report on the 47th Session of the UN Commission on the Status of Women 3–14 March 2003 UN Headquarters in New York," *Women's Voice*, September 2003.

Viguerie, Richard. *The New Right: We're Ready to Lead.* Falls Church, VA: Vigurie Company, 1981.

—— and David Franke. *America's Right Turn: How Conservatives Used New and Alternative Media to Take Power.* Santa Monica: Bonus Books, 2004.

Walch, Tad. "Richard G. Wilkins: defending the family." *Brigham Young Magazine*, Vol. 51, No. 3, Fall 1997.

Waldman, Steven and John Green. "Tribal Relations," *Atlantic Monthly*, February 18, 2006.

Wallis, Jim. *God's Politics: Why the Right Gets it Wrong and the Left Doesn't Get It.* San Francisco, CA: HarperSanFrancisco, 2005.

Walters, LeRoy. "The United Nations and Human Cloning: A Debate on Hold," *The Hastings Report*, January/February 2004.

Warren, Elizabeth. *The Two-Income Trap.* New York: Basic Books, 2003.

Webster, Paul and John Hooper, "France and Germany Seek U.N. Ban on Cloning of Humans," *Guardian*, August 10, 2001.

Weigel, George. "What really happened at Cairo," *First Things*, February 1995.

——. "Europe's Problem – and Ours," *First Things*, February 2004.

Whitaker, Brian. "Fundamental Union," *Guardian*, January 25, 2005 <www.guardian.co.uk/elsewhere/journalist/story/0,7792,1398055,00.html>.

Wilcox, Clyde. *Onward Christian Soldiers? The Religious Right in American Politics.* Boulder, CO: Westview Press, 1996.

Wilhelm, Mark. "Membership Decline and Congregational Identity in Yonkers, New York: A Case Study in the Presbyterian Church (USA)," in Coulter et al., eds, *The Mainstream Protestant Decline* (1990).

Wilkins, Richard. "Ramifications of the International Criminal Court for war, peace and social change," *Federalist Society White Paper*. Washington, DC: Federalist Society for Law and Public Policy Studies.

Willets, Peter, ed. *The Conscience of the World: The Influence of Non-Governmental Organizations in the UN System.* London: Hurst, 1996.

Williams, Daniel and Alan Cooperman. "Long-Serving and Well-Traveled Pope Persevered Despite Illness," *Washington Post*, April 3, 2005, p. A1.

Women's Media Pool. "Governments pledge to accelerate efforts to achieve equality for women and fulfill Beijing commitments, as UN Commission concludes," New York, March 11, 2004.

World Family Policy Center website, "Summary: Process and Outcomes of Doha International Conference for the Family," <http://www.worldfamilypolicy.org/intl_conf.htm>.

Wright, Wendy. "Countries Take Sides on U.N. Cloning Ban," Concerned Women for America, October 3, 2003 <http://www.cwfa.org/articles/4674/CWA/life/> (accessed on December 4, 2005).

_____."United Nations Debates Cloning Ban," Concerned Women for America <www.cwfa.org/articledisplay.asp?id=2582&department=CWA&categoryid=life> (accessed on October 3, 2002).

——. "U.S. Proposes adding Fathers to UN Document," Concerned Women for America website, March 5, 2004.

_____. "World Congress of Families Equips Delegates for Battle at World Summit on Children," Concerned Women for America, January 1, 2002 <http://www.cwfa.org/articledisplay.asp?id=1958&department=CWA&categoryid=nation>.

Wuthnow, Robert. *The Struggle for America's Soul: Evangelicals, Liberals and Secularism*. Grand Rapids, MI: Eerdmans, 1989.

—— and John H. Evans, eds. *The Quiet Hand of God: Faith-Based Activism and the Public Role of Mainline Protestantism*. Berkeley: University of California Press, 2002.

——. *Restructuring of American Religion*. Princeton, NJ: Princeton University Press, 1988.

Yardley, William. "The 2004 Elections: The Voting Process – The Minority Vote; Energized Black Voters Flock to Polls to Back Kerry," *New York Times*, November 3, 2004, p. A7.

Index